21427

D0554415

Library
Oakland S.U.M.

POWER, PATHOLOGY, PARADOX

The Dynamics of Evil and Good

MARGUERITE SHUSTER

Academie Books Grand Rapids, Michigan
Zondervan Publishing House

POWER, PATHOLOGY, PARADOX

Copyright © 1987 by
Marguerite Shuster

ACADEMIE BOOKS is an imprint of Zondervan Publishing House,
1415 Lake Drive, S.E., Grand Rapids, Michigan 49506

Library of Congress Cataloging in Publication Data

Shuster, Marguerite.
    Power, pathology, paradox.

    Bibliography: p.
    Includes index.
    1. Good and Evil.   2. Spiritual life.
3. Psychology, Pathological.   I. Title.
BJ1401.S48 1987   241'.3   87–14221
ISBN   0–310–39750–2

The Scripture quotations contained herein are from the Revised Standard Version Bible,
copyright © 1946, 1952, 1971 by The Division of Christian Education of the National
Council of the Churches of Christ in the USA, and are used by permission.

"The Divine Wit of Miraculous Conceptions," by R. Slotten. Copyright © 1971 Christian
Century Foundation. Reprinted by permission from the March 10, 1971 issue of the
Christian Century.

"If God is God. . .take the odd," by A. MacLeish. From *J.B.: A Play in Verse* by Archibald
MacLeish. Copyright © 1956, 1957, 1958 by Archibald MacLeish. Copyright © renewed
1986 by William H. MacLeish and Mary H. Grimm. Reprinted by permission of
Houghton Mifflin Company.

"Is That All There Is" by Jerry Leiber and Mike Stoller. Copyright © 1966 Jerry Leiber
Music & Mike Stoller Music. Administered by WB Music Corp. All Rights Reservad.
Used by Permission.

"Thanksgiving for a Habitat," by W.H. Auden. Copyright © 1963 by W.H. Auden.
Reprinted from *W.H. Auden: Collected Poems* edited by Edward Mendelson, by permission
of Random House, Inc. Reprinted by permission of Faber and Faber Ltd. from *Collected
Poems* by W. H. Auden.

All rights reserved. No part of this publication may be reproduced,
stored in a retrieval system, or transmitted in any form or by any
means—electronic, mechanical, photocopy, recording, or any other—
except for brief quotations in printed reviews, without the prior
permission of the publisher.

Printed in the United States of America

87 88 89 90 91 92 / EE / 10 9 8 7 6 5 4 3 2 1

BJ
1401
.S48

*To my long-time friend
RMB,
to whose integrity
I can only aspire
and through whose affirmation
I first knew experientially
the grace of our Lord Jesus Christ;
and to my new friend
Jan,
who has taught me much about
faithfulness.*

Contents

PART 4—PARADOX

"My strength is made perfect in weakness" GOD

Introduction

The central purpose of this study is to explore the problem of psychopathology within the framework of the larger problem of evil. That task is clearly an immense one and by its very nature leads to a picture drawn with broad strokes. The delimiting and boldest one will place the problem frankly within the theological framework of spiritual warfare. The lines narrow to a more philosophical and psychological focus on the theme of power, for the nature of the forces operative in our world governs what may affect us for good or ill—what may go "right" or "wrong" and under what circumstances. In psychopathology something has plainly gone wrong. How one conceives its cause, cure, and prevention is determined not by empirical indexes alone but by the world view governing one's selection of data and one's understanding of personal experience.

The study is divided into four sections. Three parts correspond to the title—"power," "pathology," and "paradox." The other, comprising the first four chapters, explores data that have been used to support various views of the nature of "reality." Can we sufficiently explain our experience by reference to material determinants alone? Or must we conceive the universe as having a "mental," nonmaterial component? If so, might that component be continuous, such that "minds" are connected by something other than sensory channels? Finally, do we need to import nonhuman spiritual entities, in addition to societal pressures, as causes for the effects we see in the world? What "powers" must we postulate? The data, intended to be provocative, are initially presented with considerable credulity, so as to make a case for each position in question. If readers also perceive a measure of cavalier skepticism seasoning the credulity of the treatment, they may attribute it both to my recognition of the probabilistic nature of all empirical affirmations and to my conviction that things are often not what they seem.[1] In any event, each of these chapters also contains a section

---

[1] This comment applies *a fortiori* to the chapter on paranormal phenomena. While I believe that something more than chance and an inflamed imagination is involved, I am

11

designed to combat reductionism by probing possible implications, qualifications, speculations, or value issues that derive from the preliminary discussion. The philosophical threads are drawn together in chapter 5, in which a general, theoretical conceptualization of "power" is attempted. Chapter 5 is a turning point, for it specifies the paradigm implicitly present in the preceding chapters and explicitly governing the succeeding ones.

In chapters 6 through 9, the data base is abruptly shifted from the empirical to the scriptural because I consider "evil"—of which psychopathology is a part—to be a spiritual and moral category rather than a scientific and empirical one. As I already hinted by mention of spiritual warfare, I take the source of evil also to be personal rather than natural, or impersonal: chapter 6, in open accord with a biblical world view, deals with Satan and demons as personal, willful beings. The following three chapters consider implications of that world view for our understanding of the major and minor evils in human experience. This shift in data base does not, however, entail a shift of theme: the focus is still on the issue of power. First, the Devil and his minions—in their basic nature, activity, and ability to produce effects in the world—may be characterized by raw power. Second, pathology of any sort produces at least some area of powerlessness. Third, powerlessness tends to lead to a compensatory striving for power and thence, directly or indirectly, into the snares of Satan, whose domain power is. Thus pathology—an area of impotence—may be viewed as demonic in its origins and as tending to provoke reconstitutive efforts that are essentially demonic. The psychotherapist may easily be trapped into promoting "cures that are ultimately as bad as the disease. The dilemma is how to remedy powerlessness without succumbing to power seeking.

The final three chapters promote a radical, paradoxical, Christian view of health whereby the power of Satan is conceived as being countered not by a like power but by the Word and Spirit of God operative through human *weakness*. Evil is seen as defeated at its roots when we are enabled not to do it, when we are strengthened to bear the suffering of others, and when it is transformed to good by the Holy Spirit. These chapters challenge every view of health that would exalt it to the level of a minor deity or would make its major prerequisites autonomy, independence, self-fulfillment, self-esteem, and the like, as over against a focus on right relationships with God and one's brothers and sisters.

thoroughly unwilling to make an all-encompassing statement as to the validity, nature, and source of the phenomena.

The question might well be raised of the relationship of experience to exegesis as a determinant of the views articulated in these pages. In one sense, that sort of chicken-and-egg question is discussed in chapter 1—a world view determines what one sees, and what one sees establishes one's world view. The best answer I can make is that, without scriptural revelation, I would have difficulty, in this day and age and culture, perceiving the course of daily life in terms of spiritual warfare. On the other hand, if there were no phenomena in the world today lending themselves to such an interpretation, I doubtless would be writing about something else! I both take the normativeness of Scripture as an a priori and believe that, since it purports to have an objective referent in the world, experience may sensitize one to its current relevance and meaning. Thus, the claim that we are engaged in spiritual warfare is first and foremost a faith statement, but I believe that there are pressing experiential reasons for conceiving that warfare not metaphorically but rather as it was conceived by the New Testament writers.

A final introductory note applies to the choice of format. The decision to intersperse dialogues in the text was not dictated wholly by mere whimsy, though I would decline to plead *entirely* innocent to that charge! One of their functions is to serve as introductory and transitional devices. Another is to provide a forum for recognizing views other than the author's without overburdening an already complex text with a thousand qualifications. A third is to give some respite from extended, convoluted exposition. A fourth is to illustrate the seductive nature of certain types of rationalistic argumentation. And finally, it is perhaps aesthetically appropriate that a radical style be adopted to express unconventional subject matter.

Part 1

The Elusiveness of "Reality"

*Whatever perspective we use
in looking at our world,
an elusive "something" seems
to lie just beyond our view.*

1

Matter over Mind?

Inquirer: Haven't I seen you somewhere before?

Stranger: Oh, perhaps. I've been around . . .

Inquirer: The thing is, I can't quite place where or when. I feel, well, as if you're always just around the corner—but that's silly.

Stranger: It certainly is. Ridiculous. I'm surprised at you! If the progress of science has taught us anything in the past few hundred years, it's the value of careful experimentation and repeated observation against mere superstition and subjective feeling. In fact, we have finally recognized that developing a true science of behavior depends upon taking a systematic deterministic position.[1]

Inquirer: Yes, yes. I suppose so. . . . I didn't mean to imply that I'm enamored of "ghosties and ghoulies and things that go bump in the night."

Stranger: No, of course not. But you really must be more precise in how you speak. I've no doubt that there are entirely satisfactory explanations of these intuitive "feelings" of yours to be found in brain physiology, chemistry, and physics. We've learned a lot about human consciousness and even altered states of consciousness. The brain is a marvelously complex mechanism, you know; we simply need to know more about how it works, how it's put together.[2]

Inquirer: Oh, I agree. In fact, I've been intrigued to learn how many factors influence our consciousness, ever since I read what William James had to say many years ago:

> Even our normal waking consciousness, rational consciousness as we call it, is but one special type of consciousness, whilst all about it, parted from it by the flimsiest of screens, there lie potential forms of

---

[1] Immergluck 1964, 276.

[2] "Brain" refers to the physical organ, as it can be described by its structure, chemistry, and physics. I define "mind" as the conscious capacity (mediated by the brain) to think, perceive, feel, and choose.

consciousness entirely different. We may go through life without suspecting their existence; but apply the requisite stimulus, and at a touch they are there in all their completeness, definite types of mentality which probably somewhere have their field of application and adaptation. No account of the universe in its totality can be final which leaves these other forms of consciousness quite disregarded. How to regard them is the question,—for they are so discontinuous with ordinary consciousness. Yet they may determine attitudes though they cannot furnish formulas, and open a region though they fail to give a map. At any rate, they forbid a premature closing of our accounts with reality.[3]

Stranger: Right! Our data are phenomenal! And we have just begun!

Inquirer: Yes; brain structures, stimuli affecting them, and on and on—there seems to be no end to unexpected determinants of our behavior.

* * *

To be human is to be aware not only of the world but of ourselves. We do not just feel and behave and perceive and think; rather we ask questions about *why* we feel as we do, *why* we behave as we do, *why* we perceive and think as we do. Partly, we ask because we would like to be able to control our lives more effectively or to change them for the better. Partly, though, we ask because every once in a while we get the unsettling sense that we may be missing something—that some people experience "reality" very differently than we do or that "they know something we don't know" about it. The questions might be sparked by the testimony of a user of psychedelic drugs, who tells of brand-new aesthetic experiences; or by a religious person, who speaks of inexplicable joy and answered prayer; or by a psychic, who seems to get knowledge apart from ordinary means. Is "reality" larger and more mysterious than we thought? Or does the human brain simply play a large number of intriguing tricks?

The first half of this chapter and the first halves of the next three chapters explore the data used to support a variety of quite different answers to the question of the nature of reality. We may grant that human beings sometimes have a powerful sense of the uncanny, of forces beyond their control or understanding, of a spiritual dimension of reality that serves as a wellspring for religion; but does that dimension *really* have an independent existence of its own? Or should it be seen as a mere by-product of physical processes? Or of quite natural, though not merely material, "mental" processes? Or of poorly understood "paranor-

[3]James 1961 (1902), 305.

mal" powers of mind? Or of sociological and anthropological forces? While these varying explanations of human experience may sometimes be complementary, at other times they quite openly compete one with another. Thus the sequence of these chapters is based not on a strictly linear progression of thought but rather on a movement from a very narrow principle of explanation (brain physiology) to increasingly broad ones (all the way to sociology and anthropology). At each point in the various arguments, however, the underlying question must be kept in mind: Does any one of these arguments, or any combination of them, *sufficiently* explain the phenomena associated with the persistent human belief in a spiritual realm?

Our answer to that latter question depends not just on data, though, as if we evaluated data in a vacuum of pure objectivity. It also depends on what alternatives we see, on factors illumined by the philosophy of science, and on an understanding of how profoundly our presuppositions shape what we see. Thus the second half of each of the first four chapters deals in an intentionally provocative way with possible problems with or implications of the preceding material.

The chapters are left rather open-ended precisely because, as will become clear in chapter 5, I do not in fact believe that purely naturalistic approaches of whatever breadth suffice to explain the depth and height of human experience. Nonetheless, these approaches do offer challenges to a Christian world view that assumes the active involvement, for good and for ill, of personal spiritual powers in our lives. Thus we have a responsibility to look seriously at the case made by proponents of these approaches, particularly at those points where we might be quickest to rush in with spiritual explanations.

ALTERED STATES OF CONSCIOUSNESS

Those who take a "matter over mind" position—that is, that conscious experience in general and unusual religious experience in particular can be attributed to the physical and chemical state of one's brain—have found so-called altered states of consciousness (ASCs) a fertile field of exploration. In recent years a great deal of research has been done to try to discover the determinants of such experiences. One clue has been provided by the fact that ASCs attributed to very different sources—drug trips, various trances, mystic experiences—are described by the persons experiencing them in very similar ways. Common characteristics include alterations in thinking, disturbed sense of time, loss of control, changes in emotional expression, changes in body image, perceptual distortions, changes in the meaning or significance of things, a sense of the ineffable, feelings of rejuvenation, a tendency to respond easily to suggestion, unusual sensations, and telepathic phenomena

(Deikman 1969b; Krippner and Davidson 1970; Lee 1968; Ludwig 1968, 1969; Tart 1969). Such similarities suggest that, however apparently different the causes, the resultant states of mind (or brain?) themselves may well have something in common, which of course raises the question of whether the experiences should be seen as having equivalent *meaning* (or lack of meaning). In any case, researchers have paid particular attention to three ways of explaining the commonalities: (1) different properties of the two hemispheres of the brain, (2) effects of certain types of stimulation or deprivation of stimulation, and (3) effects of damage to parts of the brain.

Right Brain vs. Left Brain

Patients with uncontrollable epilepsy have sometimes been treated by cutting the corpus callosum, the fibers connecting the two hemispheres of the brain, so that seizures would not spread over the whole brain. Subsequent studies of such "split-brain" patients revealed something surprising: not only did they appear to have two separate centers of consciousness (Gazzaniga 1973), but these centers seemed to function differently when confronted with the same stimulus. For instance, the left hemisphere can enable patients to name an object they see but not one that they feel while it is hidden from view, while the right brain can enable them to know what to do with an object but not to speak its name (Ferguson 1975, 182). To give an oversimplified summary of the results of the extensive research on the differences in the sides of the brain: the left hemisphere carries on verbal, linear, analytic reasoning of the sort highly valued in objective, science-dominated Western culture. The right hemisphere, on the other hand, responds to patterned wholes and is not ordered by linear time. Its only speech functions are singing, swearing, or other "automatic" responses. However, it may be dominant in religious responsiveness, imagery, sociability, and intuition. Now, the point of this brief summary is to suggest a striking correspondence. The functions of the right hemisphere closely parallel the descriptions that people who are familiar with altered states of consciousness give of their experiences (Ferguson 1975).

Could it be that "getting high" and having a "spiritual experience" are simply quite natural expressions of right-brain activity, no more intrinsically strange and ethereal than our capacity to make sense out of rows of peculiar marks on a piece of paper? Is it just that we foster the latter and ignore or inhibit the former? If so, what can activate or intensify so-called right-brain functions in those who live in a left-brain society and whose two cerebral hemispheres remain normally connected?

20

Stimulation and Lack of Stimulation

The most obvious answer is drugs. Drugs do induce altered states of consciousness. However, some have difficulty accepting, not just the protestations of some users that they are actually seeking religious enlightenment, but the fact that their reports often parallel closely certain religious ideas (particularly Hindu and Buddhist ideas) regarding the meaning of life, the nature of the human personality, and union with God (Ferguson 1975; as we shall see, meditative techniques common to Eastern religions appear to promote right-brain phenomena). Moreover, use of drugs as an adjunct to or stimulus for religious experience scarcely originated with LSD freaks: note the native Americans' longstanding use of mescaline. Even the incense formula in the Old Testament (Exod. 30:23–24) has been thought by some to contain nutmeg, a spice with hallucinogenic properties.[4] In short, similar sets of events may be initiated by either drugs or worship; furthermore, the two have often been associated in practice. One might conclude that what we perceive or experience depends simply on a particular pattern of brain activity, no matter what *caused* the pattern. For instance, we may "see" colors when we look at a flower garden in full bloom or when we press on our closed eyelids (see Eccles 1953).

Incidentally, when speaking of chemical stimuli, we ought not to stop with those manifestly mind-altering substances taken for recreational or religious purposes. Thousands of persons exist on prescribed tranquilizers, antidepressants, and stimulants. Hormonal imbalances influence mood along with metabolism. Even the diet of a person with a sensitive metabolism can alter his outlook: hypoglycemia, for instance, can mimic an anxiety attack or worse (Watson 1972). Lack of calcium in the water fosters clairvoyance (Bauer 1967). And runners get a "high" after prolonged exertion. Often we are simply ignorant of the biochemical roots of our moods and behaviors.

More than chemicals affects the condition of the brain, however. It responds with definite changes in the brain waves to almost any repetitive, rhythmic stimulus. Flickering or strobe lights, dancing, pounding drums, or reiterated syllables can induce an altered state of consciousness. At the same time they produce a brain state that is much less variable and less responsive to outside stimuli than usual (Ferguson 1975).

Curiously enough, *lack* of stimulation appears to have exactly the same effect on brain-wave patterns. The grosser varieties of sensory deprivation work best, of course, such as being immersed in a tank of tepid water or being bound up in the equivalent of cotton batting. But

---

[4] Exegetical support for this idea is not strong. While קדה can refer generally to sweet spice, it is usually translated "cassia."

21

even meditating for a half hour on a single object, covering one's eyes with ping pong ball halves, daydreaming, floating on water, or sunbathing may do the trick. Some have even attributed hypnotic induction to sensory deprivation, assuming that a subject may concentrate so completely on the hypnotist that she somehow shuts out the normal range of incoming stimuli (Van Der Walde 1968). In any case, even minimally stressful conditions, such as meditation, may rapidly produce such intense effects as feelings of depersonalization, hallucinations, delusions, and the like—changes in perception of the world and oneself much larger than we expect "normal people" to experience (Deikman 1969b, 218).

The relation of brain states associated with these phenomena to the right-hemisphere way of perceiving the world is not immediately obvious. The effects are the same—but do we have one or two converging physical routes to altered states of consciousness?[5]

Damage to the Brain

Besides the normal functioning of the right hemisphere and some rather predictable effects of certain types of stimuli, we may note a third source of experiences that Western persons generally consider atypical: damage to portions of the brain. Connections among parts of the brain are indeed so numerous and complex that few functions are controlled strictly and exclusively by a single portion. Nonetheless, epileptics with temporal-lobe lesions, *in particular when the lesions are in the right hemisphere,* often report déjà vu and *jamais vu* experiences;[6] feelings of loneliness, strangeness, and depersonalization; obsessional thinking; hallucinations and perceptual distortions (one study reports that 45 percent of noninstitutionalized patients with temporal-lobe lesions have hallucinatory experiences); and sometimes assaultive and violent impulses (Small 1973, 63). The individual may wholly forget a period of altered behavior; may vividly recall the past, as if reliving it;[7] and may have primitive visceral, smell, and taste sensations. Another linkage between structural damage and paranormal experience or abilities is the high incidence of past brain injury among gifted psychics and the evidence that hospital patients with concussions do better on ESP

[5] I return later to the thought that both routes may imply a receptive, passive stance on the part of the individual rather than an active one, which may be necessary to the occurrence of what we call paranormal phenomena (see Deikman 1973a).

[6] Such experiences are feelings of having gone through something unfamiliar before or having never before gone through something familiar, respectively. Many persons experience occasionally the eerie déjà vu sensation, which is common to almost all ASCs and increases in meditation and which may be induced by electrical stimulation to parts of the brain (see Ferguson 1975, 60–61).

[7] Penfield (1975) demonstrated that electrical stimulation of certain brain cells could produce a vivid reliving of past experiences.

(extrasensory perception) tests than a control group of patients (Ferguson 1975, 238).

Finally, we might consider the possibility that either excessive or insufficient energy or activity within the brain itself (perhaps related to how many outside stimuli it "admits" or responds to) may produce paranormal experiences. At the onset of acute schizophrenia, the patient frequently experiences overstimulation, an energizing, a heightened perception of the world, a new awakening and mystic feeling of oneness with the world, a great sensitivity to stimuli, and an apparently enhanced telepathic ability. Powers of ESP seem to be common to many mental patients; and some suggest that patients' sense of the uncanny and at least some paranoid reactions may be due to telepathic perceptions (Ferguson 1975, 214). The acute phase of heightened perception becomes too great to bear, and the patient must retreat.

In short, altered states of consciousness have an enormous number of physical sources.[8] They have something in common with normal right-brain perceptual modes, can be induced by increasing or decreasing stimuli, and are often associated with injury to or abnormal activity within the brain itself, apart from specific environmental stimulation. Strangely enough, these widely varied physical avenues can all lead to mystical and trance experiences, hallucinations, and psi phenomena.[9] How they are related to one another and to the objective world is unclear, but some of the same brain-wave patterns (or rather, interference with usual brain-wave patterns; perhaps it is not "normal" even for the right brain to function by itself?) are common to them all.

* * *

Stranger: Well now, I hope it's clear to you that your "feelings" and "experiences," however unusual, quite simply depend on which physical button we push, so to speak. Whatever people say about their own pet altered states of consciousness, they look a lot alike in the end; and whatever differences there are obviously depend on physical and environmental variations. "A very little distemper of the

---

[8] "ASC's may be produced in any setting by any agents or maneuvers which interfere with the normal inflow of sensory or proprioceptive stimuli, the normal outflow of motor impulses, the normal 'emotional tone,' or the normal flow and organization of recognitive processes" (Ludwig 1968, 70).

[9] "Psi" is a general term used for extrasensory perception, psychokinesis, and other such parapsychological phenomena, wherein a transmission of motion-producing energy (psychokinesis, or "PK") or a "communication of imagery and of impulse from one self to another [takes place] without the use of the senses or of any secondary mechanical devices, a communication which is usually independent of distance in space, and occasionally of distance in time" (Haynes 1961, 15).

23

brain . . . is enough to represent Spirits, Angels and Devils, Sights and Stories of Heaven and Hell to the Fancy."[10]

Inquirer: I grant that it's pretty hard to perceive or experience anything without our physiology being involved. Even experiences that feel "mental" are profoundly dependent on body chemistry and what is going on in the world.

Stranger: Precisely.

Inquirer: Still, I have a couple of problems with the whole "body over mind" position.

Stranger: Still? After intelligent consideration of the data? (At least, I *suppose* you're intelligent?)

Inquirer: Yes, I'm afraid so. For instance, if everything we do and feel does indeed stem simply from physiological reactions, how is it that *destruction* of parts of a person's physiology—such as damage to the brain—may enable him to do things he couldn't do before? Specifically, consider psi phenomena. They are somehow related to the "real world": telepathy involves communicating real messages without using normal sensory channels; psychokinesis involves moving real objects apart from physical means, and so forth. Of course, destructive alterations in our nervous system can change subjective experience, but how on earth do they give us new possibilities with regard to so-called objective reality?

Stranger: I hope you realize that most of the scientific community is scarcely enamored of this parapsychology business. They consider it altogether too unlikely to be worthy of serious attention. Hume[11] was right: some things are too intrinsically improbable, in the light of the uniformity of nature, *ever* to be credible. Responsible persons consider pursuing such red herrings a waste of time—and of taxpayers' money. Besides, much of this telepathy and precognition is so vague that it could apply to almost anything, sort of like horoscopes. It doesn't surprise me at all if destroying part of the brain leaves the rest of it to produce such nonsense, just as over- or underloading the circuits can produce hallucinations.

Inquirer: Perhaps. How about the idea, though, that the brain is actually a filter or reducing mechanism?[12] Maybe it serves to protect us (whatever "us" is, if not to be identified with our brains) from too many incoming stimuli. After all, we couldn't survive if possibilities

[10]Sargant 1959, 1, quoting Burton.
[11]1926 (1777).
[12]Bergson initially suggested this view (see Heywood 1961, 211).

for action weren't limited somehow. But I have a more basic objection: however experiences may be influenced, you must admit that there is a certain irreducibility about the fact of *experiencing* and of knowing. You said earlier that a science of human behavior demands a systematic deterministic position. Doesn't such a position make nonsense of the very possibility of one's adopting or rejecting the position? To reverse your argument, take, for instance, what behavioral scientist Boring has said about your behaviorist friend B. F. Skinner's deterministic bent: "Skinner is saying something more than that behavior is caused. . . . He is saying that, because behavior can be controlled, human living can be improved. . . . There . . . is a possibility that it may not be, unless the gospel is accepted. This is sheer voluntarism."[13] Or, considering our everyday lives, doesn't choice have some role in selection of the very stimuli to which we subject ourselves so that our behavior and experience may be altered?

Stranger: Choice? Experience? Simply leftovers of brain activity—epiphenomena. Mere epiphenomena. Besides, I didn't say a word about improving human living. That was Skinner's idea, not mine.

*   *   *

AGAINST REDUCTIONISM:
PROBLEMS OF CONSCIOUS EXPERIENCE

However provocative may be the data on the *influence* of physiological brain states on experience, most of us instinctively object that physiological brain states and experience are *not the same thing.* If they were, we could not transcend ourselves sufficiently to observe that our experience changes as circumstances change. Indeed, I began this chapter by commenting that to be human is to be self-aware, to be conscious of ourselves. No matter how precisely we may specify the conditions provoking altered states of consciousness, no matter how rigorously scientific our studies, we are stuck with the awkward fact that *consciousness* is altered—not *produced,* just altered. And consciousness is exceedingly mysterious. Being conscious includes thinking, feeling, perceiving, experiencing, paying attention, and—at least for humans—being convinced that one can decide, choose, will.

By stimulating part of the brain, one may make a person move—but he will report a sense of passivity quite different from his experience when "he" performs the same motion. By stimulating another area, one

13 Boring 1957, 190.

may evoke a minutely detailed description of some long-forgotten experience—but the record appears to include only that to which the person originally paid attention, not that which she ignored. Nowhere (at least nowhere on the cerebral cortex, where Penfield did his work) can one stimulate the brain in such a way as to cause a patient to believe or to decide (Penfield 1975, 50, 77).

Consciousness is indeed mysterious; and it would seem obvious that it profoundly affects our behavior in the real world. In fact, we have trouble even speaking of "our" behavior if we did something when we were not conscious in the ordinary sense—if we were sleepwalking or having a seizure, for instance. For this reason I consider it crucial not to discount conscious experience but to explore it on its own terms. Of course we may identify physical correlates of certain types of experience, as we have above. But we must also remember that our experience of ourselves includes such things as our paying attention and making choices.

Intention/Attention

"Intention" and "attention" go together. Both imply design or purpose. Furthermore, they interact profoundly in influencing our behavior.[14] Now it is obvious that, if we intend to get high, we may attend to every clue as to where we may obtain our favorite chemical. We did not *have* to get high; we chose to, and we pursued the means to our end. Intention generated attention.

But suppose a group seemingly having a grand time catches our attention. We notice that they are smoking peculiar-smelling cigarettes and wonder if those have anything to do with their mood. We decide to try one and see. Attention generated intention. To complicate matters, we find that we experience almost nothing for our efforts. Puzzled, we inquire and discover that one must perhaps *learn* to get high on marijuana (as well as accumulate enough of the chemical in one's brain), that is, learn to pay attention to certain aspects of one's experience. And so the interaction goes.

Consider a third possibility. Suppose that, instead of being ordinary citizens out for a good time, we are police. If we ask where the marijuana came from, it will be not with a desire to purchase some but because we want to catch the pusher. And our reaction to the party may not be anticipation at joining it but irritation that breaking it up will make us late for dinner. The point is that, far from a person's being simply determined by a stimulus, he will attend to the particular

---

[14] Rollo May (1969) has gone as far as to suggest that attention is the seat of the will and that intentionality is the structure that gives meaning to experience.

properties of it that further or interfere with his plans (see Polanyi 1967).

If we could stop our analysis here, with the emphasis on our ability to be selective rather than to respond mechanically to environmental stimuli, it would appear that we had given the cause of "freedom" a considerable boost. Unfortunately, matters are not so simple. We do experience a sense of will or purpose when we choose to pay attention to something. However, we are not free to reach just any conclusion from what we see or hear or feel—not even to reach every conclusion consistent with all the data before us. Rather, we are limited by our physical senses (or the limits of the instruments we use to extend our physical senses).[15] For instance, we simply cannot see ultraviolet light with the naked eye and would naturally deny its existence if unaided human vision were our only means of observation. Thus, while physical structures such as eyes make many things possible, by their very nature they make other things impossible. We have to accept our eyes for what they are, just as we must accept the fact that we cannot pick up a skyscraper and carry it on our backs or build a ten-story tepee.

Furthermore, our perceptions not only are limited by our perceptual "tools" but also depend upon past experience and learning. Different stimuli may produce the same sensations, as we have already discussed, but the same stimuli may produce different sensations, depending on past experience. In some cases actual physical capacity may be changed: cats raised from birth equipped with spectacles preventing them from seeing vertical lines apparently never gain the ability to see them in later life (Smith 1975, 24–25). More frequently, not physiology as such but the *meaning* of a stimulus is affected: Zulu Indians, reared in a culture where there are mainly curves and few straight lines or corners, do not fall prey to the perceptual illusions dependent on linear perspective that give us fits when we look at trick figures in puzzle books (Gregory 1966, 160–61). In some sense, then, the Zulu truly live in a different world than we do; analysis of the world necessarily follows and depends upon prior unanalyzed perception (see Kuhn 1970, 193–94). We are all limited in our view.

World Views (Paradigms)

Something analogous to what happens on the *perceptual* level happens on the *conceptual* level as well. Not only may physical stimuli that we experience, voluntarily or involuntarily, subsequently control our reactions, but also our choice of intellectual commitments—or the

---

[15] I argue below that physical channels are not the only channels through which we can pay attention. Nonetheless, any channel we use has its own limits, so our experience is always partial.

choice of commitments of the community to which we belong and are subject—may provide a structure, or paradigm, that effectively determines how we perceive and interpret our world. Experience, as soon as we manage to articulate it even to ourselves, is no longer *raw* experience, but experience understood in a particular framework.

Determining what experience one has "really had" or what one's experience *means* is no simple matter, although (or because) it often seems so obvious on the surface. Actually, in different cultures, different periods of history, or different schools of thought, people simply do not agree on the most basic questions, such as what the fundamental entities of the universe are, how they interact with each other and the senses, what questions may be asked, and what methodologies may be utilized (see Kuhn 1970, 4–5). These presuppositions—our paradigm, as it were, for interpreting reality—are intimately connected to what is seen as possible, credible, and worthy of exploration. As long as "schizophrenia," for instance, is correlated directly with demon possession, thoughts of administering medication would not just be tossed aside as irrelevant; they would not even occur. Conversely, if medication is considered the appropriate remedy for some hypothesized physiological problem, to call in an exorcist would be incongruous in the extreme—strictly a return to the Middle Ages. What can be connected and how is necessarily—and, usually, usefully—limited by one's world view. If possible connections, like perceptible incoming stimuli to the brain, were not both limited and consistent, we might well be trying to cook our meat by sticking pins in it or to cure the common cold by sacrificing iguanas. We *need* Occam's razor, the principle of not multiplying hypotheses but of choosing the simplest explanation consistent with the data. The problem comes, of course, when the simplest explanations no longer appear consistent with all the data. Which is to be discarded, hypothesis or data? What constitutes "real" data?

Thus we cannot in any final way separate "fact" from "theory," since what *counts* as fact *depends* on the theory, just as surely as what we perceive depends on what we have learned to see. For change to occur, the community that must live by the new way of seeing must simply give its assent. Although we blithely assume that paradigm changes bring progress (otherwise why change?), often they merely banish old problems from the realm of legitimate "scientific" discourse (such as the problem many cultures and ages have identified as the "demonic").[16]

---

[16] Indeed, sociologist Peter Berger (1969) makes clear how quickly such changes can sometimes occur by noting that modern anthropologists have to make concerted efforts—including coming home after relatively brief periods—in order to avoid "going native," or adopting the world view of the culture they are attempting to study "objectively." Cf. Kuhn 1970, 170: "We may . . . have to relinquish the notion, explicit or implicit, that

Risk

Obviously, then, to believe anything lays one open to the possibility of being wrong. But to refuse to believe anything whatever without prior assurance of its validity would be absolutely paralyzing. Imagine, for instance, insisting upon proof that a strange language means something before being willing to learn it (Polanyi 1964, 151). If one had never heard of the language before, one could presume that the supposed instructor in the language was just perpetrating an elaborate hoax by deliberately conveying nonsense. One must make the commitment to learning *before* one will receive persuasive evidence.

Of course, we all make such commitments whether we realize it or not. Often we do not realize it, since commitments of all kinds tend to be self-confirming. No amount of evidence would make most of us believe in fairies. If some among us were to argue for their existence— that is, make a commitment that was foreign, unacceptable, or not understandable to the community in which we live—we would readily label them mystics, heretics, or lunatics. Today—but not in the past— insanity is the preferred categorization for those not functioning in terms of consensually validated reality.

Perhaps it is because belief and commitment are inherently risky and because a common belief system is absolutely crucial for communication and practical community functioning that relatively narrow limits are set for "acceptable" beliefs. While "everybody knows" that Occam's razor must be kept whetted, we forget that "simplicity" of explanation is defined in terms of an agreed-upon conceptual framework that is scarcely the only one possible. If anyone doubts that we have a problem here, let him look at the statistical—leaving wholly aside the subjective, experiential—evidence for ESP. It is immediately apparent that far more impressive figures are needed to provide it with even a cloak of respectable possibility than are required to "prove" (i.e., engender overwhelming acceptance of) more intrinsically credible phenomena.

Perhaps even more upsetting to many is a concept, such as miracle, to which statistics cannot even be applied. Of course the miraculous is, by definition, conceived not even to be subject to science in that it cannot be predicted or controlled. If supposed violations of the laws of nature were actually found to be repeatable, then the laws—not our ideas about the possibility of miracles—would need to be changed. However, it is not mere nonsense to say that the "conceptually impossible" may occur. In a general sense, we have just shown that a given interpretive framework establishes all sorts of supposed impossibilities. In Euclidean geometry it is inconceivable that parallel lines should meet, but what

changes of paradigm carry scientists and those who learn from them closer and closer to the truth."

29

about in non-Euclidean geometry? With particular regard to miracle, the "conceptually possible" is defined by the laws of nature (through what paradigm we perceive them is not immediately relevant to the argument). Thus, if "nature" were not the only operative force, the fact that something had happened would *not* make it "possible" in any ordinary sense (see Swinburne 1970, 28; note also Aquinas's views to this effect, cited in Brown 1984, 12).

While such an argument for the "possibility of the impossible" may be philosophically defensible, one could say that it is scientifically irrelevant, since it explicitly transcends the bounds of science. That complaint would be valid *if and only if* science were not a *human* endeavor. Science itself will always be influenced by concerns and experiences that transcend a given age's scientific vision. Thus, even a scientist's choice of problems on which to work will frequently be determined not just by pure intellectual curiosity but by values, religious commitments, or anomalous life events for which current scientific theories have no satisfactory explanation.

Furthermore, "knowledge" can never rightly be dissociated from the fact that it is persons who know. Persons have an understandable and quite proper investment in distinguishing *themselves,* as conscious, willing, choosing beings, from the material and conceptual *structures* that so powerfully influence their consciousness and willing and choosing. I have gone to some pains to hint at the complexity of the interplay between our consciousness and those factors that affect it: what we more or less freely choose at one point in time may more or less completely determine how we will respond at another point in time, and so forth. However, if we try to *reduce* our conscious experience to the impersonal factors that have an impact upon it, we will end up with a picture of the world in which we ourselves are absent. Reductionism leaves no room for precisely what it is supposed to explain.[17]

Thus we argue that experience must itself be given status as a datum and regarded from the aspects of both the structures (physical connections and conceptual paradigms) and the intentions that govern it. People report a belief in (experience of? commitment to?) a spiritual realm that is not reducible to the natural order. What difference might it make if their belief is true?

---

[17] See Polanyi 1964, 142. Similarly, "As to the Freudian interpretation of intellectual passions as a sublimation of appetitive drives, it leaves unaccounted for everything that distinguishes science and art from the instincts of which these are supposed to be sublimates" (Polanyi 1964, 309). And again, "Contemplate some able and sincere materialist. . . . He understands everything, and everything does not seem worth understanding" (Chesterton 1959 [1908], 23).

Mind over Matter?

Stranger: Goodness, this conversation has degenerated rapidly. As if talking about a "mind" separate from "brain" weren't enough, we're right back to the "ghosties and ghoulies" with this discourse on spirits. I thought you said you weren't enamored of such fairy stories!

Inquirer: Wait a minute. I never intended to impugn fairy stories per se, and I haven't yet said a word about spirits. I was talking about a spiritual dimension of reality and about the nature of our knowledge and experience and . . .

Stranger: I know, I know. Let's not go through all of *that* again! I'm a practical sort myself; I like to stick to what's useful. This philosophy business may be amusing; but if you're so eager to talk about mind, why not talk about what it can do concretely? I personally still think that it's an epiphenomenon, of course, and that it's *brain* that really counts: have you ever seen a mind without a brain? Still, you'll miss reams of nice, empirical data, most effective in keeping scientists arguing, if you're content to stop with mere philosophy. Why not go at the problem from a different angle?

Inquirer: What do you mean? (And by the way, I never expect to *see* a mind, with or without a brain!)

Stranger: Oh, you know, all the effects of suggestion—hypnosis, placebo effects, that sort of thing. The old brain can play some rather surprising tricks.

Inquirer: Wow, you're right! Why didn't I think of that? You really do have a lot of intriguing ideas.

Stranger: Thank you. Most of my friends think so. But back to the subject—the power of suggestion, I think it was. Be literary and call it "mind over matter," if you like; but how about making some attempt for the moment to stick to the physical effects of suggestion, okay?

Inquirer: Sure—but I just had another idea. What about biofeedback? Does it count? Its effects are surely physical, even if suggestion from a second individual isn't involved.

Stranger: Isn't it? Doesn't someone else suggest that altering body processes through biofeedback is indeed possible and desirable? But that's all right—it's a tidy, measurable process of the sort that I like.

* * *

ALTERED PHYSIOLOGICAL STATES

As we have seen in chapter 1, those who object to the tyranny of reductionism can always point to conscious experience as something that cannot quite be explained by any of the factors that influence it. Mere experience, however—or even the choice of intellectual commitments that serve to interpret experience—may seem comparatively weak and passive when compared with the powerful physical events that spark it. If "mind" can only respond and not initiate, it remains open to the charge of being a mere epiphenomenon. But what if, counter to the "matter over mind" hypothesis, mind can actually make changes in matter? And, in fact, persons *can* alter the very biochemical, physiological processes that are often alleged to control them so completely; and they can do so under a surprising variety of circumstances, which I briefly explore below.

Biofeedback

"Biofeedback" means the provision of a recognizable stimulus, such as a tone, that varies in response to a normally unrecognizable (or at least unrecognized) physiological state, such as hand temperature. Even supposedly involuntary responses such as heart rate and blood pressure can be changed if people (or animals) get feedback concerning when the level or process is moving in the desired direction. How the adjustment is made we do not know: the organism can evidently "recognize" cues of which it is not consciously aware when they reliably correspond to a cue of which it *is* aware. Given a fair chance, mind—or is it brain?—can alter measurable biological processes.

In biofeedback, some sort of "intention" (produced in animals by reward or punishment) to respond to the recognizable stimulus is necessary, but anxiety or effort will subvert the process: a combination of active focus and passive responsiveness seems to be required. Results, however, are not totally regular or predictable. One somewhat skeptical investigator wrote, "Success seems to be inversely proportional to the competence of the investigator, and directly proportional to the subjectivity of the symptom. It works best on capricious psychosomatic disorders" (Smith 1975, quoting Dworkin). Does bio-feedback perhaps involve considerable suggestion or autosuggestion of the sort we shall consider below? Whatever the factors involved, though, we at the very least have evidence that the feats of bodily control that have long been claimed, for instance, by the yogis, are not impossible. (Indeed, yogis wired up to biofeedback machines do impressively well; see Ferguson 1975; Karlins and Andrews 1972; Smith 1975.) And even a few legitimate instances in which a person succeeded by conscious intention in altering physiological processes would suggest strongly that more than strictly mechanistic forces are observably at work in our world.

Placebos

Actually, it does not require a lot of fancy machinery to persuade people to make their bodies function better: the little pink pill of the country physician will do quite nicely. Placebos are substances that, unbeknown to the patient, contain no active ingredients but are administered in response to a person's psychological need for medicine. They work. A double-blind study of pain-relievers and placebos showed that placebos were approximately 50 percent as effective as aspirin, Darvon, and morphine.[1] Two pills work better than one, and placebo injections do better yet (Smith 1975, 17). This result may sound less surprising if we consider the fact that, though physicians have long been respected for their healing powers, most of what they have prescribed (until relatively recent times) has been either inert or actually harmful (Frank 1974, 138). Apparently, positive expectations helped the patient get well. Furthermore, expectations have been shown to be so powerful that they can actually *reverse* the nature of physiological response normally produced by a drug. Finally, not only relief of symptoms such as pain but also actual tissue changes can be engendered by placebos. The commonest example is wart removal: warts are notoriously responsive to home remedies, and such remedies or a physician's placebo treatment is just as effective as surgical excision (Frank 1974, 139–40).[2]

Not too surprisingly, persons who respond to placebos tend characteristically to depend upon others and accept them in their conventional roles; perhaps for this reason they are sometimes better

[1] In a double-blind study, neither the physicians administering pills nor the patients receiving them know who is getting placebos and who is getting active medication.

[2] One could argue that placebos were employed in some of the biblical healing miracles: Naaman the leper was told by Elisha to go wash in the Jordan and he would be clean (2 Kings 5:10–14); and Jesus anointed the eyes of a man blind from birth with a clay made of dirt and spittle (John 9:1–7).

able than nonresponders to adjust to the world. Surprisingly, though, persons do not appear to react *consistently* to placebos under all circumstances: response seems to depend on a fairly specific interaction of the patient's state and the setting in which the placebo is used. One of the crucial factors is the healer's belief in the effectiveness of his procedures: doubts on his part are easily communicated nonverbally and subvert the entire process (Fish 1973, 7; Frank 1974, 146–49). At some level, placebo healing involves trust in authority.

Faith Healing

The next step in achieving health without employing standard medical means is to remove all physical procedures and to rely simply on "faith healing." While the gospel accounts, for example, often depict Jesus as requiring some activity on the part of the persons healed, at other times he simply touched or spoke to them and talked as if faith or belief itself was the key to healing. Here the authority that the supplicant must trust is religious rather than medical.[3]

We need not trace the history of faith healing (and its counterpart, "voodoo death," a phenomenon firmly attested, for example, in Frank 1974, 51–53; Richards 1974, 86) through primitive culture, the early church, and modern Christian Scientist and spiritist practitioners; we simply note that belief in it persists among the educated and uneducated alike.[4] The documents produced by the early church fathers, for instance, were written by educated men at a time when pagan superstition was being explicitly rejected. These documents, unlike the New Testament itself, were contemporaneous with the miraculous events of healing they reported and hence were open to scrutiny (Frost 1954).

We have no reason for wholesale incredulity here. Rather, in view of what I have just said about biofeedback and placebos, plus the high probability of psychosomatic factors in many ailments, we have every reason for at least a limited acceptance of the phenomena. Few who have watched healers at work would deny that many persons at the very least experience a subjective reduction of symptoms, which in itself is

[3] Note Jesus' comments "according to your faith be it done to you" (Matt. 9:29) and "your faith has made you well" (Mark 10:52). In context, of course, the people believed that *Jesus* could heal; they did not believe in belief per se. Many Christians object to the term "faith healing" as inappropriate to what takes place. We shall not join that debate here. Later groups and persons have used various techniques to enhance involvement and belief; similarly, medical rituals tend to inspire confidence in the procedures to be applied. Christian Scientists enjoin *disbelief* in the ailment (or belief in health), and many occult groups emphasize elaborate rituals.

[4] Persistence itself does not guarantee validity for a belief. Intermittently reinforced behaviors, whether useful or not, are notoriously hard to extinguish; and almost no one denies that occasional dramatic healings have had some correlation with faith-healing practices.

significant. When Kathryn Kuhlman was once criticized for curing only psychosomatic illnesses, she reportedly responded, "Praise God; I understand those are the hardest to cure!"

Indeed, those who give purely subjective factors—belief, expectancy, and the like—primary importance in faith healing can cite striking evidence for their view. For instance, excepting the original cures, those who live near Lourdes have not been healed there (Frank 1974). Moreover, experiments have been done in which patients have recovered or had striking relief from symptoms at the precise time when they *believed* a healer was at work in their behalf, although one actually was not (Frank 1974, 74; cf. LeShan 1974). Extraordinary expectancy *can* achieve what the regular course of nature and modern medical treatment sometimes do not.

Hypnotism

Perhaps the most immediately dramatic results of suggestion or autosuggestion can be seen in the phenomenon known as "hypnotism." It has been employed to stop the pain of everything from cigarette burns to surgery to childbirth, to enhance performance (provided basic capacity exists), to promote healing of specified lesions, as well as to facilitate ecstatic phenomena or altered states of consciousness, automatic writing, altered time sense, and "regression." Does "hypnotic suggestion" produce a trancelike state wherein all of these unusual phenomena may occur?

Unfortunately, no phenomena or physiological signs uniquely identify the hypnotic state; there is no test for hypnosis. People often dislike admitting that they have been hypnotized and regularly rationalize their seemingly automatic following of a posthypnotic suggestion: they apparently feel as if they can do what they want, but they do not want to disobey. Furthermore, expectations of the nature of hypnosis tend to produce the expected effects, whether those effects are amnesia or convulsions. The hypnotist's belief in his powers is important to hypnotic induction, but induction is essentially easy if the subject's attention can be captured. The resistant may be as good subjects as the compliant, provided that they are paying attention. People can hypnotize themselves if they will suspend their judgment, focus their attention, and engage in visualization (Ferguson 1975; Wolberg 1972; the process sounds similar to some mystical techniques!). The barriers around what is conceived to be possible must be taken down, and then the suggestion of another person or one's own visualization may lead to phenomena that were not previously possible.

*　*　*

Inquirer: If I do say so myself, I'm rather impressed with what the old mind can do! It looks as if what we "put our minds to" makes all the difference!

Stranger: Humph!

Inquirer: What do you mean, "humph"? Looking at all of these things was your idea in the first place!

Stranger: You mean, you responded to my *suggestion?*

Inquirer: Well . . . yes; I guess so.

Stranger: Precisely. It's fine to feel all independent about what "mind" can do, but how pliable it is when it comes to suggestion! Take hypnosis, for example. Are you aware that just giving instructions that properly motivate people can produce responses to suggestions just about as effectively as any hypnosis hocus-pocus?[5]

Inquirer: But they have to pay attention first, either way.

Stranger: In response to another suggestion? But let's not go around in circles. My main interest at present is to drive home the point that, however much you dignify what you might want to call mental acts, they don't get you much farther than material ones do. Plug a suggestion into a mind and you get an altered state of consciousness. Plug a drug into a brain and you get—an altered state of consciousness. They look a lot alike. And frankly, the drugs are generally more economical.

Inquirer: I get the feeling something's slipping by me.

Stranger: You and your feelings!

Inquirer: Isn't it true, for instance, that we can't really know how healing works, and that sometimes people seem to die or recover for no particular reason, but just as if they'd decided to?

Stranger: I never said that altering one's "state of consciousness" (that is, one's brain state)—however subtly and by whatever sort of verbal stimulus from one's own head or someone else's—wouldn't change one's bodily state overall; I'm arguing precisely that it does. People have even proposed that all medical therapy is 90 percent placebo. My point is that, however you label what's happening, it's all part of one natural process.

Inquirer: What do you mean by "natural"?

[5]Barber 1969; cf. Fish 1973.

Stranger: Simply that there are certain rules that can't be broken, whether we know just how they work or not. I grant that it's silly to talk about nature without including persons as a part of it; but let's not have them trying to climb outside of nature, either. Of course, getting people to expect or to want to do something creates possibilities that didn't exist otherwise, just as putting gas in a car creates some possibilities that didn't exist with the tank empty. Pumping gas into a tank doesn't say anything new about the nature of a given car that we can't know from how the car is put together. Likewise, pumping suggestions into brains simply shows the nature of brains.

Inquirer: I'm not quite persuaded. I guess my real feeling is not just enthusiasm for "mind" as such but the sense that it can be in touch with something beyond the strict uniformities of nature. I've already made the point that it can initiate as well as respond, whatever you keep saying about suggestion; but also it seems to tap into something that sometimes violates predictable uniformities. For instance, I've read that "the evidence that an occasional cure of advanced organic disease does occur at Lourdes is as strong as that for any other phenomenon accepted as true."[6]

Stranger: Surely, but it is just as true that "inexplicable cures of serious organic disease occur in everyday medical practice"[7] without even suggestion being applied. With the millions of people who have come to Lourdes, a few such cases are not improbable. Apart from these few spontaneous cures, the only established thing your fine "mind" can do is speed up or slow down an ordinary healing process or remove some symptoms. Let me emphasize the fact that people don't regrow amputated limbs. Rarely is the origin of symptoms touched. One clinical psychiatrist searched for twenty years without finding a single case in which an organic condition was entirely cured simply by the work of a healer.[8]

* * *

[6] Frank 1974, 69.
[7] Ibid., 71.
[8] Rose 1971, 175; see also p. 128. Of interest, however, is the comment made in the author's presence by a physician, a professor emeritus at a respected medical school, that he frequently sees definite, organic symptoms in terminal patients, such as a cancerous intestinal blockage, completely removed following prayer. The patient is sent home free from discomfort but often dies, painlessly, fairly soon afterward—sooner than would otherwise have been expected. This doctor sometimes counsels relatives not to have him pray if they cannot handle losing the patient quickly. In cases of successful prayer, is the patient exhausted, though made comfortable, by heroic rallying of some untapped recuperative power—or what?

AGAINST REDUCTIONISM:
PROBLEMS WITH A NATURALISTIC MODEL

A large proportion of the evidence for faith healing fits the model of "suggestion accelerating the natural, plus a few spontaneous cures." Blood pressure rises and falls, hearts beat faster or slower, wounds heal, diseases are cured, psychosomatic ailments persist under stress or are relieved when pressures decrease and needs are met. That essentially natural processes can be altered by will or belief or in response to suggestion is interesting—even impressive—and possibly helpful. It certainly suggests that the course of biological events is not inexorable and that what we think actually makes a difference. It does not help us answer the question of whether human mind or belief or a mysterious "something else" can add any fundamentally new potential to "nature" (Frank 1974, 110).

Scripture, though, speaks of the healing of a man born blind (John 9). Does it speak nonsense? On the basis of that question George Bernard Shaw made his well-known comment that he considered Lourdes a blasphemous place: not a single wooden leg or glass eye or even a toupee is to be found among the wheelchairs and crutches kept as mementos of those who walked away healed (noted in Smith 1975, 19).

Awkward Evidence

Considering the large number of cases that fit the naturalistic model, we may find it very tempting to attribute those that do not to faulty reporting or ignorance of some important organic variable. One could argue, for example, that stories about early Christian martyrs' feeling no pain and experiencing immediate healing of torture wounds fit the model, depending on the nature of the wounds. Should we then discount the portions of the stories that describe their surviving ordinarily effective means of execution? Perhaps these anomalies are merely the result of inflamed imagination, natural under the circumstances (see Frost 1954, 347).

What, then, about modern heart-attack patients (one such known to the author) who have evidence from clinical tests of sudden, dramatic reversal-to-normal of a damaged heart following a healing service? Should we attribute the change to the fact that the patient did not depend on a healer alone but also followed a prescribed dietary regimen? What about the lengthening of a short leg? What about complete restoration of a disintegrated spinal disc (Hill 1974)? "Nature," acting either spontaneously or slowly, is not noted for this sort of

38

cure. "Suggestion" seems to have added something besides enthusiasm to the process.[9]

Furthermore, healing occurs not only when the patient manifests high expectations and believing compliance or when the healer communicates belief in what he is doing. In the Scriptures, healing is sometimes credited to the faith of someone other than the patient (Mark 2:3–5; John 4:49–52), and unbelievers may be asked to leave, even when the patient is dead and presumably not suggestible (Mark 5:39–42). In the incident in John 4, the healing was performed at a distance, scarcely the best way to arouse a patient's precisely timed expectation.

The significance of the healer's faith has been suggested by numerous modern reports of such persons' positive effects on barley seeds and growing plants (usually not credited with suggestibility) and animals (usually not credited with a concept of disease, although animals respond best when they are not agitated but in some sense receptive; Grad 1970; Haynes 1961; Moss 1974). The role of the healer may be even more evident when healing of a human is done at a distance, particularly when the person has no idea that a healer is at work (see Hill 1974, 173–77; LeShan 1974, 122; Marshall 1974, 159–64). Reports of such phenomena must obviously be taken cautiously, however credible the reporter; but the recurrence of such reports provides, at the very least, food for thought. A parallel phenomenon that may lend credibility to these distant healings occurs in hypnotism. Not only have hypnotized subjects reportedly been awakened from trance at a distance, but apparently they have even been made to fall down from a distance (Koestler 1973, 16). While suggestion of a sort is being used in all of these cases, it is not being received through anything we consider to be normal channels; and furthermore, it is not being accepted or rejected by any ordinary process of focusing attention or failing to attend.

We are dealing now, not with the question of mind as it relates to consciousness, "knowing," and the structuring of experience, but rather, to speak crassly, with the question of the mind's effects in and on the physical world. It evidently can in some sense produce or channel production of physical effects. What, then, is the source of its energy? Does it have energy of its own? If so, is it an energy of the same or of a different sort of magnitude than energy in the physical world? Or does it pervade the physical world at some imperceptible level?

---

[9]LeShan (1974) argues for at least five different types of healing, only one of which includes cures not possible by the body's normal mechanisms of repair.

The Dualist Hypothesis

Some of the greatest names in brain research have concluded that, of the two unlikely alternatives that brain action explains mind or that we must postulate two fundamental elements, the latter is the more acceptable. "Mental phenomena on examination do not seem amenable to understanding under physics and chemistry. I have therefore to think of the brain as an organ of liaison between energy and mind, but not as a converter of energy into mind or vice versa" (Sherrington, quoted in LeShan 1974, 247). In Penfield's words,

> For myself, after a professional lifetime spent in trying to discover how the brain accounts for the mind, it comes as a surprise now to discover, during this final examination of the evidence, that the dualist hypothesis seems the more reasonable of the two possible explanations. (Penfield 1975, 85; cf. Eccles 1953)

These men are saying—and Penfield says it explicitly in comparing the mind's relationship to the brain with that of the relationship of a computer programmer to a computer—that "the mind must have a supply of energy available to it for independent action"; it is "a distinct and different essence" (Penfield 1975, 46, 62).

None of these men is suggesting, however, that minds can operate apart from brains or that, once programed, the brain cannot provide for the carrying out of all sorts of automatic behavioral sequences on its own. Eccles (1953, 258), for instance, tries to show the structure of the brain to be such that its activity could be altered by very tiny forces, such as those created if "will" operated in such a way as to create a "field of influence."[10] The theory apparently assumes that "mind" is strictly an upper-story affair, serving to initiate basically mechanistic activity.

Such a hypothesis works rather well for any phenomenon resulting, as discussed above, from the setting off, intensifying, or accelerating of natural processes. Of course, for accelerations and intensifications to take place, we have to assume enough "mind influence" that physical mechanisms keep working when they would normally quit; but to affirm such a possibility is perhaps not overly difficult when we consider feats done under hypnosis or the fact that relatively frail women have been known to lift a car when a loved one was caught beneath it. Our bodies are capable of a great deal more than we normally acknowledge, given enough "motivation."

It might seem that, once we have taken the step of acknowledging that our mind can, by means of our brain, influence our own body, it

---

[10]Thus "mind influence," or "will," is itself given a patterned, spatiotemporal character. This sort of hypothesis hence covertly assumes a negative answer to the fundamental question of whether there can be energy without some sort of structure (see Penfield 1975, 79).

would not be too difficult to suppose that its "field of influence" could extend beyond our own body—to plants, animals, or other brains (or minds?). We will look at this problem more closely in the next chapter. However, we must note now the likelihood that proposing such an extension of the field of influence introduces a qualitative and not just a quantitative change in the theory.

That is, Eccles considers relatively minute and circumscribed influences whose "size" is appropriate to the size of the effect. As soon as we go beyond a single brain and mind to speak of an impact of mind on the outside world, we have said something not just about the intricacies of the brain but about world-stuff generally: namely, that something about it can both transmit and be affected by mind-stuff.[11] Let us make no mistake: we do not perceive the intricate structures of human brains in barley seeds! Thus, we must postulate either a receptive mechanism of a different sort or else an energy force, or some analogue to an energy force, very significantly larger than we have been suggesting. As we will see most clearly in looking at psychokinesis, the magnitude of energy that we can conceive of the mind's generating by means of, say, the electrical potential of the brain is disproportionately smaller by far than the effects produced. We do not currently know of a source or type of energy that can do what mind seems to be able to do.

Most problematic of all, of course—and most disproportionate to known physical energies—is the effecting of changes that known physical processes do not produce on their own. The so-called miracles most clearly exemplify such changes and give a tantalizing glimpse of a world in which, indeed, "all things are possible to him who believes" (Mark 9:23), wherein, even, "Whoever says to this mountain, 'Be taken up and cast into the sea,' and does not doubt in his heart, but believes that what he says will come to pass, it will be done for him" (Mark 11:23). In this world, a person's belief affects more than just the believer.

---

[11] Whether, when speaking of persons, we believe "suggestion from a distance" to work directly on the brain of another or on it secondarily through the other's mind is of interest; but even if we choose the second option, the possibility of the transmission of the suggestion must figure in our view of the world.

3

Paranormal Phenomena

Inquirer: I keep getting reminded—in all of our discussions, but especially now that we're talking about the inexplicable—of that whole area of investigation you so unceremoniously dismissed during our second conversation. I agree that psi phenomena don't seem very likely—maybe that's why they're so fascinating. Besides, you know what Kant said: "Philosophy is often much embarrassed when she encounters certain facts which she dare not doubt yet will not believe for fear of ridicule."[1]

Stranger: All right, so you can name-drop. Why don't you look at the facts, then?

Inquirer: But I thought you said it was a waste of time and money.

Stranger: I did. I think the scientists are a long way from considering the ideas *I* have about the majority of those phenomena. Still, as I've told you a thousand times, I'm a pragmatist. You can get value from food without knowing the first thing about digestion; scientists make use of gravity without knowing how it works; doubtless you can get into psi without understanding it.

Inquirer: Wait a minute. I didn't exactly say I wanted to "get into" it. I just want to look at the various phenomena.

Stranger: *You* were the one who said that one can't very well evaluate anything strictly from the outside. But then, directing your precious "attention" to it is at least a first step—and perhaps an irreversible one, if it's true, as our friend Penfield says[2] that everything to which we attend is recorded permanently on our brain. So do as you like.

Inquirer: I'm a little confused. First you act as if these strange happenings don't occur; then you talk vaguely of "your ideas" about them; then you talk of "pragmatism," as if my interest weren't scientific but I just expected to get something out of my exploration.

[1] Quoted in Heywood 1961, 41.
[2] 1975, 74–75.

43

Stranger: Of course; and the last point is the important one. Psychologists assume that behavior is motivated, however they conceive of motivation; and they usually infer the motive from the behavior. Your motives may be a bit opaque to me at the moment; but the further you go, the more I'll know about them—and you. So, as I said before, do as you like.

Inquirer: I think I'd like to be as objective as possible.

Stranger: My, you're defensive. *I* never impugned objectivity. Are you afraid your ghosties and ghoulies might sneak up on you? But do whatever you like.

* * *

PSI PHENOMENA

In the previous chapter we left unanswered the question whether "mind" could possibly exchange influence not only with the particular brain with which it is associated (and thence the body governed by that brain) but also with *other* minds or bodies. If, when one asks that question, one intends to exclude the use of ordinary sensory channels and the instruments we use to extend those channels, one enters the realm of what are commonly called parapsychological, or psi, phenomena.

The evidence adduced to support the reality of psi phenomena is massive and varied. It ranges from Rhine's painstaking experiments in telepathy and clairvoyance, which yield statistical evidence so impressive that some suggest that one would have to throw out the whole science of statistics before one could discount his data, to the déjà vu experiences that have happened to most of us or to the rather common event of having a friend or relative who has sensed, at the precise moment of some traumatic event, that a distant loved one was in danger. The phenomena may be physical as well as mental, as in poltergeist occurrences, psychokinesis (PK), levitation, and healings of people, animals, or plants. Other events such as ghosts, hauntings, and apparent communications are somehow connected to the dead.

Many psi experiences occur spontaneously. Some have been studied in experimental settings. Others are deliberately sought or induced, as in a mediumistic séance. I do not debate here the "validity" of some or all of the phenomena described.[3] Precisely *what* is occurring may easily

[3]The interested reader may refer to the sources cited and to their bibliographies for extensive case histories. Koestler (1973, 31–35), for example, argues strongly for the established personal and professional integrity of a large number of investigators of

be questioned or debated in any given instance. My point is simply that *something* not fitting our usual view of things does seem, at least sometimes, to be going on.

ESP and Associated Phenomena

The term "ESP" usually refers to telepathy and clairvoyance, though it can also be applied in some sense to pre- and retrocognition. As I have indicated, telepathy and clairvoyance appear—at least to those who accept Rhine's laboratory work with playing cards—to be statistically well established. (The former term refers to information transfer between minds; the latter, to "seeing" by means other than the normal perceptual processes. One can speak also of clairaudience and clairsentience.) For those who doubt the significance of evidence derived from Rhine's limited set of symbols, experimenters have designed means of studying telepathy with far more complex stimuli. In one such experiment an individual is directed to concentrate on a visual stimulus such as a drawing or picture, while a second subject sleeps in a distant room. When the latter begins to dream, as determined by EEG and rapid eye movements, he is awakened and asked to report the dream. On rare occasions the dream will correspond in highly significant detail to the stimulus that the other person was attempting to "send" (LeShan 1974, 277–83; Smith 1975, 334–35).

In another novel procedure, two susceptible subjects hypnotized each other, and, while they were in deep trance, produced shared experiences in a common dream world for which there were no external verbal stimuli. In trance the experiences of mutual activity and communication were potent and self-validating: an intense psychological intimacy was almost "forced," as if the subjects' identities were merging or fusing, and the subjects reported feelings of passing through each other. In posthypnotic discussions what they each had thought to be an individual fantasy threatened to become real when it was confirmed by the other. These postexperimental discoveries were unnerving enough (perhaps partly because they threatened the subjects' individual identities) that the experiments were discontinued (Tart 1969).[4] In other experiments involving hypnosis, subjects have even been known to taste something that the hypnotist ate (Moss 1974).

Distance affects ESP little, if at all. Mother and young child have a continuity of experience, even when separated, that can be demon-

psi. I have attempted to avoid merely sensational, popular reports. I grant, however, that the data are inherently rather sensational and prone to distortion; nor can one absolutely guarantee—in any endeavor, but especially in those in which not all the data are readily replicable—accurate, unbiased reporting.

[4]"Direct hits" in some of the experiments involving "sending" of pictures also produced intense anxiety in the receiver (Smith 1975, 335).

strated by monitoring and comparing their physiological reactions. This continuity gradually declines, usually as the child learns to read, an activity that involves controlling and directing thought (Haynes 1961, 111). A similar physiological mutuality occurs between other individuals or even animals with close emotional or biological ties, such as newlyweds or identical twins or a dog and its master: a stimulus to one will affect both (Ferguson 1975, 348–94). One rather grisly experiment demonstrated pronounced EEG changes in a female rabbit in a laboratory, corresponding with the times at which her babies were killed one by one in a distant submarine (Ferguson 1975, 346). Even more astounding, perhaps, is the "reaction" of wired-up plants to the killing of shrimp in a distant room. The plants also react if a person who has "murdered" one of their number enters the room but do not respond when some other individual enters (Karlins and Andrews 1972).

More unsettling yet, ESP appears not to be affected by time. While the experiments of the preceding paragraph purport to show some unknown linkage between concurrent events, considerable data indicate that some messages "arrive" before they are "sent." In one card-guessing experiment the subject significantly often (at odds of billions to one) guessed, not the card turned up, but the *following* card. Equally significant have been the efforts of subjects to guess which colored lamp would next light up, an event that was randomly determined by radioactive particle emission (Koestler 1973, 40–41, 44). Animals have demonstrated the same ability in predicting which half of a box would discharge an electric shock (Ferguson 1975, 353).

Again, the stimulus situations do not have to be simple. Researchers found that a man with a history of precognitive experiences could dream features of an elaborately and randomly contrived event that was neither planned nor carried out until the following day and was engineered through a series of "blind" operations (Ferguson 1975, 353–54). Could similar occurrences in dreams produce the eerie déjà vu sensation that so many persons experience?

The relation of these imprecise but nonetheless striking phenomena to quite specific "prophetic" predictions of future events is unclear, though it would certainly seem possible that they share a common mechanism or source. Anecdotal evidence abounds for persons' having a premonition of a plane crash or other disastrous event and successfully avoiding, or warning a loved one to avoid, what turned out to be a genuine calamity. (The logical problem here is indeed thorny. If something can be predicted at all, apart from ordinary analysis or speculation, it must in some meaningful sense be determined ahead of time. But if one can, by an act of the will in response to a vague premonition, withdraw oneself from the event, that determinism would appear not to be absolute. What, though, does it mean to speak of a nonabsolute but nonetheless real determinism? For the contribution of speculative physics, see Gribbin 1984, especially chapter 11.)

If we can break the time barrier in one direction, there would seem to be no theoretical reason why it might not be broken in the other. We would then have a framework for dealing with some of the complex knowledge of past events for which the hypothesis of reincarnation is popularly invoked (cf. the work of Prof. Ian Stevenson, reported in Slagle 1974). Those supposedly reincarnated seem to have very detailed knowledge of someone who is long deceased. This knowledge, however, is limited to events affecting only that one person, which is problematic if such individuals simply have an ability to "see" backward in time. (Does the knowledge come from some inexplicable "connection" of their mind with another, earlier, mind?)

Another means of being in a place or time where one physically is not is the so-called out-of-the-body experience, or astral projection, belief in which is based on the premise that persons have an "astral" body as well as a physical body. (An astral body is a ghostlike double of the physical body that can leave the latter.) An out-of-the-body experience may occur spontaneously when a person, especially one who is ill or distressed, is lying in bed and suddenly becomes aware that "he" is hovering somewhere above his body and can clearly see it below him. Others report that they have willfully projected themselves to another time and place where they have never been, have had experiences in that world, and have "brought back" heretofore unknown and later-confirmed data.

Such experiences are surely open to more credible explanations than that an individual somehow left his physical body. Some cases, though, are not easily dispensed with. A man at sea, for example, dreamed his wife, who was back at home, visited him in his stateroom on a ship—an ordinary dream. His roommate, however, was awake and observed the visit. And his wife at home correctly described the stateroom (Moss 1974). This episode perhaps involves a shared telepathic and clairvoyant experience, but even so, the effects are the same as if an actual out-of-the-body journey had occurred. Choice of explanations must thus be made on aesthetic or strictly presuppositional grounds. One could just as well argue that clairvoyance and telepathy involve an out-of-the-body experience as the reverse. Once the sensory limits of knowing are transcended, there may not be any difference.

Physical Psi

If the possibility that knowledge and perceptions can be transmitted and received apart from normal sensory channels proves unsettling, more unsettling yet is the possibility that physical effects can be produced apart from ordinary physical means. We have in one sense broached this subject already, for many would call instances of faith healing manifestations of psi.[5] At this point, though, we shall concentrate more specifically on directly observable events.

Let us begin with psychokinesis (PK). In the scientific arena, Rhine has obtained statistically significant results with attempts to influence the fall of mechanically thrown dice. In the popular arena, persons such as Uri Geller, Mme. Kulangina, and others reportedly bend forks or nails and move objects at a distance.

Such abilities are disputed and are difficult to test precisely because psychic abilities cannot reliably be called upon at will. Hence, it is easy to make accusations of fraud. When Geller was tested at Stanford Research Institute, he bent no forks—though he did generate a magnetic field, affect the roll of dice, and make numerous telepathic hits. When Geller was tested by physicist John Hasted and his coworkers, he reportedly bent a metal disk, a key, and a knife in the lab, and many striking poltergeist phenomena accompanied both the lab work and a visit to Hasted's home. Another physicist remarked, "He cheats, he cheats a lot, and also he's real" (Smith 1975, 338–39; see also Bannister 1976, 5, a source with obviously lower credibility).

Results such as bent knives may be achieved apart from normal physical means, but, apparently, not usually without physical concomitants on the part of the psychic. Persons have reported a subjective feeling like an electric current when PK will be possible and are physically exhausted by the effort required: Mme. Kulangina often suffers a headache and a five-pound loss of weight (Moss 1974). Similar effects are suffered by the Russian Mikhailova, although another Russian, Vinogravada, is reportedly relaxed (Ferguson 1975, 345).[6]

It is somewhat doubtful whether these manifestations of PK are directly comparable to the proven ability of amplified brain waves, at one's "will," to trigger a TV switch (Moss 1974, 17). While the application of the will is evident in both instances—and highly important—it is difficult to identify directly the nature of the energy in the first case with its more obvious source in the second (although we certainly do not fully understand electricity). Also, the magnitudes of energy required differ greatly.

Psychokinesis as usually defined involves some sort of concentrated intentional effort. The same does not hold for all physical psi. One of its most unsettling spontaneous manifestations is the so-called poltergeist, or noisy ghost. Poltergeist effects include a whole range of bizarre happenings, usually but not always more annoying than harmful. Most

[5]Others would explain the phenomena in terms of telepathic suggestion. Still others refuse all such categories. We will not pursue the matter further here.

[6]Stress is also common to physical mediumship. For an account of phenomena by a former medium, see Gasson 1966, 128–32.

common are apparently spontaneous movements of untouched objects in a manner that is often inconsistent with the laws of physics. Descriptions of such occurrences are remarkably similar in different situations and are difficult to discount unless we credit mass hallucinations. Rarer, though well-attested, are fire raising and traction, levitation, biting, wounding, or stigmatization of the human body (Owen 1964).

A. R. G. Owen (1964), who has made perhaps one of the most extensive and careful investigations of poltergeist activity, concludes that it usually has no features requiring intervention of an entity distinct from the poltergeist medium—the person without whose presence the phenomena do not occur, most frequently, in this case, a pubescent girl—though there may be occasional indications of possible outside influence.[7] Animals are *not* centers of poltergeist activity, and the magnitude of the effects is within the range of those produceable by an unaided adult man.

Intense conflicts, psychological crises, or family problems involving the person who is the focus of the poltergeist activity usually exist, suggesting that some form of emotional energy is involved (Haynes 1961; Koestler 1973; Richards 1974). In the life of St. John Vianney, poltergeist outbreaks seemed to occur almost as a signal that some notorious evildoer was going to repent and come to confession—had he established such a rapport with the sinner that he experienced the emotional struggles of the sinner through these phenomena (Haynes 1961, 197; cf. Cristiani 1962)? In general, sleep inhibits the phenomena; hypnosis may halt or modify them. They are unrelated to epilepsy or physical or mental defect in the focal person, but anxiety or need for attention appears to contribute. Still, whatever energy is generated has no known mode of action. Thus, we may at least deduce the existence of physical forces not contemplated within present scientific paradigms. Furthermore, the apparent connection of the phenomena with psychological factors in the medium suggests some sort of "psychic" or "psychophysical" mechanism at work (Owen 1964, 432).

A final manifestation that many would include in the category of physical psi is levitation. While spontaneous poltergeist occurrences are associated with rather negative psychological states, the levitations reported by Christian and Eastern mystics are accompanied by equally strong feelings of rapture and ecstasy.[8] Direct pursuit of other levels of consciousness may also suffice (see Martin 1976, 363). When being sought, levitation is said to require the presence of at least one "strong

[7] For a contrary opinion, see Montgomery 1975, 33–34.
[8] See Underhill 1961, 376–77 and p. 377, n. 4, for a cautious statement of the subjective versus the objective nature of levitation. See also Montgomery 1975, 56–57.

psychic," but an experimental approximation can be achieved if four persons make rhythmic movements and chant some phrases in unison: they can then lift a person using only the backs of two fingers each, expending little energy (Moss 1974, 132). Again it would appear that something belonging to the general category "psychophysical" is occurring.

Hauntings

I mention only briefly the whole area of ghosts and hauntings, and then only spontaneous occurrences, for to go into sought-out contacts is to enter quite explicitly the realm of spiritism, which is beyond the scope of this chapter.[9] Apparitions, uncanny sensations, and strange happenings seemingly linked to specific places are common enough that "ghost tours"—trips planned especially around favorite "haunts"—have been arranged to attract devotees of such phenomena. If the apparitions are mere hallucination, they are a strangely public one, for they are frequently seen by more than one person and also by animals (Moss 1974). In one fascinating case in England, motorists commonly saw a monk crossing the road. After the road was lowered, the monk was seen floating above it, as if some sort of record were definitely and spatially attached to the place where the road used to be. Some suggest that such ghosts are "impersonal traces of earlier personal action," usually either habitual or accompanied by violent emotion (Richards 1974, 195). In other instances, their presence seems more active and may affect electricity, telephones, light bulbs, and film (Moss 1974, 318); or there may be other types of poltergeist activity.

Data on "real ghosts" have been gathered most carefully by Myers and fall into the following categories of experience: ordinary death coincidences, when a phantasm appears to a living person at the moment of death;[10] apparitions seen long after death (of a person whose death was unknown to the percipient), usually wearing the clothes in which they died; apparitions conveying accurate information unknown to the percipient and often appearing in a form different from when they were

---

[9] Both Christian and non-Christian authors have proposed the hypothesis that persons deeply attached to "things" in this world may be unable fully to leave it. They may then "come back" or "stick around" and carry out unfinished business through ritualistic behaviors (LeShan 1974; Richards 1974). Of course, it may be difficult to determine beforehand what constitutes "too much" attachment; and a rather antimaterial metaphysic is implicit in the hypothesis. See also Montgomery 1975, 131–33, for a "multilevel explanatory scheme" for ghosts.

[10] An occurrence of this type happened to the author's mother, though not in strictly visible form. While she was in the yard one day in Pasadena, she was very strongly conscious of the presence of an old friend in New York, of whom she had not thought in many months. She asked jokingly, "How's your beautiful blond hair?" and received the reply, "It isn't any more." She was puzzled by the response, but put it out of her mind. Soon she learned that that day, at about that hour, her friend had died.

known by him (e.g., with a beard); and apparitions of those not known to the percipient but subsequently identified. Myers was persuaded that genuine activity and initiative on the part of the apparition—as in giving information—are involved (Murphy 1970). Usually these ghosts experienced a violent death. Only occasionally do they appear for the benefit of the living.

Facilitators of the Phenomena

Psi phenomena have a bad name in the scientific community partially because they cannot be produced or repeated at will under properly controlled conditions.[11] Nonetheless, certain generally identifiable conditions do increase the *likelihood* of their occurrence. Altered states of consciousness, for example (whether trance, drug, or mystical), contribute markedly. Another factor relates to some unknown quality of persons and even objects. On the human side, some persons show particular abilities in sending or receiving telepathic messages; and "psychic giftedness" tends to run in families (Haynes 1961, 71–72). On the nonhuman side, clairvoyance studies seem to suggest that some target objects, apparently identical to others, produce higher ESP scores in percipients, as if they either had some "psychical" property or else were reflecting something "sent" by the clairvoyant.[12]

However, several other factors seem to unite the experiences of psychics and of persons who have induced ASCs with the experiences of those who report spontaneous occurrences of psi phenomena. For one thing, powerful, self-transcending emotions appear always to be a factor in spontaneous ESP experiences; and in the large majority of cases, the emotions are negative—associated with violence, death, and the like (see Koestler 1973, 128; Moss 1974, 220). Even in Gilbert Murray's experiments in guessing subjects that others, in another room, contrived, he reported that he generally received more an emotional quality or atmosphere than a piece of information; and the tone was usually horrible, grotesque, or anxious, though occasionally delightful or abstract (Heywood 1961, 139; Koestler 1973, 37).[13] He had no success with cards, numbers, or uninteresting subjects. Similarly, for most

[11] See Koestler 1973, 293. However, it has been found that feedback regarding one's performance in laboratory ESP tasks will improve it in 30 percent of the cases (Karlins and Andrews 1972), at least suggesting parallels to biofeedback, in which doing one-knows-not-what produces measurable physical changes. It is not clear, though, whether feedback turns something "on" or "off"—whether one's brain (or whatever) starts or stops doing something.

[12] Obviously, we do not know what properties are detectable by clairvoyance or if, perhaps, some process can *destroy* clairvoyant detectability (Tart 1973a).

[13] With regard to telepathy, LeShan (1974, 184, n. 16) says that it appears that information about which one feels ashamed or guilty or really wishes to keep secret is not transmitted. Cases in which such information does seem to be revealed will be mentioned later.

laboratory subjects, ESP results decline with practice: the people get bored. On the other hand, so-called sensitives have a reputation for being highly emotional rather than rational and for being erratic, sometimes of hysterical personality style, neurotic, or even psychotic (Koestler 1973, 129, 21; Moss 1974, 184). Such a personality style may also "conceal" genuine ESP by rendering it suspect (Heywood 1961).[14]

A second factor, overlapping the first, is an affectional and/or biological tie between the parties involved. ESP is often associated with a frustrated attachment between individuals, as if the very intensity of the desire to communicate opened channels normally closed (Heywood 1961, 57; cf. Haynes 1961). As we have seen, there may be a joint physiological reactivity, even without any focal desire or intent to communicate.

Third, and intriguingly, psi activity and sexual activity seem to be somehow related. Sexual desire and menses may disappear when a sensitive's psychic powers are at their height (Haynes 1961). Contemplatives of all religions—who fairly consistently develop psi capacities—typically emphasize celibacy. Scripture directs a husband and wife not to deny themselves to each other "except perhaps by agreement for a season, that [they] may devote [themselves] to prayer" (1 Cor. 7:5). And I have already spoken of the frequent correspondence of poltergeist activity with *pubescence* in young girls. Sexual energy appears to have a peculiar linkage to the paranormal psi forces.[15]

Fourth, belief is a factor. In laboratory and classroom experiments students have been asked whether they believed in ESP and then were asked to guess the order in which some cards will fall when shuffled the next day. "Believers" do better. Other experiments have shown that "unbelievers" may do significantly *less* well than chance (LeShan 1973; Koestler 1973, 22n.). While hostility and doubt quench the phenomena, some assert that precisely what one believes is not as important as "faith of some kind in something" (Heywood 1961, 112). Those engaging publicly in PK or ESP testify consistently that the presence of skeptics

---

[14]We may recall that powerful emotions are also important in poltergeist cases, as if distress or conflict was finding concrete, physical expression. If one has unsought and undesirable ESP experiences, a good dose of Thorazine (medication commonly used to treat psychosis) can sometimes knock them out. A man brought to Stanford Research Institute "hearing neighbors talking about him" turned out to be all too accurate; he also tested brilliantly on standard clairvoyance tasks. The medication "cured" him (Smith 1975, 338).

[15]In referring to 1 Cor. 7:5, I do not identify prayer and psi activity but merely suggest a profound effect of our sexuality upon that which transcends the merely physical. Not only may abstention or budding sexual powers stimulate psi; orgy may, as well (Haynes 1961). In the latter instance we may be dealing with both powerful emotion and the suspension of critical faculties (discussed below) rather than with sexual energy per se, which appears to facilitate psi when *not* expressed. As we saw in chapter 1, insufficient and excessive stimulation may have parallel effects.

makes their task more difficult (Karlins and Andrews 1972; Smith 1975). On the other hand, an encouraging presence is facilitative, even if the person directly involved in an ESP experiment is using mechanical means to send signals unknown to him: again, as in the discussion of healing, we see that "belief" turns into a highly complex variable (Heywood 1961, 149; see Frank 1974, 131).

Finally, a certain passivity on the part of the percipient appears to contribute by leading to a suspension of critical faculties, perhaps in some sense a dissolution of self boundaries (Ferguson 1975, 102; cf. Ludwig, 1969). Sometimes, at least, verbal thinking seems to reduce psi, while persons having an out-of-the-body experience may show decreased left-hemisphere brain activity on an EEG (Heywood 1961; Krippner 1975, 263).[16] Members of Mensa do less well than chance on ESP tests (Koestler 1973, 21–22)—due to disbelief or to highly rational minds? Notice, too, that the facilitating features mentioned in this section all by-pass or supersede critical rationality. So do the induced altered states of consciousness, facilitative to psi, discussed in chapter 1, and the "belief" states of chapter 2. (Biofeedback, the most passive of the procedures mentioned in chapter 2, is also by far the most likely to enhance ESP.) So do meditative procedures such as TM and techniques such as I Ching, astrology, tarot cards, ouija boards, and the like (Weldon 1975; LeShan 1974). For psi phenomena to occur, it appears crucial that the analytical left brain be temporarily, if only partially, put out of commission. This inhibiting power of critical thinking may help to explain the greater extrasensory powers of animals and young children. If we then add stimuli processed mainly by the right brain, we may achieve yet stronger effects—with the qualifying caution that knocking out part of the right brain also enhances psi![17]

[16] I have indicated that the linkage between mother and child may begin to break down as the child begins to read. Cf. Ferguson 1975, 5, for possibly contrasting data of a mother's responding physically to a son's mental calculation of a mathematical problem. Here, however, the mother's awareness of the experiment provides an additional source of connectedness. It would also be worth testing whether stressful verbal activity was similarly communicated. Going at the connection from the other side, Krippner (1975, 153) reports a subject who had difficulty speaking after a PK session.

[17] One could reasonably argue that the excitation factor facilitates transmission, while passivity—or knocking out part of a "brain filter"—facilitates reception. This argument breaks down when considering boredom as it affects card guessing: the *cards* have apparently not become less excited. The next possibility is to alter the metaphor and speak of facilitating not "transmission" but "connection," which can be made from either side or even aided from the outside. Connection does not in itself ensure reception. Broad commented that, while telepathic interaction may be constant, it will be noticed only under particular circumstances (Koestler 1973). A statement verging on such a view is that, "though the stimulus to extra-sensory perception may come from outside a man's individual being, it draws strength from the love or hatred or self-identification that link him with other beings" (Haynes 1961, 180).

Stranger: How dull.

Inquirer: Dull? I thought all of that rather fascinating, myself.

Stranger: I really thought you'd get into mediumship and automatic writing and all. They're really much more interesting. Besides, they're sort of the logical extension of all these extrasensory abilities.

Inquirer: I'm not so sure that they are a *logical* extension. I grant that people interested in psi often derive their interest from concerns for survival after death; but if, say, Freud were to insist that my concern for being on time and my enjoyment of fingerpainting had the same source, that hardly means that fingerpainting and punctuality themselves are related. One could at least argue for differences among spiritism, automatisms that may stem from dissociative unconscious processes, and some sort of natural psi phenomena. Still, I admit that unconscious processes also appear to distort extrasensory perceptions—almost as if something like Freud's "primary process" was involved.[18] Those matters do seem to have a peculiar intertwining, I guess.

Stranger: And let me remind you that they all involve a certain passive receptivity and an attaining of knowledge or other effects without the usual means. If such matters are worth exploring at all, I hardly see how you can call yourself scientific if you stop halfway through the task.

Inquirer: All right, all right, but if you don't mind, I need a break for a moment. What we've already looked at would seem to demand a whole new view of the world—of how things hang together and of causality—and I at least need to have a stab at making sense of it all.

Stranger: Right from your armchair, I suppose. You left-brain types are all alike. And I suppose you'll use that perfectly good, material brain to argue against a strictly material reality. Let me warn you that using your left brain hardly guarantees that what you say will make sense. Let me also warn you that, if you're going to argue for a certain underlying unity in the world, you're not going to be able to tell for sure whether you're talking about the categories of your understanding, as your friend Kant thought, or about the world. Mystics have the same problem when they have one of their "intense perceptions of unity," or however they put it.[19]

[18] Heywood 1961; Moss 1974.
[19] See Deikman 1969a.

Inquirer: How did you know I was thinking about interconnectedness or unity?

Stranger: ESP, maybe?!

* * *

AGAINST REDUCTIONISM: THE INSUFFICIENCY OF SCIENTIFIC CAUSALITY

From looking into psi phenomena, we may begin to suspect that various aspects of our world are profoundly interconnected in a way that overturns our ordinary conceptions of causality. We certainly do not need psi per se to reach such a conclusion: gravitational attraction is a most mysterious sort of action-at-a-distance, and raising one's hand upon deciding to do so ultimately goes back to pure and simple psychokinesis. The ordinary is as baffling as the extraordinary. Nonetheless, the latter may highlight, at least, the former.

The first question (and the last one!) is what is connected to what, and how, and when? In other words, what is "the nature of everything"? The straightforward answers to that question that seem to suffice for daily life (until we examine it closely or until something "really strange" happens) will not quite do. Thus we may be justified in making some brief, highly speculative forays further afield, seeking hypotheses that may bear on the problem. In inquiring about *what* is connected to what, we must consider the contention of field theory (the darling of modern physics) that everything in the physical universe is connected to everything else. (And what about the nonphysical universe?) When we ask *how* things are connected, we must go beyond traditional conceptions of causal connections to consider the possibility of acausal ones. And when we inquire about *when* certain connections occur, we must explore the possibility that many different systems of connectedness may all operate at the same time. Finally, we must consider the possible impact of *choice* within or upon such systems.

Interconnectedness

To "understand" something, we generally explore its relationships to other things or the interrelatedness of its parts. The more predictable we find the relationships, the more confident we feel of our understanding. We have all sorts of useful rules about how material objects relate to one another, and these rules work remarkably well. Our hypotheses about rational and irrational processes in humans work less well but still prove useful. The so-called paranormal, on the other hand, stubbornly refuses to fit the hypotheses or follow the rules. Nonetheless, it apparently keeps occurring (or at least events occur for which persons have trouble finding another category).

If we could confine each of these processes to its own realm, our thinking would at least be a lot tidier. We could be *comfortable* dualists or posit as many independent realms as we liked. Unfortunately, as I have been at some pains to show, the processes that we might wish to confine to distinct realms have a most awkward tendency to interact. How can totally disparate things, having nothing in common, interact? To say that they cannot is to say that we are ultimately dealing *just* with permutations of mind or of matter or of some third thing, or else there is a very great deal we do not know about how "everything" is structured and about what is actually "possible." Since many data suggest that what we usually call "mind" and "matter" cannot be confined to wholly separate, airtight compartments, let us explore some characteristics and implications of their hypothesized interconnect-edness, without at this point attempting to specify an explanatory mechanism.[20]

For one thing, since animals and children appear to receive telepathic messages better than human adults, we may propose that the connect-edness leading to psi manifestations is not supra- but subrational—not a higher but a lower power, to use an evolutionary metaphor. Even on the face of it, psi is a highly inefficient, unpredictable way of communicating or producing effects in the world; and the very factors that augment it tend to interfere with what Western culture, at least, considers to be effective functioning. On the one hand, one must give up an objective, manipulative stance toward the outside world; on the other hand, one cannot fully control which stimuli will impinge upon one from the outside world.

Now let us be clear that having more information than one's neighbors does not necessarily give one an advantage. If, as noted above, many hospitalized mental patients have better-than-average ESP capacities, it is not immediately obvious whether insanity and ESP talents are related through some third common factor (such as organic dysfunction) or whether the latter causes the former. Both possibilities are likely true. But in defense of the hypothesis that ESP could literally drive one crazy, we can imagine how we would feel if we really were getting all kinds of messages—quite possibly true ones, though distorted by unconscious processes, as extrasensory messages tend to be—that no one else could hear or see. It would be as if everyone else's telephone lines were hooked up normally, but ours was hooked

---

[20] For one attempt to organize "psychoenergetic phenomena" in terms of an unconventional magnetic energy, see Ferguson 1975, 343. Regardless of the success of this attempt, the mind-body or mind-matter problem remains a problem.

concurrently to those of the people to whom we are emotionally tied. The ensuing chaotic stimuli and the fact that no one else could perceive them would indeed be enough to drive one crazy. (In that regard, we note that some paranoid persons function quite well if others agree to accept their delusions. "Insanity" is consensually defined in our society.)[21]

The point is that, if we are to survive, incoming stimuli must be limited. We need a brain that will *prevent* many stimuli from coming to consciousness (Heywood 1961). (See Ferguson 1975, 346–47 for data indicating that the brain is indeed affected by far more than comes to awareness. The perceptual paradigms we have already discussed do the same thing at another level. They, like the selectivity of our brain, operate so automatically that we do not even notice them unless they are challenged.) A few holes in the screening device, so to speak, may let more information through. When it functions properly, however, many possible connections will not occur, or at least will not come to awareness.

But notice what we are implying: if thoughts are the sorts of things that may or may not, depending on circumstances, penetrate others' screening devices, then thoughts have a sort of reality about them. That is, wholly apart from actions or verbal communication, they in themselves impinge in some way upon the rest of the universe. The rather sobering conclusion follows that "what anybody thinks has some tendency to come about in fact, just because it is thought of; and it still has that tendency even when the thought is no longer in anybody's consciousness" (Heywood 1961, 219, quoting H. H. Price).[22]

The last paragraph makes two very provocative assumptions. First, it implies that the universe must be regarded in terms of field theory,

---

[21] We should also note that therapists do not treat hallucinations and delusions as utter nonsense but ask, for instance, what the "voices" are saying, on the assumption that what they are saying has some meaning for the "deluded" individual. Pragmatically speaking, I do *not* suggest that the delusions should be credited and hence reinforced by the therapist, whether or not they are genuine psi manifestations, precisely because psi is largely dysfunctional in our society and people get along better when they ignore such stimuli (see Shulman 1968, 69, 157). Furthermore, there is considerable evidence that pursuit of psi manifestations tends to foster personality dissociation, a somewhat different issue we will explore more fully later.

[22] The second part of the statement is perhaps less intrinsically credible than the first, though not necessarily so if a thought's existence at any point makes its impact on the field. So also Cové (quoted in Wiesinger 1957, 200): "Every thought strives toward its own realization." Such a possibility gives added depth to scriptural warnings about the impact of our thoughts and words and the metaphor that God's thoughts and words create all things. (The various mind-cure movements have capitalized on this idea in a way that seems to have enough truth to keep them alive and too little for their doctrines to be universally accepted—or perhaps it could be argued that they are too difficult to practice consistently for the truth that they contain to be manifested consistently; see James 1961 [1902], 108.)

meaning that the whole determines the parts but also that not a single part can wiggle without somehow affecting the whole. Planck and Einstein have commented, respectively, "According to modern mechanics [field theory], each individual particle of the system, in a certain sense, at any one time exists simultaneously in every part of the space occupied by the system"; and "physical reality must be described in terms of continuous functions in space" (quoted in LeShan 1974, 65–66).[23]

Second, it suggests that "thoughts" and "consciousness" are every bit as much aspects of that field (as we have seen Eccles postulate in his mind-brain model) as are atoms and apples. If these assumptions are in any significant sense correct, all sorts of important interactions (such as psi phenomena) must indeed be taking place that cannot be explained using traditional cause-and-effect categories.[24]

Causal and Acausal Connections

Most of us have been taught to view and to manipulate the world in terms of cause and effect. The billiard ball moved because he hit it with a cue. The baby cried because her mother spanked her. You got the message because I telephoned you. To be called a "cause," something must occur before its presumed effect, and we must be able to posit some sort of physical or psychological mechanism by which it can produce that effect. Of course, in any given instance we might be mistaken: perhaps a sudden gust of wind and not a cue moved the

---

[23] Such statements leave considerable room for psi phenomena when the concrete objectivity of material reality is concomitantly dissolved (see n. 22). For a discussion of the functioning of any "thing" as both a whole in itself and part of a larger whole, see Koestler 1973, chap. 4.

[24] The "objectivity" of atoms and of energy is itself open to question. Koestler (1973, 55) cites as a trend in physics "the constant emphasis on the theme 'atoms are not things'; 'on the atomic level the objective world ceases to exist'" (cf. Smith 1975, 371; Gribbin 1984). Similarly LeShan (1974, 63): "One asks a physicist the question 'If light travels in waves through a vacuum, what is waving?' The answer one gets will be something like 'What makes you think that because there are waves, something must be waving?'" See Deikman 1973b for a discussion of the place of belief or thought in what he calls the biosystem. An example of what appears to be an interaction of these two assumptions is scientists' increasing recognition that the observer affects the observed—even that our observation "creates" a reality *on the physical level* that did not exist apart from the observations (Gribbin 1984)—and that no part of the universe can be tidily separated out. Hence the necessity of a holistic approach (see Koestler 1974; Smith 1975, 370; also DeCharms 1968, for a treatment on the interpersonal level). LeShan (1974, 64) argues powerfully that mediums, mystics, and physicists have by their varied routes all come to basically the same, field-theoretical view of the world. This view of reality he characterizes by four central ideas: (1) the central unity of all things, wherein relationships are the most important consideration; (2) the illusoriness of sequential time, in which moments are parceled out; (3) "evil" as a part of the whole and hence not to be judged as contrary to "good"; and (4) the insufficiency of the senses as a means of gaining information. So-called clairvoyant reality thus contrasts directly with our everyday sensory reality, which assumes discreteness, sequentiality, moral judgments, and predominantly sensory awareness.

billiard ball. Still, cues do reliably move balls. Most of the time our assumption will be correct. Problems arise, however, if the supposed cause comes after the effect (e.g., we have a detailed and correct premonition of a plane crash) or if we can see no sufficient mechanism joining cause to effect (as in PK or telepathy or faith healing). Space and time and physical energy are basic to a causal understanding of events.

The concept of causality, however, has always been problematic. It implies more than can ever be empirically demonstrated between two objects or events (Koestler 1974; Hume 1926 [1777]). Furthermore, we may not properly speak of a "sufficient *external* cause" (Chein 1972, emphasis added), for such a postulate denies the properties of what is being acted upon (for instance, what if our billiard ball weighed fifty pounds and had a flat spot?—a "sufficient" cause is sufficient only with respect to something having its own particular characteristics; it involves a *relationship* to what is acted upon, not something simply *external* to what is acted upon). Even (or especially) in modern physics the notion of causality is in trouble, for the laws of probability are acausal connections; and Heisenberg's Uncertainty Principle and the laws of quantum mechanics have made probability, rather than strict causality, foundational to subatomic physics. But even in so trivial a procedure as throwing dice, there is no causal linkage among throws to ensure that making a large number of them will result in a strikingly even distribution of results. The odds of any given number appearing are in no causal way changed by past throws. Thus, as Jung writes,

> If the connection between cause and effect turns out to be only statistically valid and only relatively true, the causal principle is only of relative use for explaining natural processes and therefore presupposes the existence of one or more other factors which would be necessary for an explanation. (1973, 446–47)

What sort of factor might do? Could events be connected not just by proximity in time and space, as usually perceived, but by *meaning*?[25] This view would suggest, first of all, that spatial and temporal clusterings of causally unrelated events—coincidences—may actually be not merely coincidental but "meant" in some unknown manner and, second, that meaningful connections are not limited to that which is temporally present or spatially contiguous but embrace and may enable such events as telepathy and precognition. (Jung is clearly saying more than that we selectively perceive coincidences and attribute, *post hoc*, "meaning" to their occurrence. Drawing upon research into psi phenomena, Jung

[25] See Jung 1973; cf. Koestler 1973, chap. 3. Insofar as space and time are nothing in themselves but rather postulates of the conscious mind, Jung considers it natural that they should be relative to psychological conditions.

posits an intrinsic—not just a *post hoc*, or imposed—connectedness by meaning.) This acausal connecting principle Jung calls "synchronicity."[26]

A principle such as synchronicity posits a more than merely psychological power for the items of psychological significance (purposes, emotional attachments, intentions, choices) that make life important to human beings. These things that *matter* and that fit together may find expression in the physical world apart from the use of physical means. We could of course object that to conceive hidden affinities functioning as a sort of glue for the universe is a brazenly occult notion; but in doing so we should at least remember that it was also a theme of many early scientists and philosophers (Koestler 1974). As I noted earlier, "scientific progress" does not always solve old problems but rather dubs them useless, irrelevant, or "unreal" and then throws them out.

Coinherent Systems of Connections

Let us attempt one more very large leap. When we ask why a given event occurred, we normally expect a single (causal) answer to our query. What if that expectation is fundamentally mistaken? What if, instead of one, there are a multitude of different, potentially "true" answers? If so, which answer is *actually* correct for a particular individual may depend on that individual's relationship to the event. Or more precisely, it may depend on the *system of relationships* in which the event impinges on the person.

Let it be clear that we are *not* talking simply about different levels of explanation for the same event. We are talking rather about different sources or reasons or causes of an event, all operating at once— overdetermination, in psychological language—but only a limited number of which bring it into relationship to a given individual. As an inadequate analogy, we may consider three families in an elevator, all of whom pushed the button for the third floor. If we were concerned merely about levels of explanation, we would rightly note that one level of explanation for the progress of the elevator upward is its mechanics;

[26]Koestler would extend the interpretation of acausal events from an illustration of a basic but poorly understood interconnectedness of the universe to a principle of integration and a tendency to build order and complexity—"evolution" of a sort—quite in contrast to the second law of thermodynamics. He terms such events "confluential" to avoid an emphasis on time alone and considers the principle governing them to be equal in importance to mechanical causation (Koestler 1973, 122; 1974, 62). He does, however, recognize that we must be cautious about assuming acausality when we may be dealing with unknown causes—or perhaps, we might add, undeterminable (e.g., because of the impact of the observer) but by no means necessarily indeterminate ones. It is still intriguing to consider within this framework the ultimately *destructive* nature of the merely causal (the second law of thermodynamics assures us that the universe will indeed eventually run down, that randomness must increase), a theme to which we will return later in another context (chap. 7).

another is each family's intention to go to the third floor. However, our current point is that, while any one person's intention could "cause" the elevator to rise, the only intention relevant to a given child is his own parent's particular intention, which does not depend on—nor is it even necessarily related to—anyone else's intention.

Lest such speculation appear excessively brazen, we may note a suggestive fact from physics: wave equations for particles of very high energy have an *infinitude* of possible solutions. What if "not only are there some respects in which the universe is infinite but *there is no respect in which the universe is not infinite*" (Melhuish 1973, 57, 97)? What if "we ourselves actually live, not in a universe, but a pluriverse consisting of more than one Space. One star may exist in one Space and another star in another Space, there being no spatial distance between them"? (Melhuish 1973, 72–73, quoting Benardete; see Gribbin 1984). Analogically, we are implying that the wave equation may have more than one solution *at the same time* ("time" also being used only analogically) and that in the pluriverse there may be any number of systems of connection operating concurrently, any one of which may or may not impinge upon a given entity.[27] That is, energic, spatiotemporal, or causal connections; "meaningful" and acausal connections; and any number of other sorts of connections might compose a whole series of what we could call "coinherent" fields.

Positing a series of coinherent fields has wide-ranging implications. First, it is convenient in terms of dealing with the law of contradiction: logically, we do not violate the law, provided we do not posit contradictory sets of events *in the same sense,* just as the axioms "parallel lines do not intersect" and "parallel lines do intersect" can both be true, but in different frames of reference.[28] Second, it allows many metaphysical systems to operate at once, making way for a much more richly textured universe. Third, it provides for the possibility of "broken fields," the possibility that *not* everything is connected and interacting in the same way but that even the interrelationship of things is affected by the fields and metaphysical systems of which they partake. Fields may

[27] In an entirely different philosophical context, Mackay (1967) has demonstrated that there are cases in which two persons' beliefs must be different if both are to be correct. Specifically, a person may correctly predict a particular behavior on my part by believing that my actions are determined; but I act in that way on the belief that I am free to choose what I shall do. Mackay, then, is arguing that subjective decisions are "free" because of the *logical* indeterminacy of choice for the chooser. I argue that determinacies and indeterminacies and potential for more than one "right" opinion based upon beliefs go beyond merely logical analyses.

[28] Melhuish (1973) goes beyond this sort of reasoning to speak of a "contradictory complementarity" embracing identity and pure change. Reality is thus intrinsically paradoxical: "Even a basic logical principle occurs adequately only in consequence of conceivable antithesis" (p. 21); "a thing is never only what it is" (p. 23). He is saying that a single mode of being can never be determinative; I suggest that it may be.

have boundaries that are variously permeable and impermeable (e.g., note the factors facilitating or inhibiting psi phenomena). Certain causal or connecting systems may then be put *out* of commission as well as *into* commission. Fourth, the "same" act or occurrence does not necessarily have the same meaning in different fields. The commonplace analogy here is a motivational one: it is patently not the same thing to stick a hook in a worm to catch a fish in order to feed one's family as it is to hook a worm for the purpose of seeing it squirm. The problem then becomes not just what the various fields might be but also what determines in which field a person is functioning.

Chosen Connections

To suggest that more than one field may be operative and that "meaning" or "mental" connections may be as determinative of events in our world as "causal" connections leaves room for the importance of *choice*. Choice may become a candidate for the role of selecting (consciously or unconsciously, actively or by default) the field that defines relationships composing our lives, and therefore the sorts of action that are possible. LeShan comments,

> There is no metaphysical system that "correctly" describes reality. Each valid system (and who knows today how many of these there are?) includes different "basic limiting principles," different definitions of what is "normal" and what is "paranormal" within them. . . . The metaphysical system you are using is the metaphysical system that is operating. (1974, 152–53)

Radical as such a view seems, it is apparent that we have really just shifted our argument for the determinative importance of paradigms to another plane. While in chapter 1 we were considering persons and communities who make sense of the world in terms of selected aspects of a single reality, thus producing incommensurable world views, here we face the possibility of alternative forms of consciousness (paradigms of relating to the world) yielding incommensurable "realities" (different modes of being and knowing).

Since we customarily speak as if the physical cause-and-effect world is the "real" world, we have difficulty conceiving other "real" fields. Psi phenomena, though they may seriously shake our certainty about the completeness of our paradigms, are unpredictable enough (at least to our perceptions) to leave us more uneasy than informed about the relationships they represent. Let us consider here another set of relationships that may compose a field, namely, the church as the body of Christ (not to be identified with the visible church).[29]

[29]The true church includes all persons who have been called by God and have responded in faith. The example is particularly useful in that it illustrates a field with

By definition, the church is complete in itself, present in, but not limited by, time and space and not perfectly discernible by any means known to us. It has a unique source of power: "It is no longer I who live, but Christ who lives in me; and the life I now live in the flesh I live by faith in the Son of God" (Gal. 2:20). It is profoundly interconnected:

> Just as the body is one and has many members, and all the members of the body, though many, are one body, so it is with Christ. . . . If one member suffers, all suffer together; if one member is honored, all rejoice together. Now you [Christians] are the body of Christ and individually members of it. (1 Cor. 12:12, 26–27)

It is *not* linked in the same way to the "world" (all that is not the church): "They are not of the world, even as I [Jesus] am not of the world. . . . I have sent them into the world" (John 17:16, 18). What if such assertions were not mere metaphors but sober fact?

To press the example further, remember that, since we conceive will or choice to be a factor in what systems are operating, the possibility of one system capitulating to another or being impinged upon by it is always present. Hence the continual warnings to God's people that they are not to love the world, and also the initial physical separation of the Jews from the surrounding culture that would undermine their faith. However, events ostensibly determined by one field can also be incorporated constructively in (or, better, can also be determined by) another, as in the case of Joseph's brothers: what they meant for evil, God meant—and used—for good (Gen. 50:20).[30] But if Joseph had been operating in a simply worldly way, he could have failed to see God's hand at work and have proceeded to execute his brothers. He had to choose which field defined what had happened and then make the appropriate response.

The visible church has only clues badly followed as to what it would mean to be the true church. Fields, like paradigms, entail indwelling and commitment. There are conditions—any field we choose as determinative of our lives imposes conditions. "No one can serve two masters" (Matt. 6:24).

---

extension in time as well as space (the "communion of saints" is by no means limited to those physically alive at any given time). Interestingly, Paul—counter to his usual style—uses concrete, physical, nonspiritualized language in speaking of the body of Christ, *not* moving to the abstract and intangible (Kallas 1966, 93–99).

[30]To propose "God's plan" as a field is possibly confusing in that it, unlike any other, must incorporate all the others. (At the eschaton, anything not so incorporated might be defined as hell.) I assume that all the others, including the church, might vary in relative dominance for each component and at different times.

4

"Possession" Phenomena

Stranger: If you don't mind my saying so, this conversation is getting pretty heavy. Not only do you get carried away with some speculative and radical metaphysics, but then you have to drag in religion. Not that I have anything against "religion" as such, you understand, but to conceive of a God who could create all sorts of delightful "coinherent realities" as options, to use that barbarous term of yours, and then declare them off-limits—well, he'd have to be a sadist, a bigot, or a prude. Or, of course, a colossal egotist, demanding that people just "serve" him. But that thought is less than original; and as I was saying, theology isn't exactly my favorite topic. Can't we get into something a bit more popular?

Inquirer: Popular? Well, how about demonology? That's popular!

Stranger: Altogether *too* popular for my taste.

Inquirer: I really am serious, though. "Possession" is perhaps the way most of the peoples of the world have understood altered states of consciousness. You yourself said we shouldn't go just halfway in our explanations. You suggested we talk about mediums and the like: that's not so far from possession, since mediums believe they contact spirits and have spirits speak through them.

Stranger: True, but the whole topic breeds such perfectly hysterical reactions: "When in doubt, cast it out"—that sort of thing. What's more, it holds back science, scaring people away from really investigating things like psi phenomena, since some pastors seem more eager to attribute anything they can't understand to the Devil than to God. I call that the "Devil of the gaps" world view. It's the latest thing. Nobody's really interested in the "God of the gaps" anymore. Perfectly ridiculous, of course; but it can inhibit the advance of knowledge and control of the universe, which are obviously of prime importance. The only bright spot is that the extremists have managed thoroughly to disenchant a lot of people with the narrow sort of viewpoint I thought I heard you edging toward in that "one master only" line.

Inquirer: Don't you think it must say something about our culture that we have become so obsessed with demonology? It would be useful to know why. In any case, I still believe that we have a responsibility to look at so-called possession phenomena, and not just in our society. Not that we can exhaust the anthropological literature, but we can at least sample it.

Stranger: My, you're sounding stuffy and self-righteous. If you don't mind my being frank—I'm speaking as a friend, you understand—I find that tone of voice disagreeable. And please—*don't* exhaust the literature; you'll exhaust me first!

* * *

THE NATURE AND FUNCTION OF POSSESSION STATES

In each of the preceding chapters, we have considered circumstances in which persons have felt themselves to be in touch with powers or forces, or to be experiencing aspects of reality, that were new to them. Speaking of such experiences, they might be tempted to say, "I was just not myself," meaning the remark entirely metaphorically. That metaphor, though, like "I don't know what possessed me," originates in a belief almost universal to humankind that external powers or spirits can take control of a person in such a way that the person's actions must subsequently be attributed not to him but to those powers or forces. Such a person is said to be "possessed." To inquire into possession phenomena is to ask whether they can reasonably be reduced to their physical, psychological, psi, and (adding a fourth dimension) social components or whether a "spiritual" component should be postulated as well.

Characteristics of Possession States

Many moderns wrongly assume that "demon possession" is a primitive, catch-all category applied indiscriminately by the ignorant to all disagreeable, inexplicable, or variously abnormal conditions from insanity to illness. As early as 1893, Nevius established the fact that the Chinese distinguished demon possession from idiocy, insanity, epilepsy, and hysteria, all of which they attributed to physical causes. The same is true of other cultures (Oesterreich 1974; Unger 1953).[1] Dissociation or

---

[1] See Matt. 4:24; 10:1; Mark 1:32–34; 6:13; Luke 7:21; 9:1. It remains common to

trance may or may not be interpreted as possession.[2] And even to believe that demons can cause disease is by no means necessarily to equate disease and possession: demons may do people harm without possessing them (Lewis 1971; Nevius 1893; see Luke 13:10–16).[3] In fact, presumably primitive people may be quite sophisticated and discerning in the categories they apply.

Considering the care with which the label "possession" is used, it is curious that, while reported subjective phenomena remain remarkably constant throughout history, specific behaviors manifested by those who are considered possessed vary widely from culture to culture.[4] States labeled as "possession" by a given culture range along a continuum from complete dissociation through semilucid conditions to apparently complete lucidity. During lucid possession states a person may even watch his own violent physical manifestations as a passive spectator (Oesterreich 1974; cf. Lhermitte 1963) or give a message allegedly from God or the gods.[5] Possession may be an individual or a collective experience and may be voluntary (sought, as in some shamanism) or involuntary.

Nonetheless, in the dissociated state, certain common changes prevail, whether the individual lived in the first or the twentieth century; in Africa, China, or America. First, there is the automatic presentation and persistent, consistent acting out of a new personality, manifested in facial features, voice timbre and pitch, and behavior. The demon may speak in the first person and use the third person for the possessed. The spirit is evidently fully conscious of the individual he possesses, while the individual knows nothing of the demon and cannot recall the

interpret the biblical manifestations of possession as simply epilepsy or insanity (e.g., McCasland 1951), despite the fact that writers of Scripture clearly distinguish them.

[2] See Bourguignon 1968; Tippett 1976. Instances of trance possession were found in 90 percent of 488 societies studied in 1934 (Tippett 1976).

[3] If it seems to be multiplying hypotheses to suggest that demons could cause an "ordinary" physical illness, we might remember that we call an ulcer an ulcer, whether its source is physiological or psychological.

[4] Mystical experience generally produces a remarkable uniformity of language and symbolism; cf. Lewis 1971; Oesterreich 1974; Unger 1953; James 1961 [1902]; Laski 1962. I do not necessarily equate ecstasy and possession, but experiential statements may overlap in various altered states of consciousness, as we have seen; and some ecstasies are indeed negative ones, or "desolations."

[5] Lest we be tempted to go too far afield too quickly, we might remember the range of belief about, and experiences of the working of, the Holy Spirit in our own Christian tradition. Consider, for example, the dissociative states and physical manifestations in Holy Roller and snake-handling cults; the controlled (in terms of volume, tempo, and duration) utterance of nonrational speech, or "tongues," by neopentecostal groups, often accompanied by affirmation and exercise of other gifts such as the "discerning of spirits" and healing; the sometimes highly rational, moralistic, political utterances of the Hebrew prophets, who prefaced their words with "thus saith the Lord"; and the conviction common to all Christians that the Holy Spirit indwells everyone who is truly a believer (see Rom. 8:9). To compare phenomena is not, of course, to identify their source.

possession state. Second, knowledge or intellectual abilities not ordinarily possessed by the subject appear, often manifesting themselves in powers of oratory, poetical expression, new languages spoken, or clairvoyant or telepathic knowledge.[6] Third, extraordinary bodily strength is sometimes accompanied by physical contortions that cannot be imitated voluntarily. Fourth, moral character often changes completely, the person's speech usually becoming coarse and filthy, expressing ideas opposed to all traditionally accepted ethical and religious ideas.[7]

Furthermore, different possessing spirits manifest different behaviors, which may alternate in a single individual but are self-consistent (Jacobs 1966; Tippett 1976).[8] Other characteristics frequently mentioned include strange physical ailments, self-destructive impulses, poltergeist phenomena, animalistic possession, quick relief with exorcism, and a distinctive stench coming from the possessed.[9] (The latter was observed in the early nineteenth century by the eminent psychiatrist Esquirol [Oesterreich 1974, 190] and could suggest some physical, metabolic disorder. Perhaps it is similar in nature to that which some psychiatrists claim to be able to distinguish in schizophrenics.) In short, characteristics run the gamut from physical to psychological to psychic. They may be at least partly explained from any of these perspectives, as exploration of how such states may be induced will show.

Induction of Possession States

Many possession states are induced in ways almost precisely parallel to the means of altering brain states that we investigated in chapter 1.

---

[6] Sargant (1974, 28) quotes Binet and Feré to the effect that "instances have been given of subjects who could, during somnambulism, perform intellectual feats of which they were incapable in the waking state" (cf. Heywood 1961, 107, who gives the same datum for mediums in trance). Sargant holds that hypnoidal states may lead to the remembering of forgotten languages or construction of new ones. He finds no proof that languages totally new to the individual are spoken. I would argue that, even if a person, say, many years previously traveled through a country for a day or two, so being exposed to a language, it is scarcely credible to think that from that experience he could draw the vocabulary and grammar that would enable him to express himself coherently and meaningfully in a totally different situation. An interesting case of another sort, in which possession as such was not involved, was that of some women in Africa who had a gourd of demons in their house. If anyone came and stole, the gourd would speak and tell the names of the thieves and what they took. Anyone, not just the women, could hear the voice (Jacobs 1966).

[7] See Koch 1965; Langton 1942; Nevius 1893; Oesterreich 1974; Richards 1974; Tippett 1976; Unger 1971; Mark 5.

[8] Compare multiple-personality data that indicate that different personalities may have different and self-consistent scores on psychological tests and physiological and neurological measures, though there may be a practice effect on some tests (Ludwig et al. 1972). Mediums, too, may have very different metabolisms for themselves and their guides (Moss 1974).

[9] *Demon experiences* 1960; Koch 1965; Martin 1976; Nevius 1893; Oesterreich 1974; Richards 1974.

Some groups use drugs; and the popular imagination readily conjures up images of "natives" engaging in rhythmic dancing and drumming. There may be intense concentration and hyperventilation—or, in our society, a closed room in which physical activity produces a hot, stuffy atmosphere and corresponding biochemical changes (Alland 1962; Lee 1968; Mischel and Mischel 1958). Individual experiences often follow upon a period of fasting and physical stress, joined with an intense expectation of receiving a vision, revelation, or some special sign of, say, a shamanistic calling. When a person is "recruited" to such a calling, the event is usually marked by some disorder or illness or affliction. This initial trauma may be accompanied by a sense of spirits that are intruding on the person. Some societies presume that the shaman must surrender his own soul (become passive?) in order to fulfill his role. Such symbolism of surrender may also be accompanied by sexual symbolism of union with the possessing spirit.

Often, too, something interpretable as suggestion and/or contagion occurs as persons in a group "transfer" their possession to another by touching, rubbing, or spinning; and shamanistic gifts are often transferred from an older shaman to an initiate or may be passed on in a hereditary system (see Langton 1942; Lee 1968).[10] While the above instances involve largely voluntary possessions, we should note that an innocent spectator may give way to a communal experience and manifest the behavior of the regular participants (see Tippett 1976, 166).

Whether a given form of mass or personal possession is desired or not, and whether the setting is another culture or ours, a hysterical disposition or other psychopathology is by no means a *precondition* for involvement. The individuals affected often show no prior hysterical symptoms and indeed appear to be in perfect psychological health, as attested by a large number of researchers (Oesterreich 1974, 190; Alland 1962; Eliade 1957; Langton 1949; Lewis 1971). One comments, in fact, that possession phenomena seem "about as highly correlated with 'character structure' and personal history as the measles" (Gregory 1974, xii).[11] However, it appears that group phenomena and the more

---

[10] Contagion certainly seemed apparent at Loudun (see Oesterreich 1974). We have already seen that psychic abilities appear to run in families and that they may emerge after a physical trauma, particularly to the head.

[11] Gregory substantiates this opinion by looking at the widely varied character structures of the possessed at Loudun (see Huxley 1952, or the summary in Oesterreich 1974). Numerous anthropologists agree that shamans are basically healthy, though admitting that the social role may also give room for sanctioned outlet of various symptomatic behaviors. Sargant (1959, 1974) believes that possession—as well as conversion and hypnosis and indoctrination of all sorts—occurs most easily and frequently in "normal" people because they are adaptable and open to suggestion and because their brains are functioning so as to provide relief for themselves. Psychotics and severe neurotics (and sometimes, but not always, those with burning, obsessive beliefs) are the hardest to influence because they do

extreme dissociative states are sought after only when fairly explicitly sanctioned by a culture or subculture, to the influence of which I now turn.

Social and Psychological Functions of Possession States

Whether a culture officially approves or disapproves of states called "possession," having the category available makes possible the interpretation and relief of certain stresses that could otherwise threaten the social structure. Such a category provides sanction for cathartic expression of intense emotional excitement (Sargant 1974). It gives room for the acting out of socially unacceptable behaviors, such as role reversals and those associated with hostile impulses and sexual feelings. Thus internal psychological pressures find an outlet.

At the same time, belief in powerful spiritual forces at work helps give meaning to daily events. Is there disease or physical suffering? Perhaps the spirits or natural forces have been offended or are displeased by some social disorder or disharmony (Lee 1968; Prince 1968b; see 1 Cor. 11:17–34). What can be done? Provide possibility of confession in a nonpunitive setting; and perhaps sanction some slight, self-inflicted harm, as if the offender were doing penance (Lewis 1971; Mischel and Mischel 1958; cf. Frank 1974, chap. 3). Is there social tension? Maybe a mass trance performance can transform the pressures into a common struggle against external sources of malevolence. Or perhaps group possession may be used much like group psychotherapy, with the added advantage that the really serious problems can be

not adapt and are less likely to attend to stimuli. More specifically, Sargant hypothesizes that strong, focal excitation in one part of the brain—which he believes characterizes hypnosis and hysteria—inhibits other parts, small or large, leaving that ideational field clear for the first comer. Charcot, he notes, by suggestion produced hysterical states that look for all the world like possession (Sargant 1974, 53). Or, if stress is great enough to produce what Sargant terms an "ultraparadoxical" phase of inhibition (a construct taken from Pavlov's experiments with dogs), the very ideas an individual most strongly rejects or struggles against may come into ascendancy. Thus fears of possession could bring feelings of possession. (In contrast, most contemporary students assume that, if a person *thinks* he is possessed, he almost certainly is not, but needs a psychiatrist.) If stress is more intense and widespread, a radical transformation of personality could occur, the resulting personality structure being diametrically opposed to the old. The requisite focal brain activity may be produced by strong stimulation, perhaps enhanced by anxiety and guilt and physiological stress, or by relaxation and sensory deprivation. These alternatives, of course, encompass most of the techniques for inducing possession that we have mentioned above. Sargant would attribute "involuntary" and solitary experiences of possession to particularly powerful anxiety and psychological conflict. In any event, the normal critical processes are short-circuited. Sargant has been roundly criticized by Prince (1968a, 133) for trying to "paper the crack between the functional and the organic with arbitrary assertions, rather than with experimental evidence." In his own study of "psychomotor amnesic states," including psychomotor epilepsy, hysterical fugue, sleepwalking and hypnotic somnambulism, and some forms of multiple personality, Prince finds that some do and some do not alter the EEG, which is at least a measure of brain activity, even if not a wholly reliable one.

referred to the "powers" for resolution instead of remaining the responsibility of individuals or the group. Some researchers feel that, in such settings, so-called possession seems more an extension and distortion of everyday behavior than a state radically discontinuous with it (Mischel and Mischel 1958, 253; cf. Ebon 1974, 222).

At the individual level, data prove even more complex. When dissociative states are culturally disapproved, the afflicted individual usually seems genuinely to suffer and to desire release. Nonetheless, possession provides enough possibility for gain—attention, an outlet for hostility, profit from fortunetelling or healing activities—that conscious fraud may occur (Lewis 1971; Nevius 1893). Both the personal inconvenience of seemingly genuine possession and its potential benefits and paranormal power may combine to produce such social institutions as shamanism.[12]

In shamanism, supposedly "tamed" spirits, to which the shaman is "in hostage," are thought to protect him against other spirits and in a sense allow him to control their manifestations. Possession thus becomes useful and fairly nonthreatening. Shamans may induce it almost at will, manifesting less motor activity and behavior change than do those in less close touch with the powers; and they can learn to "turn it off" by autosuggestion when it is undesired (Alland 1962; Mischel and Mischel 1958; Nevius 1893). It is a common belief in China that those who do yield to a possessing spirit or demon will be helped, given healing and occult powers, but that those who do not yield will suffer (Nevius 1893). In fact, the reality of extrasensory powers among shamans, though always questionable, seems well attested: everything from clairvoyance to fire walking has been repeatedly observed (Eliade 1957; Oesterreich 1974).

Is a shamanic vocation a way of expressing or of resolving a psychic crisis? Insofar as a society allows the vocation, the distinction may remain moot.[13] One longtime researcher commented, "I cannot

[12] Lewis (1971) distinguishes what he calls "central" from "peripheral" possession cults. The former, which are frequently ancestral cults, function to uphold and maintain the moral integrity of the community. The latter, which may exist side by side with the "central" variety, generally involve persons who are downtrodden, odd, or particularly ambitious; they are amoral or evil and obliquely aggressive.

[13] We should note, though, that the most extreme or enthusiastic manifestations, group or individual, thrive on instability in a subculture or an individual. A group may be under attack; a person may be underprivileged, ill, or distraught. When social stability is attained, even possession becomes ritualized: a religious cultus and a professional shamanism, both relatively orderly and circumscribed, develop. Thus, "What is considered to begin with as an uncontrolled, unsolicited possession illness readily develops into an increasingly controlled and voluntary religious exercise" (Lewis 1971, 93). At the same time, Lewis, who does not identify shamanism and mental illness, comments, "In our culture the absence of acceptable and realistically valid labels for the feelings which the shaman and the schizophrenic are presumed to share leads in the case of the latter to a heightened sense of guilt and to further mental alienation" (p. 181).

remember a single shaman whose professional hysteria degenerated into serious mental disorder" (Nadel, quoted in Eliade 1957, 78). Another way of looking at the occupation is that "those who had previously been ill have become shamans just because they succeeded in getting well. . . . The acquisition of the shamanic gifts indeed presupposes the resolution of the psychic crisis brought on by the first signs of this vocation" (Eliade 1957, 77). Anton Boisen (known as a primary founder of the pastoral counseling movement) reported a similar personal experience with an episode of insanity in his own life. He hypothesizes (1936) that functional mental illness and religious experience both arise out of inner conflict and disharmony and that both are attempts at reorganization.

Indeed, wholly apart from any paranormal powers to which a possessed individual might have access, various mystical experiences may result in a felt calmness and well-being that looks a lot like good mental health (Prince 1968c, vi). Some would say, then, that we in our society unfairly denigrate altered states of consciousness generally, out of fear of the unknown and of loss of defenses against socially unacceptable impulses (see Tart 1973b, 58; Van Der Walde 1968; Weldon 1975). Thus we lose a means of individual relief and the stability a community gains by having a category enabling them to interpret and accept otherwise-threatening behaviors or physical symptoms as valuable signs of a special gift.

One more question must be raised, however. We noted above that an experience with psychologically positive results seems to demand a yielding to the power or spirit in question: Is it always or even usually helpful to do so? Continuing with a psychological perspective, we could propose that an alternate personality arising in a dissociated state is simply a manifestation of powerful, repressed urges in an individual. The fact that these urges would normally be socially unacceptable or unacceptable to the individual is precisely why they have been repressed.[14] This type of explanation is widely applied to "multiple

[14] "When the Christian patient is filled with the fear or horror of 'bad thoughts,' he easily slips from the scruple of obsession to the delirium of possession by materializing in the diabolical being the representations, feelings and tendencies which he detests and wishes at all costs to reject" (Lhermitte 1963, 101). It is also notable in this context of unacceptable wishes being expressed that persons often experience their first symptoms of possession after a fit of anger or grief or *in a dream* (Nevius 1893). However, the meaning and source of dreams of various kinds have never been totally clear. In 1913 a Dutch physician analyzed his dreams and described nine types, among which are the following: (1) vivid—dreams that seem to mean something, such as bad dreams had in the room of someone one does not know is disturbed; (2) symbolic or mocking—dreams giving a consciousness of waking and sleeping bodies (similar to astral projection), sometimes symbolic, sometimes giving a fake feeling about the world, sometimes predictive, sometimes allowing one to "talk" with dead people, though without getting any information about the other side; (3) demon—dreams where demons are seen, usually

72

personality" cases in our society, the disorder in its full-blown state often being considered to be iatrogenic. (That is, a therapist may react to conflicting trends in a patient's psyche as if they belonged to separate personalities. The patient then obliges by acting out the discrete personalities.) The cure, then, is to reintegrate the personality (yield to the powers? see Bowers et al. 1971; Gruenwald 1971; Ludwig et al. 1972). Unfortunately, in "multiple personality," as in "possession," the original personality, if weak, may vanish; or fusion with the other(s) may produce a change for the worse (see Ludwig et al. 1972; Nevius 1893).[15]

Conversely, pursuing activities that encourage personality dissociation may indeed produce it, to the extent that an individual's life may seem to be directed, against his will, by another personality system (see Bowers et al. 1971; Erikson and Kubie 1939). Auditory hallucinations judged evil by the individual may follow, to which the person's personal sentiments and facial expression may gradually be assimilated (Oesterreich 1974, 60–66). Complete breakdown of the person is not infrequent. In fact, the dangers of such practices as automatic writing and playing with a ouija board (in terms of correlation of use with psychological breakdown) are so well substantiated that Christians and occultists alike warn against their use (Richards 1974).[16]

One could argue that cause and effect are being applied in the wrong direction—that only intrinsically unstable and unconventional persons tend to engage in such activities—except that children who quite innocently get involved at a friend's house may also suffer adverse effects. Not surprisingly, considering the passivity necessary to engage successfully in such manifestations, persons who become involved also

following lucid dreams ("These beings are always obscene and lascivious, and try to draw me into their acts and doings. They have no sex and appear alternately as a man, or a woman. Their aspect is very various and variable, changing every moment, taking all the fantastic forms that the old painters of the Middle Ages tried to reproduce, but with a certain weird plasticity and variability, that no painting can express" [Eeden 1969, 155].); and (4) wrong waking up—dreams like demon pranks, seemingly uncanny, vivid and bright, with an ominous sharpness and clearness, bad dreams for which the terror disappears when the demon is seen. Of these dreams Eeden says, "I would maintain that it is not *my* mind that is responsible for all the horrors and errors of dream-life. To say that *nobody* is responsible for them will not do, for there is absolute evidence in them of some thought and intention, however depraved and low. A trick, a deceit, a symbol, cannot be without some sort of thought and intention. To put it all down to 'unconsciousness' is very convenient; but then I say that it is just as scientific to use the names Beelzebub, or Belial. I for one, do not believe in 'unconsciousness' any more than in Santa Claus" (p. 157).

[15] The alternate personalities are not *always* inferior, although they most generally are: they may sometimes be "better" in culture, genius, sanity, morality, and/or health (Taylor and Martin 1944; cf. Erikson and Kubie 1939).

[16] Moss (1974) suggests an interesting test: if one cannot engage in an automatism while reading a book, practicing it at all is dangerous. Is the implication that inability to keep the left brain in gear, or processes that put it out of gear, may foster grave psychological difficulties?

often begin to have other extrasensory experiences in their daily lives. In any event, even if the alternative personalities a person may manifest are simply sides of himself, fostering their expression apparently does not necessarily improve social and psychological health. A negative trend may be enhanced or a conflict sharpened rather than there being a helpful catharsis or a resolution of a psychic struggle. The evidence remains ambiguous.

* * *

Stranger: Well, I hope you're persuaded by now. It took you long enough.

Inquirer: Persuaded? Persuaded of what?

Stranger: Of exactly what you set out to demonstrate—that "possession" is a catch-all label for all sorts of altered states of consciousness. You surely do get off the track in a hurry. As if one explanation for a person's strange behavior weren't enough, you've provided explanations ad nauseum—physical, psychological, social. . . . Whew! And then you don't even know what you're persuaded of.

Inquirer: Off the track . . . ? Yes, I guess so. I guess I was thinking that some of those data just felt really strange.

Stranger: Wonderful. Your *feelings* have suddenly become evidence again?

Inquirer: No—I mean yes—I mean, I don't know. There's a lot I still don't understand. Oh, I know about the possible effects of physical stimulation and of suggestion—we've been through all that. I can see the effects of internal conflict and social pressures and expectations. That all fits. But other things don't. I've got lots of questions, but especially the exorcism business bothers me at the moment. Why do Christians here or in other countries seem to find possessed people so reactive to the name of Jesus?[17] How come possessed people often know ahead of time, when nobody's told them a thing, that a Christian is coming to pray for them; or get all agitated when, unbeknown to them, somebody prays for them at a distance? Sometimes they even get delivered that way! And why does exorcism work so well that people can be immediately and seemingly

[17] I am not dealing with simple word-magic, however important words may be. The conviction and commitment of the person using the name "Jesus" is of prime importance (see Gasson 1966, 94, for the testimony of a former spiritualist; his carrying a Bible in his pocket before he was converted scarcely prevented any phenomena from occurring).

permanently delivered even after suffering torments for years?[18] I don't get it!

Stranger: Sometimes you make me weary. Positively weary. Not so long ago you spent ages talking about all the things that could happen from a distance, and here you go forgetting every one of them. Mix your precious psi phenomena with some Christians' narrow little world view ("paradigm" was the five-dollar word I think you preferred), and of course you'll see "demons" jumping out of everyone around at the thought of Jesus. It makes me ill to think about it. Do you suppose it would matter if they were using the name "Peanuts," provided they put enough hocus-pocus around it or generated enough psychic energy to get involved at a distance? And it's true, a few of these Christians can get unconscionably single-minded. Unbalanced, I call them. But enough of that. Would you mind if I gave you a little lecture on exorcism?

Inquirer: Why no, not at all. I guess I really don't know much about it. But I do think the name of Jesus makes a difference.

Stranger: You certainly don't know much about it. So let me tell you a few things.

* * *

INTERLUDE ON NON-CHRISTIAN EXORCISM

First of all, Christians hardly have a corner on exorcism.[19] Long before New Testament times, people in ancient cultures not only believed almost universally in demons but used remarkably similar means of dealing with them. They all thought that incantations using sacred names and knowledge of the demon's name were important. They all had rituals and music and special, sacred herbs (McCasland 1951, 102). In later times pagans used needles or burning pills, charms and incense, sacrifice to gods, conjurers, and calling upon other demons. In fact, the idea often seemed to be to make the possessed person so physically uncomfortable that the "demon" had to leave—a strange sort of reasoning it would seem, that extended to Christians and reached positively barbaric depths in the Middle Ages, particularly in the treatment of the insane (Nevius 1893; Bonnell 1956; Montgomery 1975, 219, n. 30).

Today, mediums, rituals, magic, and physical means such as static

[18] Jacobs 1966; McAll 1976; Nevius 1893.
[19] This point is also affirmed in Scripture (Matt. 12:27; Luke 11:19; Acts 19:13). Even using the name of Jesus effectively does not prove that one is a Christian (Matt. 7:22–23).

electricity are employed (Richards 1974). The latter is not to be confused with shock treatments (which some persons consider to be a form of electrical exorcism) but rather refers to the implanting of electrodes in the supraorbital region of the brain—apparently a special "devil spot"—and running a current through it. In one such case the "devil" shrank in apparent size, became more polite, and changed shape into a gentlemanly figure over a series of treatments (Ebon 1974, 108).

If physical stresses can produce "possession," it is not too surprising that they can relieve it. The same goes for suggestion: often enough, the strange clinical symptoms of possession do not even show up until exorcism is initiated.[20] Even a neurologist who believes theoretically that possession is possible cautions that "imaginary possession is one of the most easily induced maladies" (Lhermitte 1963, 102), a point illustrated by the history of a fourteen-year-old American boy who overheard the conversation of a minister and missionary, concluded that he was possessed, and proceeded to act accordingly—more so when the minister was out of town and not attending to him (Kildahl 1964)! Naturally enough, what suggestion produces, suggestion can cure. If people do not believe they can be possessed, they are not.[21]

Likewise, faith by both possessed and exorcist in the possibility of cure is important (Ebon 1974; Oesterreich 1974). That faith "works" proves nothing about the existence of demons.[22] In fact, in cases where individuals believe that exorcisms will be long and arduous they are; whereas some people of a simpler faith just read their Bible, pray a bit, sing a few songs, and the task is done (see Martin 1976; *Demon experiences* 1960; Nevius 1893). It is not surprising that, if the demon is conceived as subtly material, persons should hallucinate something leaving (Oesterreich 1974).[23] And as we know from modern psychotherapy, an intense emotional experience can be cathartic, whatever the content (Sargant 1974).

Actually, comparisons of exorcism and psychotherapy are fascinating.

[20] While the obvious conclusion is that the disorder is iatrogenic—which, I agree, may often be the case—it may also be argued that symptoms of possession are most likely to appear as a response to spiritual confrontation. The above-noted consistency, bizarreness, and strength of symptoms suggest a peculiar uniformity of the human mind in its reaction to the very thought of possession, if not the intervention of some outside power.

[21] This assumption is patent. If people do not believe in possession, there is obviously no possibility that *any* set of symptoms would be given that label.

[22] See White 1976a. However, if there were demons, quite possibly little could be done about them apart from faith. The scientific method, limited enough (as our look at paradigms has shown us) for the material world, collapses for the immaterial. A good scientist cannot believe or assume the hypothesis he is trying to test; but there is no way of exorcising demons without believing they exist (White 1976b, 282).

[23] Exorcists have indeed reported seeing something leave. One Episcopal priest in the United States was terrified when he saw something black proceed from an exorcee's mouth and dive into a lake (Woodward 1974). See also Hill 1974, 196, for an incident in which two persons are reported independently to have seen the *same* "something" leave.

Similarly, it has been said that shamanism is more than psychotherapy, since shamanism takes more data into account; but psychotherapists resemble shamans in that psychotherapists use all sorts of ritual and other "witchcraft" (see Frank 1974; Lewis 1971). I have mentioned the group-therapy atmosphere of mass possession phenomena and implied the alliance of patient and helper, struggling against an unseen antagonist, but I have given less attention to the "talking cure" aspect and the *naming* of demons (believing that we know what something is gives us a feeling of power over it).[24] In short,

> exorcism, to put it simply, is a special form of healing a human soul in distress. . . . Is the "possessed" man or woman suffering from diabolical intrusion, from hysteria, schizophrenia, unresolved aggressive impulses, manipulation by a "hungry ghost," an evil, unclean, or ignorant spirit? (Ebon 1974, 221)
>
> The history of exorcism is full of evidence that tells us, "If you're looking for devils, devils you'll get; and if you look for evil, malignant, ignorant or earthbound spirits, for hungry ghosts or spirits of foxes, those are precisely what you'll get!" The Freudian psychotherapist encounters an Oedipus complex, the surgeon a much-needed appendectomy, the nutritionist a vitamin deficiency. (P. 211)

Cures seem to be as much by common consent as anything else. If the "possessed" person does not wish to be released, he most likely will not be (*Demon experiences* 1960; Martin 1976). Of course, enough discomfort can do something to produce consent, too; though we grant that most of the self-proclaimed exorcists today abstain from physical techniques, with the possible exception of suggesting in some cases that the possessed person and the exorcist fast.

* * *

Inquirer: I guess you're right.

Stranger: Of course I'm right. But right about what, specifically?

Inquirer: Right that, just as there isn't any manifestation of "possession" that can't be attributed credibly to other causes, even the effective-

---

[24] To return to the idea of "word-magic," it and the power of names as participating in the reality of a thing are of course common ideas in primitive societies and linked to our prior suggestion that thoughts—which take shape by means of words—are far from nothing. The fact that our theoretical language today is enormously complex may effectively obscure its magical quality. Like incantations used against unknown forces in earlier ages, it gives us a sense of control over reality in the face of increasing evidence of how scant is our knowledge and how inadequate are our theories. In saying that "much of the verbiage in academic journals might as well be the language of alchemists" (Ebon 1974, 224), we should perhaps mean to give more honor to alchemists rather than less to our academicians!

ness of exorcism doesn't establish that the person was possessed. To say that penicillin can cure pneumonia hardly proves that everything penicillin cures *is* pneumonia.

Stranger: Precisely. I couldn't have put it better myself.

Inquirer: I don't want to try to prove too much, though. Exorcism doesn't always work, and it's hard to say why suggestion is so much more effective in some cases than others. On the other hand, I've heard that Christian exorcists had a reputation even among non-Christians for being the most effective in the ancient world, although they employed no ritual or special procedures besides the name of Jesus.[25] Some missionaries have reported universal success—despite finding some demons harder to cast out than others—deliverance being maintained if *and only if* the person who was healed became and remained a Christian.[26] Psychiatrists as well as lay people today list cases in which Christian exorcism succeeded after a whole series of psychiatrists, psychiatric hospitalizations, or courses of electric shock treatment failed.[27]

Stranger: Yes, of course. These Christians' naiveté sometimes serves them well. A fresh and vivid faith, absolute certainty of victory—when people haven't the sense to be cautious and prudent, their enthusiasm can really do a lot for their persuasive power.

Inquirer: But sometimes a Christian who has never exorcised before may be scared silly and have no idea whether a simple command will really affect a demon; and the exorcism still works.[28]

Stranger: In those cases, the person "exorcised" was probably so shocked by the implication that he had a demon that the suggestion worked by virtually overwhelming him, as does the technique psychologists call "implosion." Listen, you were right the first time. There are always alternative explanations.[29]

Inquirer: One more thing, though: I still think we've dropped some data through the cracks. Sometimes the explanation given for phenomena

[25]Oesterreich 1974, 107 et passim. We may note also Justin Martyr's comment that numberless demoniacs were healed "though they could not be cured by all other exorcists, and those who used incantations and drugs" (quoted in Frost 1954, 58). Tertullian used as an argument for the very existence of demons the singular effectiveness of Christians in driving them out.

[26]Nevius 1893, 145, 256, 258. The difference among demons here seems *not* to reside in the exorcist's expectations alone.

[27]Richards (1974) cites a girl who had been in four hospitals and seen seventeen psychiatrists; cf. Martin 1976; McAll 1976.

[28]See Basham 1972. Note also the disciples' surprise in Luke 10:17.

[29]See Wilson 1976; White 1976a, 1976b for the opinions of persons who both believe in the reality of demon possession and affirm the possibility of alternative explanations.

that some call "possession" doesn't fit very well with explanations given for the effectiveness of exorcism. If one is correct, something must be wrong with the other. It's not fair for the skeptics to have it both ways at once. Take, for instance, presumed psychosis or epilepsy. Whether or not people have differentiated these states from possession, it is still true that persons diagnosed today as psychotic sometimes respond to exorcism, as I just said. Furthermore, the case of the boy described in Mark 9 fits rather precisely a description of epilepsy; is the cure, then, also reported accurately? Not that these disorders never remit strikingly, but hardly in immediate response to simple verbal entreaty.[30] What is happening if they do yield seems at least as mysterious as if possession was the initial explanation. In fact, no elaborate suggestive procedures or arousal of expectations seems necessary for cure. Besides, placebos have been shown ineffective with epilepsy.[31]

Stranger: Which, as you said before, is far from proving a thing about demonic causality. But I bet you'll start arguing that the etiology of psychosis is debatable or that two-thirds of epileptics are idiopathic, that one-fifth get no benefit from known drugs, and that the nature of the aura is suggestive, with its pains, strange sensations, tremor, mysterious and usually foul smell or visions not related to the environment, and feeling of panic.[32] And yes, I know, when the disorder isn't focal, it may produce alterations of consciousness, impairment of recall, disorders of orientation, intellectual deficits, disturbances of drive, disorders of attention, and emotional disturbance.[33] Sounds as if demons would be as good a cause as any, right?

Inquirer: How did you know what I was thinking again! Look, I know that we could argue over data forever and not come to any conclusions except that, whatever the ultimate causes of problems affecting people, their bodies and minds will be involved; and manipulating bodies and minds will make at least some sort of difference. Agreed? Furthermore, most of the "supernatural" effects can be interpreted in parapsychological categories, even though the controlled research in that area hasn't yet produced evidence of powers great enough to account for all of the phenomena we've discussed. That doesn't mean that more research won't yield more evidence. So we're back to where we started, amalgamating so-called possession and altered states of consciousness. Just remember what one researcher said: "To reduce the supernatural to the paranormal

[30] See White 1976b; Wright 1960.
[31] Small 1973, 67.
[32] See Richards 1974, 100; Schmidt and Wilder 1968; Small 1973.
[33] Small 1973, 216; cf. Schmidt and Wilder 1968.

necessitates the predication of all demonic, spiritual, and poltergeist attributes to man—which leaves us with the same burden of phenomena under a different name" (Montgomery 1975, 38). The concept of possession is virtually universal precisely because persons have experienced these phenomena as alien to themselves and beyond the simply human. They have been consistently unwilling to attribute that experience to themselves alone. That's why I want to follow one more thread, the relationship of "demonic" phenomena to pursuit of pagan and occult activities.

* * *

AGAINST REDUCTIONISM: POSSIBLE DANGERS OF PAGAN AND OCCULT PRACTICES

I group pagan religions and the occult together because both are ways of attempting to go beyond human understanding apart from a relationship to a single, sovereign, beneficent deity.[34] They are ways of dealing with the forces of the universe, of trying to gain a measure of control or power, of trying—particularly in the case of the occult—to attain hidden or secret knowledge by esoteric practices and studies. Furthermore, they seem to come together negatively in the practice of witchcraft. (Whether witchcraft in the West stems from nature religions or directly involves Devil worship is debated, though in either case pagan and occult aspects are apparently present; see Lovelace 1976.)

The question is whether those engaged in pagan worship and/or occult practices tend to suffer symptoms of possession because they tend to be superstitious, suggestible, unstable people or whether there are dangers in these pursuits in and of themselves. This question may have no clear, empirical answer, though cautions against the pursuits abound. The apostle Paul warned, for instance, that sacrifices made to idols were really to demons—implying that there are demons behind the pagan deities (1 Cor. 10:20). Many—including persons who have themselves been mediums—believe that the spirits, familiar or not, contacted by mediums are demonic (see Gasson 1966). Many also hold that even innocent and good-intentioned experimentation with anything

[34] According to *Webster's New World Dictionary*, "pagan" now refers to any religion other than Christian, Moslem, or Jewish; it once referred to any non-Christian religion. We are here considering primarily polytheistic, idolatrous, and Eastern religions. Precisely what is to be included in the "occult," beyond specifically occult sciences such as magic, alchemy, and astrology, is fiercely debated by Christians. A few go as far as to include essentially Eastern practices such as TM and yoga. Many include any investigation of parapsychology. Most include personal experimentation with or deliberate seeking of paranormal experiences, and virtually all would include spiritism, mediumship, divination, and the like, practices explicitly forbidden in Scripture (see Deut. 18:10; Lev. 19:26, 31).

from hypnosis to yoga, astrology to ouija boards, can leave one open to demonic influence.

One person's caution is another's enticement. In our own country, interest in the demonic—and concomitant discovery of numerous "possessed" individuals—has burgeoned in recent years, as has practice of the occult. People seem bored with a mechanistic (or probabilistic), rigorously rationalistic universe and eager to affirm almost any alternative, however titillatingly dangerous or unlikely. Our current purpose, though, is to investigate not the roots but rather the fruit of such attractions. And before turning to our own culture, we must return briefly to those not our own.

Effects of Possession in Pagan Societies

We have already noted the numerous stimuli and varied social and personal conditions operative in many primitive and not-so-primitive societies that could be sufficient to induce symptoms of possession. I further implied that possession could serve some useful purposes, without stating clearly enough what an enormous trial it can be.[35] Among peoples as different as those of China and Sumatra, those strongly possessed are known to die early, perhaps due to the great stress of the possession state. Nevius (1893) reported that persons in China who yielded to demons and worshiped them found money starting to come in mysteriously or were healed or benefited in various ways—but the family ended up in poverty or other misery. The general pattern seems to be the classical Faustian one: powers are gained for a time, but only for a time. Death and destruction follow. In fact, demons have been known to say that they want not just to indwell but to destroy a person. In other words, in many cases the apparently benign face possession may show in its early stages changes radically over time.[36]

---

[35] Oesterreich 1974; Nevius 1893. I am not prepared to say whether there may be some shamanistic roles that yield no adverse effects besides a certain isolation from the community—an effect that is far from negligible in itself (see Anshen 1972). I have cited anthropologists who do not see mental illness either as a necessary precondition or as a necessary or even probable consequence of this role. This factor supports rather than undermines my point that something besides mere psychopathology appears to be operating, however much the latter may be fostered by some occult practices (in particular, mediumship and its kin). We must also remember that the social context of shamanism makes even its mediumistic aspects less likely to foster sustained dissociation: everyone presumably "understands" and sanctions the role. Finally and most important, anthropologists making positive evaluations are certainly not confronting shamans with a Christian witness; and very frequently a "demonic" reaction is aroused only by approach on a spiritual level (Richards 1974, 136).

[36] *Demon experiences* (1960, 40) records the comments of presumed demons. Similar sentiments are often expressed by one or more of the alters in multiple personality cases (Gershman 1975). One can easily hypothesize that a person is simply vocalizing self-hatred. A thus-far fairly trivial contemporary illustration of this changing character of possession comes from the experience of an American couple known to the author. One

Furthermore, the phenomena associated with possession respond strikingly to confrontation with Christianity. An illiterate East Indian woman who spoke English to a missionary could no longer do so after deliverance (*Demon experiences* 1960, 34). An eighteenth-century native American completely lost his widely acclaimed "spirit of conjuration" (with attendant miraculous manifestations) just by "feeling the word of God in his heart," apart from exorcism, and claimed he no longer even knew how to charm or conjure (Edwards 1949 [1817], 299). Apparently mediumistic gifts may also simply disappear, though in some cases converted persons (who show no psychopathology) are distressed by the return of states in which will and thought seem suspended by an extraneous power (Oesterreich 1974). Such occurrences are said to become less frequent with appeal to Christ.

On the other hand, possession may return full force if a person again worships idols or fails completely to destroy pagan deities, charms, or fetishes (Koch 1965; Nevius 1893).[37] Those seeking specific relief, however, may obtain it. In one case a woman was freed in the name of Jesus after ineffectively seeking help at various temples for nine years (*Demon experiences* 1960). More curiously, persons apparently *unaware* of the incompatibility of their contact with demons and their newfound Christianity have reported, for instance, a familiar spirit with healing powers returning with the message that it must go because Jesus is Lord of all. Similarly, one man whose sister-in-law had a demon carried on the following conversation:

> "What does the demon say?" I asked. He replied, "It said: 'If you believe in, and worship Jesus, this is no place for me. I must leave.' I said to it, 'I was not aware that I was interfering with you, or your interests. I believe Christianity to be the true doctrine. . . .' The

morning, what they thought to be angels told them that something was wrong with their car and that they should have it checked. They were surprised, as they had not been having difficulties, but followed the suggestion. Sure enough, there was a problem that could shortly have caused them considerable trouble. After a period of being helpful, the "angels" came more frequently and became more and more annoying, even pulling the covers off the bed at night and making this couple write poetry for them by automatic writing. (Koch [1965] comments that mandates from spirits start out rational but become increasingly irrational, eventuating in compulsions.) The couple were exhausted by the time they contacted the author's father, a pastor. Do we have simply a case of stress, accompanying poltergeist phenomena, and progressive personality dissociation? Martin (1976) comments similarly that spirits appear to gain entry through a trait of character or special need or interest; may help a person in his work; and may give physical protection, power with people, and prosperity or a chance to pursue satisfactions. However, the affected person's judgment, principles, and outlook are also touched, possibly resulting in loss of self-control and even of awareness of actions.

[37] The obvious argument here, if one assumes that possession phenomena express psychological conflict, is that return to idolatry or failure to destroy relics of one's old ways indicates a remaining psychological ambivalence that militates against conflict resolution.

demon replied: 'It may be very good for you: but it is very bad for us!' "
(Nevius 1893, 39)[38]

The upshot of the matter appears to be that, when a person is truly converted, not only contact with pagan deities and spirits must be cut off, but the powers seemingly mediated by those spirits or demons must sooner or later be given up as well, whether or not the person may find the powers desirable in themselves.

Effects of Seeking Contact with Spirits

Lest we assume that American and European culture protects us from such unsettling experiences, we must turn to the effects of practices all too common in the West, beginning with mediumship and its ilk. Even those involved in the occult (for instance, Rollo Ahmed and Dennis Wheatley) admit that many circles and séances attract undesirable spirits that lead to moral degeneration in adherents (Richards 1974). If immoral spirits fail to corrupt séance participants, the participants may yet succumb to their own psyche. One European psychiatrist has shown a high correlation between involvement in spiritualism or occultism and schizophrenia (cited in Montgomery 1975, 138). Also consider a thirteen-year-old girl with precognitive dreams who spoke in different voices in séance trances: "She hated the trances, because while waking up, she would find herself 'walking through hell, with devils all around, and it was *horrible!*' " (Moss 1974, 220). She became psychotic.[39] These comments equally apply to those who experiment with ouija boards. Suicide and mental breakdown commonly follow upon their use, even

[38]Here it could perhaps be argued that some telepathic communication of the missionary about the unacceptability of contact with demons was conceptualized by the new convert as a conversation with the demon. It is not immediately evident, however, that such an explanation would be the simpler of the two hypotheses.

[39]Note, further, the words of a German psychologist from Freiburg: "People who try to discover what life after death is like through spiritism and superstition are in danger of falling prey to the dark and hidden side of their own minds and souls. . . . I have quite a number of patients who have suffered serious psychic disturbances through the misuse of such practices. Their personalities have been split and they have been utterly confused by the spirits on which they have called" (quoted in Peterson 1973, 58–59; see also Koch 1965). The words of Boisen (1936, 198–99), whose resolution of his psychotic break was ultimately religious, are also significant: "I visited eight different mediums. . . . The outstanding impression left upon me was the disorganizing influence of their séances. Each medium assumed that he was under the control of some particular discarnate spirit, in each case a different one, and whenever he gave a message, that message purported to come from other discarnate spirits whom he saw hovering about the head of the person for whom it was intended. The whole thing was conducted in an atmosphere which was pervaded with the sense of the uncanny and mysterious. What struck me was the inevitable tendency of such performances to make for a disorganized universe. These discarnate spirits were nothing more than a conglomerate horde of supernatural beings of a low ethical order, some of them being distinctly diabolical. I was not surprised to find that the mediums themselves recognized the danger, especially to the beginner, of 'sitting in the silence.' "

by children: ignorance or innocence is no protection. Mediumistic and poltergeist phenomena affecting even neighboring residences may also follow such experimentation (Richards 1974).

Again, we have not established the source of such manifestations. Whether one believes mediums actually to be demonized (e.g., Unger 1953; cf. Langton 1949) or simply to be persons who dissociate easily and have considerable extrasensory powers, one should remember that the messages that they get from the spirits they supposedly contact are notoriously trivial, even if sometimes quite accurate. They do somewhat better with diagnosing diseases and occasionally make remarkable hits with prognostications.[40] It is at least peculiar that the spirits contacted or the "guides" or "familiars" of mediums and spiritualists seem universally to deny the divinity of Christ; and even spirits supposedly those of departed believers may blaspheme when asked about Christ (Cassidy 1975; Nevius 1893; Richards 1974).[41]

Effects of Other Occult and Pagan Practices

What about practices in which contact with spirits is not the explicit intent—astrology, dowsing, healing with charms, pursuit of telepathy

[40] Jeane Dixon's work, for instance, has been judged accurate enough to appear preternatural and inaccurate enough not to be of God (Lovelace 1976, 75). Lovelace concludes, "Examining Edgar Cayce and Miss Dixon, one is left with a sense of bafflement and pity for human beings who are straining to be altruistic, but are quite apparently being used for purposes and by forces which are beyond their comprehension. . . . It is apparent by this time that a common feature of most forms of occult behavior is the influence, and sometimes the total control, of alternate personalities over the minds of those involved" (pp. 74–76). This comment, of course, is a theologian's judgment and is based both on the ways these people receive their knowledge and the way that they depart from an orthodox confession of faith, despite a connection with Christianity. It is of interest that Jeane Dixon was made aware of her gifts by an old gypsy who gave her a crystal ball; and Edgar Cayce's father was a water witcher who could make brooms dance and plants grow. He obtained his gift while hypnotized (Lovelace 1976; Moss 1974). It is also interesting, though proof of nothing, that Cayce misperceived Hitler as essentially good (Peterson 1973).

[41] From this reaction to Christ one could conclude: (1) spirits have been contacted, and they are telling the truth; (2) demons have been contacted; or (3) mediums and persons interested in spiritism have a strong, unconscious hostility to Christianity that gets stronger the longer they engage in spiritism. (Theology tends, from a Christian viewpoint, to degenerate progressively as one pursues spirit contacts. See Douglas 1971 for the theological unorthodoxy of Canon Pearce-Higgins, an exorcist who consorts with mediums.) An acquaintance of the author experimented for a number of years (1967–71) with a ouija board and noticed widely different personalities coming through, as if different spirits were involved (all said they were dead, were in an intermediate state, and would be reincarnated). In various experiments, the board was rather good at card guessing and finding the cup under which a coin h ad been hidden. It refused to answer questions about the future, saying that the truth would hurt—thus the "spirit" seemed benevolent. After this acquaintance became a Christian, having had no teaching against the board, he continued using it; but on two occasions when he dropped a cross onto the board, the planchette moved to "good-bye" and would not return. The last time he used the board, the tone was suddenly different. Never before had it been evil or dangerous, but this time the message was that the experimenters were surrounded by evil. Badly frightened, they never used the board again and later burned it.

and clairvoyance, transcendental meditation (TM), and the like? I cite only an instance or so each, realizing that thousands upon thousands of people are engaged in these pursuits with, for all one can tell, no ill effects. (We may remember, however, that they remain involved because they are persuaded that somehow the practices work; and few care how [see Peterson 1973]. Perhaps, of course, the behavior is maintained by intermittent, strictly chance reinforcement.)

A striking case in the realm of astrology has been noted by Koch: a minister had an elaborate horoscope cast in order to prove astrology to be mere superstition, but then he found it coming true, detail by detail, for eight years. He was startled; and it came to him that perhaps the experiment was sin. He repented and found to his surprise that the horoscope was no longer true (cited in Richards 1974, 52).

Dowsing has been used by the United States Army to locate not water but land mines; and some believe that, used for either end, it exploits human sensitivity to low electromagnetic fields—a quite natural process. Moreover, it sometimes works better than complex instruments (Ferguson 1975, 13; Moss 1974). What do we say, though, when dowsing causes a green twig to bow strongly in such a way that the movement cannot be stopped or when effective dowsing is done over a *map* instead of "on location" (see Koch 1965)?

Healing by charms or conjuring is fairly common in Europe, especially in rural areas, and is applied to persons and animals alike. Koch (1965, 1973), after extensive study, is persuaded that, when such healing is successful in humans, distress is actually transferred from a physical to a psychological level. Furthermore, in many cases those who have been conjured become clairvoyant themselves, as if latent abilities were activated.

Telepathy and clairvoyance do occur spontaneously from time to time, as we have seen, and as such bring no side effects. Pursuing an aptitude for them, however, tends to increase their occurrence (Koch 1965, 58). The activity becomes less a lark when one begins to receive messages against one's will (Philpott 1973, 141).

TM seems innocuous enough, though it is known that meditation may lead to profound changes in personality, usually thought to be for the better (Ferguson 1975, 78–81; Moss 1974). However, TM teachers caution that prolonged meditation may lead to contact with spirits at their initiative and warn against involvement with them as a low form of consciousness. (TM might be considered more essentially pagan than occult: the initiatory Sanskrit prayer involves bowing down to Hindu deities.) Too much meditation has been known to lead to loss of contact with the real world and thence to insanity (Weldon 1975; cf. Sargant 1959, 1974).

As a matter of fact, it is perhaps significant that mystics of all faiths experience various psychic phenomena at a certain level of consciousness. All of them, whether Buddhist or Christian, warn against pursuing them. Mystics consider them dangerous temptations, deceptive, and obstacles to progress in the religious life.[42]

Witchcraft and Satanism

Thus far we have looked only at the "soft-core" occult and have ignored the "hard-core"—witchcraft and Satanism. We must at least mention these latter, for by the judgment of history, occult practices tend to be of a piece and to gravitate toward serious witchcraft (Lovelace 1976, 66).[43] Furthermore, the allure of power here, as elsewhere, does appear progressively to corrupt, just as white witchcraft seems to lead virtually inexorably to black witchcraft. ("White" witchcraft differs from "black" witchcraft in that it is supposedly practiced for benevolent rather than destructive purposes.) Nugent (1971, 78) quotes Sybil Leek, "Among my acquaintances are witches from all over the world. I do not know one whose first idea is a desire to serve humanity to the best of her ability." Or Satanist Anton LaVey: "No one ever pursued occult studies . . . without ego gratification and personal power as a goal"

---

[42]Eliade 1957; LeShan 1974; Lhermitte 1963. "A man in whom the pull towards preoccupation with his own will-power and his own achievements is marked may gradually become so much absorbed in psi-phenomena, and in his own glory as a wonder-worker, as to lose real interest in his ultimate goal, relaxing instead into the enjoyment of admiration, the exertion of power, and the deep satisfaction of being his wonderful self. The pride which has deflected him from his original purpose and made him from a contemplative into a clairvoyant may stop here, leaving him blinded with self-satisfaction, or may consume him completely, so that like a drug addict he is always craving for more, more recognition, more power, savouring the pleasure of ordering other people's lives until he comes to regard them as puppets (the more reluctant, the more satisfying), relishing the awe which he inspires until he has to pepper it with fear, and developing a fierce malevolence against those who do not yield him their tribute of admiration and obedience" (Haynes 1961, 116). Similarly, proponents of the contemporary "charismatic movement" within the Christian church are increasingly cautioning against preoccupation with the impressive, clearly supernatural "gifts" of the Holy Spirit (1 Cor. 12) at the expense of the "fruit" of the Spirit (Gal. 5:22–23) in a reshaped life. They neither discount nor devalue the former—much the contrary—but perceive dangers of pride and a looking to the gift rather than the Giver. (This sentiment was expressed, for example, in an address by classical Pentecostal David DuPlessis at the Fifth International Presbyterian Conference on the Holy Spirit, June 1976.)

[43]The relationship holds for other societies as well as ours. Lewis (1971, 124, 126) diagrams neatly the intrinsic relationship of witchcraft beliefs to shamanistic power: societies need to be able to discriminate genuine from spurious inspiration and to discredit shamans that abuse their power. "Both these requirements will be satisfied where two alternative and mutually incompatible theories of possession exist. Thus, if the same ostensible symptoms, or behaviour, can be seen either as intimation of divine election, or as a dangerous intrusion of demonic power, this will provide an adequate basis for acknowledging the claims of some aspirants while rejecting those of others" (pp. 170–71). The shaman is by no means an unambiguously benevolent figure.

(p. 71).[44] Witchcraft epitomizes the occult with the veil of innocent curiosity stripped away. What does it look like, unclothed?

It is utterly self-centered. "Almost all the cases of witchcraft in the literature, not only in Africa but also elsewhere, can be understood as centering on a breakdown in the flow of reciprocity" (Zuesse 1971, 227). In Africa, witches are seen as parasitic, gaining power from the divine flow but turning it back against the divine order for their own purposes. They wish to escape the ravages of evil by becoming one with it. Witches are usually the jealous, the isolated, the pained, the despairing, the weak—and hence, historically, most frequently women, though both sexes, all social strata, and many young people are involved today (Nugent 1971; Zuesse 1971).[45] Conversely—perhaps showing the depth of suspicion and hard core of evil in the human soul—the weak are more likely to be accused of witchcraft on the assumption that they have hidden powers of resentment and hatred (Zuesse 1971, 235). The result is encouragement of hatred, divisions, fear, purges—whether in Africa or Salem (Williams 1959; Zilboorg and Henry 1941; Zuesse 1971). The symbolism and the acts are sexual and oral. Sex and drugs tend to be part of the ritual today, and African witches speak in terms of incest and cannibalism; after all, the attempt to define one by oneself is an incestuous, cannibalistic urge (Nugent 1971; Peterson 1973; Zuesse 1971, 236).[46]

Is witchcraft a real issue today? One evangelical scholar asserts that in America the serious witchcraft movement not only is organized but is growing as vigorously as evangelical Christianity (Lovelace 1976, 81). In Germany, master sorcerers are said to outnumber Protestant pastors; in France, sorcerers outnumber doctors (estimates range from forty thousand to seventy-five thousand sorcerers). Swiss police have found worshipers of magic spirits behind an electrified fence in a sanctuary that had torture chambers (Evans 1970).

How does one become a witch? WITCH (Women's International Terrorist Conspiracy from Hell), substantiated by the writing of the infamous Arthur Waite, says, "You are a witch by saying aloud 'I am a

[44] Curiously, many contemporary witches justify their activities and search for power by the belief that humankind is essentially good and innocent; and they may be so sophisticated as to see their dancing and chanting rituals as a means of focusing psychic power (Chandler 1975; Peterson 1973; Woods 1971). However, Rollo Ahmed says that people are first drawn into black magic by "an insidious undermining of moral standards by the teaching that evil is only a relative term, that sin has no reality, and that one should give way to one's impulses" (quoted in Richards 1974, 85); occultists of integrity such as Arthur Lyons admit to the dark side of witchcraft as practiced.

[45] A significant part of the contemporary women's movement seems (unfortunately, in my view) to be replaying old themes by turning—aggressively, this time—not only to goddess worship but also to witchcraft as a way of affirming and asserting female identity.

[46] Note that the demonologies such as *Malleus Maleficarum* were also obsessed with lust, though antierotic; cf. Nugent 1971; Zilboorg and Henry 1941.

witch' and thinking about that" (quoted in Nugent 1971, 76).[47] As I have already commented, what one thinks and says *matters*.

Does witchcraft work? Doreen Irvine, named queen of the black witches (and later converted to Christianity), won her title by walking unharmed through a bonfire of seven-foot flames, calling on her master Diabolos (Richards 1974). Richards has a private manuscript telling of a person who became very good at killing others without any autosuggestion (as in most "voodoo deaths") involved. Historian Chadwick Hensen, evaluating in 1969 the Salem affair, concludes, "Witchcraft actually did exist and was widely practiced. . . . It worked then as it works now" (quoted in Peterson 1973, 65). And Nugent (1971, 78), more symbolically and ambiguously: "Witchcraft—even 'white' witchcraft—is dangerous. That is one reason why the alchemists of old laid it down that no one should devote himself to alchemy unless he is 'pure in heart and inspired by the loftiest intentions.' Otherwise, he might turn gold into lead."

In the long run, the pagan and the occult prove dangerous—and not just for those such as Aleister Crowley, who deliberately pursue evil (he wished to be the wickedest man alive) and, perhaps not surprisingly, end up bound by the powers they wanted to use to manipulate others. Dr. Harmon H. Bro, himself a psychic researcher, warns that those pursuing the psychic for selfish motives most often become distraught and alienated from friends and family, with their behavior and personality deteriorating sometimes to the point of suicide (cited in Richards 1974, 42). Of twenty-two cases in his files, half show social or psychological deviation. Dr. Kurt Koch, a Christian counselor with twenty thousand cases in his files, consistently finds those having symptoms of possession to have had contact with the occult. However—and of the first importance in thinking about the direction of causality between symptoms and practices—that contact need not be by means of personal experimentation or "occult transference" (the apparent passing of demonic power and influence from one person to another). Rather, the occult contact may be purely incidental and innocent, by way of a relative who is unknown to the patient and as many as three or four generations removed (Koch 1965, 1973). Furthermore, relief may be obtained by religious means (contrast the psychoses, also seeming to have a hereditary component but *not* assimilated en masse by Koch into the category "possession").[48]

[47] Williams (1959, 9) says the same thing differently: "No one will derive any knowledge of initiation from this book; if he wishes to meet 'the tall black man' or to find the proper method of using the Reversed Pentegram, he must rely on his own heart, which will, no doubt, be one way or other sufficient."

[48] See also Unger 1971. Does this family connection represent the sins of the fathers

The pagan and the occult are dangerous. Many of the phenomena are spurious; many symptomatic behaviors have quite sufficient alternative explanations. Nonetheless, there appears to be some sort of power tapped from unknown sources and some danger beyond that which is easily attributable to initial psychopathology. The "why" of the danger may seem as mysterious as the "whence" of the power and may—or may not—ultimately prove to be the same question. But, "Who are the casualties in warfare? The disobedient, the unarmed, the weak, the undisciplined and those with illusions about the war being somewhere else!" (Richards 1974, 134).

> There shall not be found among you any one who burns his son or his daughter as an offering, any one who practices divination, a soothsayer, or an augur, or a sorcerer, or a charmer, or a medium, or a wizard, or a necromancer. For whoever does these things is an abomination to the LORD. (Deut. 18:10–12)

being visited on the children to the third or fourth generation (Exod. 20:5)? Naturally, Koch's sample is biased by the very fact that not everyone would come to a Christian counselor and that only those having difficulties are looking for help at all. Koch (1965) recognizes that many stable people may be involved in the occult without manifesting any symptoms except perhaps a drift away from the church. Furthermore, one could argue that, if Koch covers three or four generations, it is hardly surprising that he can turn up some occult contact. Still, the size of the sample gives his observation of this correlation a certain amount of weight.

Part 2

Power

Power by its very nature has a spiritual component; and when we deal in the realm of power or impotence, we always deal, consciously or unconsciously, either with God or with the Devil.

5

The Nature of Everything—
with Special Reference to Power

Stranger: You know what I think?

Inquirer: No, what?

Stranger: I think you are superstitious—every bit as superstitious as one of Skinner's silly pigeons!

Inquirer: Why? I don't get it.

Stranger: Because you see occult practices and an indeterminate range of problems occurring together and simply assume they have something to do with one another. The most elementary course in statistics would tell you that spurious correlations are myriad, and *that* one is certainly spurious. I'm ashamed of you.

Inquirer: Maybe.

Stranger: No, I'm *definitely* ashamed of you. And then, after that initial indiscretion, demonstrating that you don't know much about *anything,* you presume to talk about "the nature of *everything.*" Where on earth did you come up with *that?*

Inquirer: Well, the issue is implicit in everything we've been talking about. The data don't fit together very well—or rather, they fit together in altogether too many ways. We seem to need a different world view for every fact we consider.

Stranger: Not that you like to exaggerate or anything! I've noticed that we've made a lot of progress with the world view we already have— which is obviously the point.

Inquirer: Besides, we indicated in our last conversation that people are looking for control, for power. They look anywhere for it, whether science or witchcraft—remember, we started out with the one and ended with the other. Not that the two are unrelated, of course, or that knowledge itself doesn't have a magical quality.[1] But anyhow, we

[1] See Russell 1938.

hardly know what we're tapping or how to tap it or what to avoid without some idea of how things are put together.

Stranger: Avoid? Draw fences around scientific investigation? Positively irresponsible. And besides, I, for one, doubt that you could even give a decent definition of power, much less talk about how it relates to "everything"!

* * *

THE CONSTITUENTS OF POWER

Definitions

"Power" can indeed be defined in myriad ways: one medium-sized dictionary provides fifteen different meanings. We, however, will be interested only in three general categories of power: (1) capacity to exert physical force or energy; (2) ability or capacity to act—to perform or produce; (3) ability to control or influence others. Each of these implies production of some sort of movement or change, whether physical or mental; each implies some sort of energy.

If we conceive movement and change in basically concrete, physical terms, such as when we speak of the power of a river or of a turbine, we may see the energy involved as essentially constant in the universe (though subject to the second law of thermodynamics) and may reasonably deal with movement or change by using such categories as "force" and "determinism," understood in a mechanistic sense. The first definition fits here. If we conceive movement and change as natural and inevitable properties of living organisms, as when we speak of the power of a horse to run a race or the power of a seed to produce a tree, we have moved to the level of open systems that, unlike nonliving things, can increase in organization and complexity. We have not succeeded in describing life wholly mechanistically, but we can apply such categories as "growth" and "decay." The second definition can be largely encompassed here. If, however, we conceive movement and change not as inexorable but as something that an intelligent being can promote or fail to promote, with or without the use of concrete controls (for instance, not only a person who can lock another up but also one who can inspire guilt in another may have a very *powerful* influence for change), we take in our third definition and enter the realm in which we may speak of a person's seeking or desiring power. After all, to talk in that way would be nonsense if power resources could in no way be distributed or directed but were fixed for all time.

When we speak of "power resources," we may be as physicalistic or as mentalistic as we like, moving all the way from pure force or constraint to the subtlest persuasive skills, but we should notice that the resources are sought precisely because they are *variously* applicable: we may use money, for instance, to buy any of a number of things or use education to be either a better crook or a better scientist.[2] In that sense power resources are a vehicle pointing beyond themselves. We rarely speak of power in the abstract; we speak of power to *do* something. Obviously, no one would care a fig about having power unless it could be used for one's own purposes (see Russell 1938, 274).

To mention purposes is to enter the realm of intentionality and will and hence, presumably, of some sort of freedom. However, we must observe immediately that no purpose on our part can be carried out unless we assume and rely upon a stable interconnection of events—a determinism, if you will (see Hobart 1934). It would be most disconcerting to flip the light switch, intending to read the evening paper, and instead have the water faucet suddenly start running. On the other hand, it would be equally disconcerting for the lights to go on suddenly *without* our having flipped the switch. I thus define "power," in the sense meant when we speak of someone seeking power, as *a union of structure and will*.[3]

I define "structure" as *any set of ordered relationships*. The structures may be physical, biochemical, psychological, interpersonal, political, and so on. Some structures appear more stable and reliable than others— perhaps intrinsically so, or perhaps because of the state of our knowledge. All structures are, from our standpoint, empirically derived constructs, not absolutes.[4] They are useful, not universal. As we have seen in chapter 3, we may construe them as acausal as well as causal, and we may to a greater or lesser extent choose which one(s) will operate. However, if we do not interfere or if we make no explicit choices, processes will continue quite deterministically "on their own": even though structures are not absolutely fixed, whichever ones are operating give at least a provisional path for getting from here to there and for defining what "here" and "there" mean.[5]

---

[2] I am not dealing here with what may influence or determine our *application* of the resources but am saying simply that their "nature," unlike the "nature" of a river or a tree, does not narrowly circumscribe what they may do or become.

[3] This definition, though foreign to our usual ways of thinking today, is not unprecedented. Indeed, Wink (1984, 3) remarks that "the ancients always understood power as the confluence of both spiritual and material factors." (I do not identify "structure" with "material factor," but I do affirm the necessity of the material if power is to find expression. Thus even demons seek *bodies*. See chapter 6 below.)

[4] "Any judgment which asserts the final validity of a certain structure of natural reality is a mythological and metaphysical opinion which rests on nothing by way of proof" (Heim 1953b, 140). Heim is speaking of natural or physical reality; surely other structures are even more ambiguous.

[5] A trivial (in the sense of being unidimensional and highly circumscribed) example of choice of structures is provided by transactional analysis and "games." Certain types of

I define "will" as *an ordering and choosing (that is, selective) consciousness.* In a sense, to establish or perceive any order is to make a choice, since we are not in touch with any single, absolute order. We focus on certain relationships as significant and ignore or fail to notice myriad other relationships or possibilities. Thus, even to will something as simple as going to the store means that I am conscious of not presently being at the store, of choosing to go to the store rather than remaining where I am or going elsewhere, and of knowing about a world in which movement from "here" to "somewhere else" is possible. (Physical locomotion is not possible, for instance, for a tree or for persons in certain states of consciousness or operating in transsensate realities.)

Now I clearly do not have *power* to go to the store unless both *structure* (path to the store, means of transportation, and enough cerebral neurons to keep the necessary sequence of actions in order) and *will* (perceived possibility and decision) are available and operative. Sheer physical ability does not give one the power to do something: a phobic may have all the necessary physical means but absolutely no power to pick up a snake until he is also able (through desensitization or whatever) to will to do so. More obviously, at least in our ordinary reality, all the will power we can muster will not turn the moon to green cheese: the structures to permit it are not available.

We may note that, on the force or constraint end of the power continuum, we tend to attribute changes to structural necessity (you made me fall by pushing me), while on the persuasion or influence end, we are more likely to attribute them to will on the part of the recipient of the power play (I decided from listening to your argument to lie down). We further infer that a person who is subject only to persuasion is *freer* than the one who is controlled physically, thus implying that physical structures are more rigid than mental ones.[6] In either case, however, the one employing power is utilizing *chosen means:* will plus structure.

Notes on Structure

To elaborate for a moment, I must quickly affirm the obvious: not all structures are alternatives, or interchangeable, or operative on the same

interactions have fairly reliable outcomes unless one party "refuses to play." Her choice of responses may break the pattern and institute a new one (see Berne 1964). This example illustrates how interpersonal power rests on interpersonal structures, but it of course has few of the metaphysical implications of the possibility of different cosmic-scale structures of reality that we discussed earlier.

[6]Skinner contends in *Beyond Freedom and Dignity* (1971) that this implication is both absurd and pernicious, leading to harmful means of control. The nature of my disagreement with Skinner will emerge in the course of the discussion and is founded on the belief that phenomena cannot be reduced to a single level of understanding.

level, or constraining in the same way—as I have already argued contra reductionism.[7] Rather, there are whole systems of structures in which each type is both a unity in itself and determined by those "below" and "above" it (see Koestler 1973, chap. 4). Consider language, for example, and the progression from phonetics to vocabulary, grammar, style, and content. Grammar is not possible without vocabulary, but in itself it does not produce content: we all know persons who use impeccable grammar to say nothing. The type of grammar chosen, though, will be determined "from above" by the style and content purposed by the speaker. Or consider physics and chemistry, which are essential to but can produce neither sentience nor a machine.

I must emphasize three points here. First, wrong functioning of lower levels can account for the failures of higher levels, but right functioning of lower levels does *not* ensure the success of higher ones. Thus, rusty components can prevent a watch from working, but shiny, new ones will not make it work unless assembled properly; or improper pronunciation can make a person incomprehensible, but perfect pronunciation of, say, nonsense syllables or an unknown language cannot produce comprehensibility.

Second, operational principles for machines or higher levels of explanation provide "rules of rightness" that account for successes but not failures. For instance, we can use logic to demonstrate (logically) correct reasoning but not to pinpoint precisely what is wrong in (logically) faulty reasoning (i.e., logic does not show which of two conflicting premises is untrue).

Third, once we have reached the highest level we can perceive in any given system, that level does *not* change its nature and suddenly become—unlike any other level—self-explanatory. Nor does the structure of a given level either automatically produce the next higher one or reveal what its nature must be. Thus a "flatlander" accustomed to only two dimensions could not fathom what a three-dimensional object would be like. Or given one-dimensional items such as five straight lines of equal length, we cannot tell from looking at them what they might mean in a two-dimensional world: they could be assembled to form a five-pointed star or a pentagon or an asterisk, for example. The components of our world are like those five straight lines: from a higher level, inaccessible to us, they could mean any number of things.

On the one hand, then, *meaning* always comes from beyond any given system (just as mathematical axioms cannot even be shown to be consistent without going beyond the system in use). On the other hand, we never fully know what is implied in what we say and believe. To add a further complication, not only do we always say and believe more than

[7] The discussion in this section is based largely upon Polanyi 1964, 1967.

we explicitly mean (that is, more than we intend), we also mean more than we say, as no vehicle of verbal or body language can fully and accurately express our intent. Structures on any level, then, are both absolutely necessary and entirely insufficient *vehicles* for meaning: they express it (point beyond themselves) but limit it by the very mode of expression (encapsulate it within themselves).[8] Every "explanation" or "reduction" assumes something larger that it explains or reduces.

Notes on Will

We have seen both how the constructing and choosing of paradigms leaves us wide open to error and how "will" can be influenced by physical and psychological techniques, such as when a person "chooses" to carry out a posthypnotic suggestion and rationalizes his doing so. I certainly do not argue for any absolute autonomy of the will, for to be wholly autonomous is to be unrelated to anything else. As soon as there is relationship, "something else" impinges upon us and influences us. I do assert, however, that our will is not to be identified with what impinges upon it. Regardless of our state of body or mind, in a profound sense *it* is not *we* until we own it. But what does the owning if not the will?

That the will is neither what has an impact upon it nor what results from its activity is intuitively obvious (see Heim 1953a, 71; Oesterreich 1974, 68). However, attempts to demonstrate this point falter because "will in itself" is discussed in terms of (and thus is obscured by) its lower-level determinants. In that sense, will is like structures in general. Will, though, is active in a sense that structures—which carry or channel activity—are not.[9] Will initiates; structures can only react, function, or grow—referring to physicochemical, mechanical or linguistic, and biological structures, respectively. (Thus we must differentiate will from

[8]C. S. Lewis approaches this problem in his sermon "Transposition" (1949) by noting that both love and lust are expressed by the same act, or that to transpose a large vocabulary into a smaller one involves using one word in many senses. (Sargant [1974] comments that the same conversion techniques can be used for good or evil ends. We could further note Schacter and Singer's experiment with injecting adrenalin into subjects: the same physiological response was interpreted as anger or euphoria, depending upon the context [Brown 1965]. Bodies have a limited number of possible physiological responses, and each can mean more than one thing.) Lewis goes on to suggest—and I will develop his idea in a slightly different sense shortly—that the "higher" may be related to the "lower" not just symbolically but sacramentally: what is symbolized is in a sense present, as a picture both represents and is a part of the visible world. Similarly, we could consider "body" to be a lower-level transposition of "mind." He concludes, "It is no good brow-beating the critic who approaches a Transposition from below. On the evidence available to him his conclusion is the only one possible" (p. 17).

[9]DeCharms (1968) uses the term "personal causation" to indicate that human beings are the origins of their behavior. He notes that a person's feelings of being an origin are more important as predictors of behavior than are objective evidences of coercion.

mere consciousness, which may be passive-receptive, though we cannot have will *without* consciousness.)

To initiate is to employ means with a view to some end. For instance, to think about a problem is to use the means of one's education and memory and creativity as mediated by one's cerebral neurons to aim at a solution. Both means and end are chosen (willed) from among whatever other possible means or ends one perceives. However, choice of either may bring unexpected and undesired consequences. If we recall from our discussion of structures that malfunctioning lower levels can affect higher ones and cause them to fail, we can see that, analogously, wrong means can destroy right goals: means are proximate ends and have a connection with ultimate ends. From the other side, wholeheartedly willed goals may entail aversive means, as when a desire to gain patience is fulfilled through the necessity of enduring a very trying situation. Thus our choices—even when made in good faith—are plagued by a profound ignorance of their consequences. Furthermore, we often fail to initiate what we truly believe we want to do: for whatever reason, we seem unable to do "the good that we would." We find ourselves impotent. When we add to this ignorance and impotence the error implicit in the "consciousness gap" (knowing and ordering always separate us from participation in a thing's reality and are always in some sense selective and arbitrary), our "will" seems to be a very feeble thing. Yet it *must* choose: if the existentialists have taught us anything, it is surely that everything we do or refrain from doing is in some sense a choice.

How "free" a choice appears depends upon whether we are looking back at its lower-level determinants or forward to that which emerges from but can never be encompassed by them.[10] Looking forward, though, brings into view a new issue. To make a choice or initiate action because of its anticipated future consequences implies that one supplies some basis, some standard of meaning, to guide one's choosing. Why make one decision rather than another? Reducing everything to "survival value" clearly will not do. Every martyr or suicide puts to lie the notion that mere survival has ultimate value. But if not survival, then what? Willing in itself, just like structure, does not supply meaning.

Notes on Power

When we put structure and will together, the result is power—structures are activated, and some impact is made on the world or other people. Naturally, in the light of all the uncertainties I have mentioned,

---

[10] Thus Chein (1972) says that we are dehumanized by that which prevents us from looking to our future. That is, a "will" specified only from below or from the past has none of the human quality of "willing."

people will tend to utilize first as means what can be most reliably predicted to produce particular outcomes; and the lower levels (except for indeterminacies of individual particles) are more limited and thus more predictable than higher ones. Hence the continual trend toward reductionism, the desire to make power to be bounded and controllable. Science, or "knowledge," pursues this route, and there can be no doubt that science has made whole nations powerful.[11] However, this route has two inherent problems.

First, by continually pouring will into knowing and operating that which is less than human, a person both defines herself in those terms and becomes a slave to those structures that she sees as crucial to her existence and to "progress." In valuing and choosing to live in terms of lower structures, we devalue what is distinctively human. It does not matter that we wish those structures to serve us: they will, but only by demanding more and more of our time and energy so that we end up serving them. On the simplest level, we note the housewife with so many beautiful vases—which she really likes very much and wants to show off to best advantage—that she must spend all her time dusting them. She may end up hating them in the end—though of course she has put far too much energy in them and they are far too valuable to consider giving them up. To move to relationships between humans, just put "personality" or "sex" in the place of "science." The more we polish our personalities or work on becoming great sexual athletes, the more the means again become an end in themselves and the human quality of a relationship is lost.

Second—and coordinate with the first problem—we have noted that neither structure nor will has any inherent meaning. It does not really matter whether hydrogen combines with oxygen or helium or both or

[11] It is by no means incidental that knowledge has the same components—structure and will—as does power, though in the case of knowledge, will's first step is in attending to and conceptually shaping structures rather than in acting directly through them to produce effects in the world. Obviously, we have to know something about how things are or can be connected before we can use them. Thus, knowledge is potential power and sought for precisely that reason. The problem is that knowledge can be shared indefinitely, whereas power is a limited quantity that exists precisely in the creation or manifestation of unequal relationships (see Libassi 1974). The one can be increased indefinitely, the other cannot (except by devising more and more ways of ranking, more and more ways of creating or perceiving inequalities). Since that which is potential strives for its own expression and realization, knowledge breeds a frustration that more knowledge cannot alleviate. Witness what happens when oppressed people find out how oppressed they are and know what they could do if only they had more resources, etc.; helping them just to know more about those things will scarcely make them feel any better. Thus the powerful are quite right in their instinctive awareness that to proclaim good news to the powerless is to proclaim bad news to themselves. Only those whose needs are fully met can afford to pursue knowledge supposedly for its own sake. Fewer still avoid using even knowledge so obtained to produce the power of snobbery and intellectual elitism, which is simply to demonstrate again that something of intrinsic value is lacking in "knowledge for its own sake."

neither, provided we know what it combines with and what happens when it does. It does not matter whether one is an "introvert" or an "extrovert," except as it impinges on particular relationships. It makes no difference at all whether I choose apple or cherry pie—unless there is only one piece of apple pie and someone else wants it.

Now then, zero plus zero equals zero: there is no more meaning in power (or knowledge) as such than in structure or will. It simply does not matter how much we can affect the world or others until we import some external criterion by which to evaluate the effects. For a little boy lighting firecrackers, a great big bang is much more impressive than a piddling sputter; but they both mean exactly nothing. However, who has ever known a small boy to be *satisfied* with a sputter? So it is with power. We can never get enough of it precisely because it is inherently empty; we keep believing that, somehow, *more* of it would finally do the trick. The final absurdity is the little boy getting a big enough firecracker to blow off his hand.[12] But we are moving too quickly.

It is a commonplace to note that we can destroy ourselves with our technology and even to see the absurdity of multiplying power resources until we can destroy everyone on earth ten times. When we have proved to our satisfaction—or rather, to our profound dissatisfaction—that all the power over the world or people that we can muster by manipulating every structure we can discover does not produce meaning, does not provide any basis for making new choices, what do we do? There are three alternatives. We may despair and call the world absurd, as it has shown itself to be, in itself: that is the existentialist solution. (In the words of Peggy Lee's song, "If that's all there is, then let's keep dancing, and bring on the booze, and have a ball, if that's all there is.") We may believe that the world is encompassed by a larger system that defines what is and is not meaningful and that we may find meaning and a basis for our actions by looking to higher-level determinants rather than lower-level ones, a "pull" rather than a "push": that is the religious solution. Or we may believe that there is power on a higher level than any we know and that attaining that power is the solution to our problems, since it is greater than the lower-level determinants of our problems; we hence commit ourselves to bringing the gods down to our level: that is the demonic solution.

* * *

Stranger: My, my, my; back to a nice, tidy, three-story universe again.
Though it looks as if you've given the Devil a place upstairs instead of

---

[12] Similarly the comment of Robert McAfee Brown (1976): "If knowledge cannot quite save us, it can very well destroy us." The words surely apply as well or better to realized knowledge, or power.

101

down, for a change. A definite improvement. Still, I thought we'd finally outgrown all that!

Inquirer: I wish we had—but I'm not sure that I mean the same thing you do in saying so.

Stranger: Meaning, schmeaning. Why are you so preoccupied with *meaning*? Everything from helicopters to human hearts runs quite nicely whether it means anything or not. I think we're wasting our time.

Inquirer: Haven't you heard a word I've said? I've been trying to make the point that human beings really don't run very well without meaning, that some standard of meaning is implicit in every choice that they make, and that there is no way they can stop making choices until they're dead. However many helicopters they build and however long their hearts keep beating, they're not satisfied.

Stranger: Ungrateful of them.

Inquirer: No, not ungrateful. I think it's part of "the nature of everything."

Stranger: So we're back to that again. I'd much rather talk about power.

Inquirer: That's what I want to do too, but how can we talk about it without knowing what sort of power is operating?

Stranger: I thought you were trying to say what sort with your little will-structure schema, until you got off on that "meaning" kick.

Inquirer: If you'll be a little patient, I'll try to show you how it all fits together. I have some ideas myself, and I also want to reflect a bit on Scripture.

Stranger: Oh no, here it comes. As soon as you can't buttress a demonstration empirically, you drag in "God" and "revealed truth" so that nobody can argue with you. I think that's a pretty cheap shot, myself.

Inquirer: I never noticed that "revealed truth" prevented people from arguing! Seriously, though, you'll have to admit from what I *have* demonstrated that, if there is no such thing as revealed truth, we're in a pickle for a way to derive values or to find any firm basis for decision down here. Not only do we need a system larger than ours to give it meaning, but we have to know at least something about it if it's to make any difference to us. Right? And we've shown that we can't figure it out from below. I don't see what we have to lose. We surely can't make the world any *more* absurd.

Stranger: Unless your "God" uses the world for a cosmic joke. That's possible, you know. "Meanings" aren't always positive for the guy who's one down.

Inquirer: True. I already implied that not every way of looking toward another level was helpful.

Stranger: Oh, when you brought in that "demonic" label? I thought that what you were talking about there, in terms of making a higher power relevant to real life, was certainly reasonable. In fact, your "demonic" solution seemed by far the most reasonable of the three. It's the only way that people can really enhance themselves.

Inquirer: We're going in circles again. Look, why is human life worth enhancing? Don't answer that, please. I really want to show you how that question and power fit in my little "nature of everything" schema. I promise it won't be elaborate, but I think it fits a lot of data, okay?

Stranger: Oh, all right. But I don't like your trying to sneak all of this Christian business by me.

* * *

MEANING AND THE SPIRITUAL DIMENSION

A Model

We must now look directly at the problem mentioned earlier of how such different "things" as mind and matter could influence one another. To construct a model, we shall return to the analogy of dimensionality as a way of describing how the various components (matter, mind, spirit) relate to one another. Then we shall superimpose the concept of levels of determination to suggest that higher dimensions have a certain priority over—and, of course, a certain dependence upon—lower ones. Thus, a two-dimensional figure such as a square gives significance to four one-dimensional straight lines but cannot be formed without those straight lines.

Let us suppose that matter is to mind as a line is to a plane—included in it, necessary to its expression, but wholly inadequate to produce it.[13] In its hypothetical pure form, matter would have no consciousness at all, just as a line has no breadth and hence is not a plane figure. But just as we have no "real" infinitely fine lines, we have no "real" matter that does not, so to speak, have some extension in the "plane" of consciousness.

---

[13] Note that we are talking of the created order and do not intend to attribute assorted necessities to the divine Mind.

As we start to move up the scale of living things (and considering the data presented in chapter 3), we would surely hold that a plant is more conscious than a rock. We need, then, to think of wider and wider sectors of a plane of consciousness as we progress from rocks to plants, animals, and human beings. In each case, everything is as "filled" with consciousness as its own being or nature allows it to be. The mental is coextensive with the physical—but not the reverse. (Our problem thus becomes not explaining how things like psychokinesis can occur—for mind is no longer conceived as making an impact on something quite other than itself—but rather why they happen so seldom. We will leave that problem for a later chapter.)

Taking the two dimensions of mind and matter, we can encompass the first two kinds of power we considered: sheer physical force, such as an explosion from combining chemicals, and the possibility of growth, as by a plant or animal. Structures of some sort are involved in each case— chemical valences, the structures needed for photosynthesis or metabolism, and so forth. In like manner, I would claim, the roots of will are involved. We have trouble seeing the propensity of hydrogen to unite with oxygen as involving choice; rather, their structures foster the combination. A bit less completely determined might be a plant's "selection" of nutrients from the soil. And then we have a given cat's preference for mouse rather than lizard for dinner—surely a "freer" choice than the plant's. As perceived consciousness increases, so does perceived ability to choose or will, to impose order rather than simply submit to it. Matter has the property of being orderable: within the limits of its structure, it "submits" to the order imposed. Mind *adds* the property of ability to do the ordering. (Mind remains, at the same time, orderable; otherwise we could have no science of psychology or process of psychotherapy.)

The roots of will, then, lie in the ordering function of consciousness. However, I suggest that consciousness alone does not *fully* account for will—for the ability (1) to choose with regard to the future and (2) to use structures variably to fulfill purposes rather than just allow them to fulfill themselves in an inexorable, determinate fashion. In order to will, and thus to have power in the third sense, another dimension and level beyond the plane of the mental (consciousness) and material is required, a level supporting not just process but purpose, or meaning. Furthermore, since such a level is not a necessity for the mental and material to sustain themselves, our very experience of willing is an indication of the incipient presence of that other level and dimension—namely, the spiritual. Like consciousness with respect to matter, the spiritual is as fully present as it can be in both mind and matter but is in no way derivable from them. Will is anchored from below in consciousness, without which it is impossible, and suspended from above by meaning, without which it would have nothing to do. In other words, when will purposes or chooses, it always draws its energy (or possibility for action) from the spiritual dimension.

Is the basis of our choosing always "good"? That is, what is the nature of our posited spiritual reality? A quick look at ourselves, and a quicker look at the world and at others, suggests that absolute virtue does not pervade all our decisions. We must admit the possibility, then, of a source of energy for willing (for ordering ourselves and our world) that, though it gives a basis for choice, is evil.[14] (I do not argue that evil may not *appear* good on some basis, but only that the consequences show it to be evil.) There can be no neutral source of energy for will because such a source could not do precisely what it must do: give us a means of choosing one thing as preferable to another. If there is a meaningful order to our world, our choices are right or wrong, not indifferent. Insofar as they are indifferent (as between apple and cherry pie, when there is plenty of both and one is not overweight), the choice is so truly meaningless that one might as well flip a coin.

Still maintaining that, taken alone, human willing provides no meaning, we must now say that there is no way, except in the most limited number of purely arbitrary cases, that human willing *can* be taken alone. Another dimension is implicitly present. It follows that power as a union of structure and will, power as an ability to exert control or influence, the power that men and women seek, is *never neutral* but either good or evil, dependent on what is energizing the will that is involved (and effective or ineffective depending upon the soundness of the structures involved).

We may diagram what I have been saying as in figure 1. I consider here the world only as human beings exist in and experience it; I do not by the diagram intend to deny the possibility that the divine or demonic will might work *directly*—not just through the human will—to produce effects in the world.[15]

[14]This is an argument for a limited dualism, a dualism limited by a fourth dimension and level: the overarching purpose of God, which encompasses even the demonic will. Whereas the other three dimensions can be derived to some extent from our experience, the fourth is an item of faith for which either divine revelation or a limitless human optimism and need for resolution is necessary. "In eternity there is none but the will of God; in time there is more than one will" (Barnhouse 1965, 29).

[15]I am not presenting a traditional trichotomist view of humankind, as if we could dissect three separate and discontinuous parts. No more can we separate a person's body and mind than we can have a plane with a single dimension. Furthermore, it is entirely possible in this view to refer to a person by using any one of the dimensions, for we have seen that higher levels are incipiently present in lower ones, even though lower ones cannot account in themselves for what is distinctive in human beings. (See Baumgartel and Schweizer 1968, who discuss σάρξ, ψυχή, and πνεῦμα as used for human beings as a whole.)

Dimension	Manifestation	Result When United

spirit—divine
  or demonic
  (meaning) — *ordering*

ordering → will

mind ←
  (consciousness) *orderable* — power (also knowledge;
             see n. 11)

orderable → structure

matter
  physical reality)

Fig. 1. Relationships Involving Will, Structure, and Power

A Reprise

Before making a few theological remarks on structure and will, I need to indicate more clearly how figure 1 reflects the discussion in previous chapters. Those chapters presented ways of producing effects in the world (and especially in persons); they were aimed at looking empirically at the nature of power. In chapter 1 we concentrated upon the material and noted two things: first, altering matter does indeed affect the higher level, consciousness, but cannot produce con-sciousness—just as we can destroy, speed up, slow down, or disrupt the functioning of a watch by tampering with its parts but need machine principles and a normative principle of accuracy to permit and then define its proper working. Second, while not just any arbitrary order fits the nature of matter, many quite different ones do: the order of which they will make use is established by an observer and agreed upon by a community.[16] Matter and mind are similar in being orderable, but the mental differs from the material in its capacity to be aware of order and its drawing upon the spiritual in the process of ordering.

Chapter 2 focused on the ordering aspect of mind as it affects body, illustrating my point that things are determined from "above" as well as from "below."[17] I argued that the apparent ability of mind to affect

[16] In physics, the principle of complementarity implies that observations that may contradict each other are neither complete nor totally correct views of nature. Blackburn (1973, 31) presents seven characteristics of complementarity: (1) a single phenomenon manifests itself in different modes; (2) description of the mode depends upon the mode of observation (interaction of observer and observed); (3) each description is "rational," not an appeal to revealed truth; (4) models cannot be subsumed by one another; (5) models are not independent because related to a single reality [we may agree with this statement even if we *also* believe in coinherent "realities"]; (6) not mere contradiction but rather different types of experience are indicated—incompatible predictions are not generated; and (7) neither complementary model is complete in itself.

[17] "Ordering" should be understood to imply both the imposing of an order or structure

other beings as well as its own body would suggest that it is not just an upper story but an intrinsic part of the whole of things—a dimension. Finally, we wondered how certain seemingly disproportionate effects of mind could occur and hinted that they might have something to do with the nature of belief. I would now say that in such cases, belief points not to a lower level but to a higher one where the "ordering" partakes of greater resources than we can muster and an energy is given to mind that it does not have in itself. Again, all of our levels are involved. (If I seem to have jumped here on the spiritual level from an ethereal "meaningfulness" to a very concrete efficacy, one must remember that an order that cannot maintain itself is futile or absurd, not meaningful. Thus God is always considered omnipotent by the orthodox, one who can enforce his will and not just pass out suggestions.[18] Power of a lesser but also forceful sort is attributed to the Devil, as we shall see shortly. We could thus place another power arrow on our diagram going down from the spiritual to the material. People do not have direct access to this type of power, however; we must use the channels of structure and will. We cannot command a miracle, though one may be worked through us. We cannot even mentally command matter directly but must utilize its structure.)

In chapter 3, looking at psi phenomena, I suggested again the possibility that the mental world is not only not discontinuous with the physical world but is not necessarily discontinuous with itself, with the result that physical channels may not always be required for communication. The overall thrust was similar to that of chapter 2 in emphasizing the reality of the mental, but I implied that connections could be just as real whether they were physical (cause and effect), mental (awareness), or spiritual (meaningfulness—or perhaps "coincidence"). Furthermore, I speculated about a series of coinherent worlds, or systems of relationship and meaning, in many or all of which the three dimensions could operate. The will would then have something to do, not just with establishing and choosing physical and mental structures in a single reality, but with establishing in which world both it and those structures will participate (what rules of relationship and meaning they will follow) and perhaps with determining how much willed discontinuity (or natural continuity) the various coinherent worlds will have.[19] "Willing" differs

---

and the commanding (or perhaps we should say energizing or empowering) of a structure—as if mind were to tell matter to grow or to heal.

[18] Eliade (1957) goes as far as to say that, though "the sacred always manifests itself as a power of quite another order than that of the forces of nature" (p. 124), yet manifestation involves limitation to the possibilities for expression present in lower levels, and hence manifestation of the sacred is always a manifestation of force (p. 126).

[19] This point speaks analogically, at least, to the problem in physics of whether we are dealing with discreteness or continuity, particles or force fields. At present, both languages are necessary (Aaronson 1974). I would suggest rightly so, because the determinant of

depending upon the reality within which it functions, and insofar as it is a higher-level determinant of lower levels, it follows that those lower levels are not the same—however they may appear—for persons with differing wills.

Finally, chapter 4 presented evidence from lower levels to explain the overt phenomena connected with so-called possession states and yet left us with the nagging question of whether something might be happening that simply cannot be inferred from considering lower levels alone, something that in the experience of all peoples has pointed them toward that which transcends themselves. The issue here, as at one point in chapter 2, becomes not just the abstract imposition of meaning by putting an unaltered world in an interpretive context, but the dynamic involvement—possibly even intervention—of the larger context: we are again dealing with dimensionality as well as levels of explanation. It follows that even activities not intended to have spiritual repercussions may have (or perhaps better, that *everything* in one way or another has spiritual repercussions). As just noted, not everything that looks the same is the same, because the spiritual and mental dimensions are not visible.[20]

what is discrete and what is continuous may be grounded in will, not physical nature, and hence may not be discernible by examining physical nature. Note also Deikman (1973b, 325), speaking on a "mental" level (lower than the willful, in our conceptualization): "Beliefs and assumptions act as barriers because they are mental activities, action currents transforming the still water of awareness into waves and eddies. To extend the metaphor even further, it would seem that some type of spatial correspondence exists such that the belief that one is a part of all mankind locates the delimiting barrier at a 'wider' periphery than the belief that one is totally separate from other persons. This effect of a belief occurs because the psychological event is an event in the biosystem, not an event isolated in a 'mental' world. Thus, a belief has substantial existence, although that existence is not to be defined as physical."

[20] Heim (1953a, 70–71) argues for a suprahuman and possibly evil source of will: "What we call the will . . . is not an energy within the narrow field of our human organism, existing side by side with the other, far more powerful energies in the world. . . . If it were that, the will of us puny human beings would be of no consequence at all for the course of world events. But the invisible force which we designate with the word 'will' is not comprised within the narrow confines of our tiny human existence. For since the volitional ego is not objectivisable it transcends the whole objective world space and all its spatial dimensions; so the will cannot be localized in the human body, this limited, objective structure—neither in the brain nor in the heart. . . . The will itself transcends three-dimensional space and the uni-dimensional objective flow of time. This supra-spatiality of the will can be recognized especially in the fact that in many cases one and the same will can gain possession of different human bodies which are spatially located far apart from one another and can use them as its instruments with demonic force." Consider also a psychologist's comment on the "messages from the gods" given by twentieth-century Hindu priests: "The impression is given of a strange objectivity intruding upon the consciousness. . . . It is naturally an assumption extraordinarily fertile in consequences to admit that there is not only a divine and transcendental power able to enter the human consciousness, but also lesser powers—it brings us perilously near to belief in the devil" (Oesterreich 1974, 349). Finally, Wayman (1968, 177) observes that "one can dream naturally, or by drugs; but who claims the dream is the same? . . . One can see visions through fasting on the desert, and then converse normally with men; and one can see

Some Biblical and Theological Remarks

Having related figure 1 to our previous discussion, I now wish to anticipate the topics of later chapters by making a few comments from a different perspective—namely, that of Scripture—on structure, will, and power. Dealing first with structure, we have already noted our human need for stability and our fear of the unpredictable and unknown. Very early in the Old Testament and throughout the Bible, we are given clues that God honors that need; that he has not mandated a chaotic, purely arbitrary universe; that he has established underlying structures prior to any that human beings may construct conceptually.

God said to Noah, "While the earth remains, seedtime and harvest, cold and heat, summer and winter, day and night, shall not cease" (Gen. 8:22). There is a natural order.

God gave the law for the good of his people (Exod. 20) and the prophets to proclaim his righteousness. Jesus said, "Think not that I have come to abolish the law and the prophets; I have come not to abolish them but to fulfil them. For truly, I say to you, till heaven and earth pass away, not an iota, not a dot, will pass from the law until all is accomplished" (Matt. 5:17–18). There is a moral order.

God has consistently provided leaders—kings, prophets, governors, bishops—for his people. Paul said, "Respect those who labor among you and are over you in the Lord and admonish you" (1 Thess. 5:12). There is—often ambiguously and yet truly—a sociopolitical order.

God said through Moses, "If your heart turns away, and you will not hear, but are drawn away to worship other gods and serve them, I declare to you this day, that you shall perish. . . . I have set before you life and death, blessing and curse; therefore choose life" (Deut. 30:17–19); through Elijah, "How long will you go limping with two different opinions? If the LORD is God, follow him; but if Baal, then follow him" (1 Kings 18:21); through his Son, "No one can serve two masters. . . . You cannot serve God and mammon" (Matt. 6:24); through Paul, "You cannot drink the cup of the Lord and the cup of demons" (1 Cor. 10:21). There is a spiritual order.

All of these structures are quite explicitly for human good. None but the spiritual order is absolute; in fact, the other orders would not be fully for our good if they *were* absolute. Every miraculous act of God breaks into the natural order.[21] Jesus said, regarding the law, that the

visions through delirium and converse abnormally with men. And who knows that the visions are the same? . . . Or are these judgments made simply through skepticism of any abnormal powers of mind [or spirit], refusing to admit those powers to anyone when the researcher himself lacks them?"

[21] As a possible further commentary on God's involvement in the whole of the world, consider Matt. 10:29, referring to sparrows: ἓν ἐξ αὐτῶν οὐ πεσεῖται ἐπὶ τὴν γῆν ἄνευ τοῦ πατρὸς ὑμῶν. This clause is usually translated, "not one of them will fall to the ground

Sabbath was made for man, not the reverse (Mark 2:27). Peter and John, in the sociopolitical arena, boldly proclaimed that, when the mandates conflicted, God and not man must be obeyed (Acts 5:29). The last, also for human good, *is* absolute because not to choose God is to choose death. We may be free to choose, but we remain free only when and if we choose God.

With respect to will, the biblical usage fits very closely the understanding at which we have arrived. We should be careful to note, however, that the sense of volition as such is primarily Greek, whereas the Hebrew concept emphasizes "desiring" or "taking pleasure in." The two ideas together give a motivational tone that is not simply abstract or representative of some segmented mental portion of a person's being but includes the whole person. The broad New Testament usage includes everything from readiness or inclination to desire, intention, resolve, and commanding will (i.e., God's or an administrator's). Both verb and noun are used of God and Christ, of human beings, and of Satan. God's will, with all its absolute efficacy, is spoken of with reference to the divine sovereignty, God's will in creation and salvation, and what he requires of the righteous. Strikingly, when used of God, the noun is singular (God's will is unified) and all but once refers specifically to his will to save. By contrast, though Satan's will asserts itself with at least a pseudosovereignty, it aims to destroy (Luke 4:6; 2 Tim. 2:26).[22]

To do God's will is presented as the essential goal, condition, and content of the Christian life (Col. 4:12; Matt. 12:50; Mark 3:35; John 7:17; Rom. 12:2; Phil. 2:12; Heb. 13:20–21; 1 Peter 4:2). Human willing, however, is marked by its impotence and failures: "I can will what is right, but I cannot do it. For I do not do the good I want, but the evil I do not want is what I do. . . . Wretched man that I am! Who will deliver me from this body of death?" (Rom. 7:18–19, 24). No amount of resolution or desire suffices. In fact, the human will is always presented as either arbitrary and (falsely) autonomous or expressive of

without your Father's will" (RSV) or "without your Father's leave" (NEB). The KJV, however, translates simply, "without your Father," adding no logical implications to the literal words of the text. Is it possible that we should see here God's personal, participating presence in the whole of his reality? Such an understanding is implicit in our diagram but is emphatically not to be confused with an independent "divine spark" in nature or in humankind. (See Marshall 1974, 14.) The whole passage, Matt. 10:26–33, is a key one in terms of the echoing of earth in heaven and the whispering of heaven in earth. God *will* manifest himself, but the acknowledging of him is absolutely crucial.

[22] The noun "will" is used of Satan only in 2 Tim. 2:26. Grammatically the word here could refer to God rather than to Satan, although the natural sense of the text makes Satan the referent. In the Old Testament, Isa. 14:12–20 and Ezek. 28:1–19 are also widely believed to refer to Satan's willfulness, his desire to exalt himself to be like God, though in the historical context they are addressed to kings of Babylon and Tyre (see Freeman 1971, 68–70; Barnhouse 1965).

sexual desire.[23] However—and of absolutely primary importance—the higher will, or spiritual dimension, expresses itself in time, if not in eternity, precisely *through* this fallible human will. (Figure 1 diagrams this relation, one that is illustrated in Jesus' human will, which reflects the divine will, or in the kings of Tyre and Babylon, who manifested the demonic will.) Thus the energizing force, or power, of the human will, and not just its isolated impotence, *seems* to come from within rather than being something imposed from the outside (see Heim 1961a, 93). Both the divine and the demonic wills take hold of one's inner being, engage one in such a way that one's responsibility remains (as if one's own will were analogous to parts of a watch that must be free of rust as a necessary condition for the watch to work). But to identify responsibility with independence is to make a fundamental mistake (like shaking up shiny watch parts in a bag and expecting them to keep time). The human will—which expresses the human spirit—is essentially related to a greater, a spiritual, dimension.[24]

Coming finally to the concept of power, we must consider three basic New Testament ideas: (1) the idea of power as a sort of cosmic principle implying that the whole of life is dynamic; (2) an overlapping idea entailing ability, authority, power, and freedom in the political sense; and (3) the sign or manifestation of power.[25] All of these terms apply to divine and satanic power, and only derivatively to that of human beings. To take first the most physical of the concepts, we see that, even in the Old Testament background, there is no sense of capricious natural forces but of the willful might of a personal God of history (Grundmann 1964). This fundamental presupposition does not entail that everything taking place in this world is *directly* willed by God,

---

[23] For the preceding comments on will, I am indebted to Schrenk 1972.

[24] In speaking of the human will and spirit, we must remember that "the πνεῦμα, though always God's Spirit and never evaporating into the πνεῦμα given individually to man, is also the innermost ego of the one who no longer lives by his own being but by God's being for him." Yet, "this πνεῦμα which abides in man is not described as more than something which, related to God, is set in him. It is not the soul perfected by God's πνεῦμα" (Baumgartel and Schweizer 1968, 436). Thus there can be no neutral ground between the πνευματικός and the ψυχικός. The latter is *not* bereft of spiritual input; however, he is controlled by the πνεῦμα τοῦ κόσμου (1 Cor. 2:12–15; cf. 15:44–46), a demonic force, instead of by God's Spirit. The "spirit of the world," when pervading a person, may give him a basis for decision making but provides no link to God. The point, though, is that a person's will functions only as related to something greater than itself. Similar is the Old Testament usage of רוח, carried over into the New Testament understanding of God's Spirit as the principle that gives life to the body and as that which, divinely effected, gives, upholds, takes away, and hardens (Baumgartel and Schweizer 1968). "Spirit" is then by no means absent from any level of human life (see note 15 above).

[25] Δύναμις, ἐξουσία, and σημεῖον, respectively. The concept "miracle" or a word strictly translatable in that way is not to be found in the New Testament, though δυνάμεις, "mighty works," like σημεῖον, "sign," verges on it, as do τέρας, "a wonder, omen," and θαῦμα, "a wonder."

but it does entail assurance that even satanic rebellion can continue only by God's power and that any power *not* in active communion with God is not neutral or harmless but demonic. (See Heim 1961b, 37. Note Grundmann's [1964, 307] comment, "There are no cosmic powers which are not spiritual or angelic." This sense of the power of demons—and angels, on the positive side—and their interest in humankind, developed first in rabbinical and Hellenistic Judaism; but Jesus' power too, the power of the Holy Spirit, is exercised specifically in relation to demonic forces.)[26]

Now God could have no enforceable authority without having power in the cruder, more physical sense. However, at another level, no power of any sort can be allocated in the first place without God's authority—not even the power utilized by the Antichrist (see Foerster 1964b). Thus, whatever concrete power or authority under Christ may be given to the disciples or the Christian community (e.g., Luke 10:19; 1 Cor. 12) belongs fundamentally no more to them than to the demonic forces. Ultimate authority rests with God.

However, a complicating factor arises in that one cannot tell simply from its surface manifestations whether a given sign or instance of power has been demonically channeled—that is, whether its immediate source of energy is good or evil (see Heim 1961b, 38). Thus some attributed even Jesus' power to the Devil (Mark 3:22), and in the end times "false Christs and false prophets will arise and show great signs and wonders, so as to lead astray, if possible, even the elect" (Matt. 24:24; see also 2 Thess. 2:9–10 and Rev. 13:13).[27] The quality of a sign, particularly as connected to the person *doing* the sign, is crucial (see Rengstorf 1971), not the mere quantity of signs or even their apparent "goodness." There would be no deception if demonically channeled power did not appear to work desirable effects.

We have come by yet another route to the conclusion that things may not be what they seem. A reductionistic set of explanations, whether to physical nature or to conscious life, may not suffice. If there is a spiritual dimension to reality, then we may find that value as well as fact becomes crucial not just to our living but even to our understanding (insofar as

---

[26] " 'Chez les Stoïciens la puissance a avant tout une signification cosmique. Il s'agit d'une explication physique de la nature. Nous avons vu, au contraire, que les puissances acquièrent ici leur plein sens par le rapport à l'âme humaine' " (Grundmann 1964, 298, quoting Brehier). Note also the "classical" theory of the Atonement, in which the death and resurrection of Christ are interpreted as a victory over the demonic forces. This position has been powerfully expounded by Aulén (1935).

[27] For a more exhaustive treatment of Jesus' spiritual power and ways it was misunderstood, as depicted in the Gospels, see Brown 1984, chap. 11.

"understanding" of the higher by the lower is possible) of the world in which we live and how it operates.[28]

"Power" is a very basic concept. Suppose it is grounded in will as well as in structural relationships. What, then, if more than one will does operate in our time-bound existence, even if not in eternity? Then the nature of the will involved in any manifestation of power, from the simplest to the most remarkable, might be of absolutely the first importance. But if things are not what they seem, how can we tell their nature?

Even logic forces us to admit the insufficiency of strictly empirical differentiations on such an issue. The inner core cannot be seen from the outside. To suggest that there may be something to see, and more, that there may be a way of seeing it, is in this context to say that we seek to go where science by itself cannot go—a risky business, for by abandoning its constraints, we also abandon its protection. We move into realms in which we can easily deceive ourselves—or be deceived. Nonetheless, we are surely deceived and lose our humanity by taking the reductionistic route. The Bible claims to show us something of that which is greater rather than less than we are. To attempt to take Scripture seriously may prove a lesser risk.

---

[28]Scientist M. R. Cohen said, "The category of reality belongs not to science, but to religion" (quoted in LeShan 1974, 83).

Part 3

Pathology

Satan may be characterized by raw power. The more we lack power—the more we suffer from weakness or pathology in some area of our lives—the more tempted we may be to fall into his snares.

6

The Personal Springs of Evil

Stranger: May I give you some advice?

Inquirer: Of course.

Stranger: What you are about to do is extremely dangerous. I'm older than you are; you really should listen to the voice of experience.

Inquirer: Well, I'll at least listen.

Stranger: You are leading us straight back to the Middle Ages as far as science and progress are concerned—a terrible mistake. Worse yet, it looks to me as if you're simply trying to get out from under what all those philosophers call "the problem of evil" (I gather that that is really what you're concerned about?) by importing alien spiritual entities as an explanation. Now, to do that obviously interferes with people's first of all taking responsibility for their own actions and, second, their going about solving problems that come to them through perfectly natural processes. For instance, if we still attributed pneumonia to the Devil, a lot more people would be dying of it today. Surely you wouldn't want to return to those days!

Inquirer: Of course not.

Stranger: I'm glad to hear it. I was beginning to wonder for a minute there. People are really quite capable of inventing by themselves all the evil they have wrought; they hardly need outside help.[1] Even plenty of theologians treat the demonic as something approximating "original sin," whatever that is. At least the demonic understood that way remains part of the nature of human beings and creation.[2] And

[1] See Kelly 1970.

[2] More precisely, Tillich (1963, 102–6) treats the demonic as a symbol characterized predominantly by "splitness" rather than "centeredness" of persons. The problem as he sees it lies in the ambiguity of human self-transcendence: looking but being unable truly to reach beyond themselves, people elevate the claim of something finite to absolute or divine status and so split it off from the rest of finite reality. This creation of false absolutes is "demonic" but virtually inevitable, as even divine revelation could only be expressed by human beings in finite—and hence distorted—terms. Evil is thus unavoidable not so

then if you add institutions and all sorts of collective entities, the possibilities for what you call evil are positively boundless (even without mentioning the fact that everyone destroys simply to live: did you have meat for dinner last night?).

Inquirer: Yes.

Stranger: Point proved. You see, "evil" is also a purely relative term. It's simply a label for situations disadvantageous to some person or group. I grant that what hurts the individual may help the group, and vice versa: it might be to my benefit to be cowardly, but not to my country's benefit. Thus my point is again proved—values are relative. And every ethicist knows that any rules you make are sometimes— probably often—going to come into conflict, so they put people in the awkward position of doing some "evil" all the time. I don't think that's fair. The most practical choice should simply be called "good," so that people aren't always feeling guilty and having to go to psychologists because they get so upset. The lines we draw between "good" and "evil" are positively pernicious.

Inquirer: The Bible teaches us to draw them, and not to get them mixed up. It says, "Woe to those who call evil good and good evil, who put darkness for light and light for darkness, who put bitter for sweet and sweet for bitter!" (Isa. 5:20).

Stranger: Lovely poetry.

Inquirer: But you're distracting me. I'm quite aware of the problems you're raising—natural evil, human responsibility, conflicting values. From the very beginning, good and evil have been the province of God (Gen. 2:17; 3:2–5). Maybe our very relativism and our difficulty in judging well demonstrate that we *aren't* gods.[3] We are stuck with having to differentiate between good and evil without really knowing how to apply the categories[4] and without being able to foresee all the consequences of our choices. And maybe the whole tangle makes it all the more striking that the Bible speaks more about the Devil than about evil in the abstract. On the face of it, one would think that making those difficult differentiations is precisely where we need help. Instead, Scripture talks about the Devil and his minions, about a rebellious will and not about a recalcitrant fate.[5]

much because of any intrinsic wickedness in humankind or the operation of an evil will external to their own but because self-transcendent yet finite beings cannot but attempt to express ultimates in the nonultimate modes they have available to them.
[3] See Rougemont 1945.
[4] Anshen 1972, 24.
[5] See Heim 1961a, 89.

Stranger: Oh, come on. Now you're not just hiding from ghosties and ghoulies yourself but are dragging them in to frighten others. Misery loves company, provided the company is miserable enough. Your miserable myth should just about do the trick. Leaving people with their problems completely beyond their control, and spooks in the corners to boot—a dreadful doctrine.

Inquirer: On the contrary. It has been well said,

> One of the reasons why confusion is gaining ground in the world is that we are afraid to face its real causes. We believe in a thousand evils, guard against a thousand dangers, but we have ceased to believe in Evil and face the real Danger. To demonstrate the reality of the Devil in the world is not to increase fear, but to restore to fear its proper object.[6]

Stranger: Proper object? A *new* one then. I'll bet you don't even know your Scriptures. I'll bet you don't even realize that Satan is scarcely mentioned in the Old Testament—on three occasions, I believe. Not very impressive for the supposed source of all the world's problems! Or didn't people need a scapegoat then? (Or could they make do with a *real* scapegoat? A nice symbol, I must admit, but what a cheap trick to proceed to symbolize the *Devil* as a goat![7] Talk about projection!)

* * *

THE BIBLICAL DATA

The reader who comes to Scripture expecting to find a single, coherent picture of Satan, a picture of the sort that would be a reasonable model for the great devils of literature, will likely come away confused, frustrated, and uncertain. There are data, but they are varied and do not easily lend themselves to systematization.[8] The Old Testament, diverse in itself, does not sound much like Paul; and neither sounds like the Gospels. The settings differ, and so do the vocabularies and focuses of attention and ways of conceptualizing spiritual forces other than God. There is a historical development of the idea of Satan.[9]

---

[6] Rougemont 1945, xi.

[7] As a matter of fact, the scapegoat has long been associated with the Devil. It has been identified with Azazel, who, in the apocryphal book of Enoch, led the rebel angels and seduced humankind (see Brown 1984, 315).

[8] This problem is scarcely limited to the subject of demonology. Subjects as central to Christian theology as the Trinity, the relationship of the divine and the human in Jesus Christ, and the relationship of divine sovereignty to human freedom are nowhere given a clear and systematic formulation in Scripture itself. No doubt such formulation would betray a fundamental mystery and lead us to assume that we understand what cannot be fully understood by finite beings.

[9] For an argument that the idea of evil itself changes over time, see Ricouer 1969.

But the common thread in the varied tapestries is acknowledgment of an unseen spiritual reality that can be harmful, dangerous, or evil. Scripture does not in fact attribute all evil to human perversity but posits an outside, willful source of temptation and attack. We must survey biblical ways of picturing this demonic reality before attempting a synthetic or interpretive approach.

The Old Testament and Intertestamental Writings

One of the most striking features of the Old Testament is that, though written in a culture pervaded by animistic and polytheistic beliefs, it pays virtually no attention to any spiritual powers other than Yahweh himself (see Morosco 1974). It leaves no place even for an ultimate dualism in which God is matched against a similarly powerful devil, much less for a raft of competing, coequal deities. This point does not imply, however, that there *are* no spiritual beings other than God himself: rather, he is pictured as surrounded by a host through which he rules indirectly, including angels of wrath that do his will (e.g., Exod. 12:23; see Kallas 1975). Satan, to whom we shall return shortly, is apparently one of this host. Other indications of an unseen, potentially threatening, spiritual reality are found in suggestions of "theriomorphic" demons (demons in the form of animals), in prohibitions against magic, and in certain passages referring to ancient kings that many believe point beyond the actual reigns of those kings (Isa. 14; Ezek. 28).

Most of us, in thinking of Satan, are likely to start with the subtle serpent in the Garden of Eden, who is assumed to be the prototype of the Devil. However, that connection is not made in Genesis, nor anywhere else in the Old Testament.[10] Indeed, the whole passage is curiously neglected.

We find Satan—a rather insignificant servant of God—mentioned only in the first two chapters of Job, Zechariah 3:1–2, and 1 Chronicles 21:1; only in the last case does the word appear without the article, as a proper name.[11] The word itself means "adversary." The "satan" functioned as an accuser, seeking to separate a person from God. Thus the concept is basically a legal one, though we must not forget that the Adversary also had physical power over Job. But whatever power he

---

[10]The connection is made explicitly in Rev. 12:9 and also in rabbinic and apocalyptic writings (see Langton 1949).

[11]The English "Satan" and Greek σατανᾶς are simply transliterations of the Hebrew שׂטן. 1 Chron. 21:1 is a late passage (cf. 2 Sam. 24:1), attributing to Satan what is apparently thought to be unworthy of God (Caird 1956). But see also 1 Kings 22:20–22; Judg. 9:23; 1 Sam. 16:14; 18:10. Whether or not the latter two "evil spirits" should be conceived as personal agents, the fact that a proximate evil is unabashedly attributed to God must be noted. The case of Saul in 1 Samuel is the only case of possible spirit possession as such mentioned in the Old Testament, but note Lev. 20:27, describing a medium as one in whom there is an אוב, or spirit (Langton 1942).

had, he had it from God; there is no suggestion of a second fundamental source of power in the universe.[12] Other faiths provide no analogy for such a being. And this emphasis on the sole sovereignty of Yahweh means that one cannot escape him by turning to other religions or seeking out other forces.

Even so, forces not conformed to Yahweh's holiness do appear. Theriomorphic demons may be much more prevalent than the modern reader recognizes (see the thorough discussion in Langton 1949). Isaiah 13:20–22 and 34:13–15, for example, describe animals consorting with demons, and Leviticus 17:1–7 suggests that demons reside in the desert. The Septuagint (the early Greek translation of the Old Testament) frequently uses the term δαιμόνιον—a diminutive of δαίμων, "demon"—with respect to phenomena that could appear to be simply natural (Morosco 1974) and also as a contemptuous term for heathen gods, as if to suggest that the heathen worship dreadful spirits (Foerster 1964a; see Gruenthaner 1944).[13] In any event, it was perhaps the very pervasiveness of belief in such spirits that led the Old Testament writers not to emphasize demons (Kinlaw 1976). They did not deny demons but rather instituted specific prohibitions against all dealings with them, whether magical or directly spiritual.

Prohibitions against dealings with spirits or demons are not a denial that such dealings are possible. If anything, one would have to say that the reality behind magic is accepted: witness the feats of Pharaoh's magicians, Exodus 7–9, less mighty to be sure than the miracles of God, but impressive all the same.[14] Still, magic is always condemned in Scripture (Kitchen 1973; Smoker 1961), including the use of charms (Isa. 3:18–23; Ezek. 13:17–23) and all forms of divination: astrology (Isa. 47:13; Jer. 10:2), hydromancy (Gen. 44:5, 15), and, above all, necromancy (Deut. 18:11; 1 Chron. 10:13; Isa. 8:19–20; cf. Rev. 9:21; 21:8).[15] "Black" and "white" magic are not differentiated.

[12] I do not deny the possibility of later dualistic influences, but only of an original dualistic background (see Caird 1956; Foerster 1964b; Gruenthaner 1944).

[13] The Hebrew שָׂעִיר may be translated simply "hairy goat" but equally—and in these instances very probably—means "satyr" or "demon" (see Brown, Driver, and Briggs 1972, 972; Morris 1973; also Caird 1956; Langton 1942). In classical Greek, prior to the Septuagint, δαιμόνιον is used only as an adjective meaning a supernatural sign (Langton 1949, 94).

[14] See Zuck 1971 for a listing of Old Testament references to witchcraft or magical practices; see also Kitchen 1973 and Wright 1973a.

[15] The Bible does relate some events—for example, that of the mandrakes in Gen. 30:14–18 and peeled rods in vv. 37–41, as well as casting of lots and use of Urim and Thummim (Motyer 1973) and use of dreams for knowledge—that seem magical or spiritualistic yet are not reproached (see 1 Sam. 28:6). Dreams were used when they occurred spontaneously, but there is no instance of deliberately asking for knowledge through them. Though the other cases may have naturalistic explanations, they apparently do not differ in intent from actions that Scripture plainly condemns and perhaps should be seen as descriptive and by no means normative accounts.

Likewise condemned are approaches to a "wizard," or "soothsayer" (יִדְּעֹנִי). Such persons' knowledge is seen as illicitly obtained: the Hebrew word comes from the verb "to know" (יָדַע) and always appears with the word for "medium," or one having a spirit or ghost (אוֹב). (Even the magical has a personal element, implying the cooperation of spirits and the belief that a given cause does not necessarily have the same effects at all times; see discussion in Langton 1942.) But the point is that seeking hidden, superior knowledge in these ways is forbidden. *The Old Testament data imply that there is indeed more spiritual power available than we are permitted to explore.*

Before leaving the Old Testament, we must at least note two controversial passages that, while they do not mention Satan or demons as such, seem to imply an early rebellion against God: Isaiah 14:12–20 and Ezekiel 28:11–19. The debate continues over whether these texts should be limited to their historical reference to the kings of Babylon and Tyre respectively or whether these kings in some sense typify Satan. If the latter, we find here the only hints Scripture provides as to the Devil's origin, hints used to full advantage by authors such as Goethe and Milton in their depictions of a supremely prideful and jealous creature.

The Old Testament is simply not concerned with an elaborate, well-integrated, theoretical treatment of evil or of evil spirits, as can readily be seen even from this brief survey. Even in Job, which centers specifically on the problem of evil and on its cosmic roots, there is no countenancing of the speculative theodicies of Job's friends and no prying curiosity into the mechanics of the Adversary's workings and authority. The whole focus remains on maintaining a right, obedient relationship to the one sovereign God.

People were not satisfied to leave the matter there however; thus demonology developed considerably in later Judaism and the intertestamental literature. The Devil comes to be seen as destroyer as well as tempter, accuser, and thwarter; and demons are seen as functioning to harm life and limb (though they were not believed to be the cause of all sickness). Elaborate angelologies and cosmologies are constructed. The bridge between good and evil spirits disappears; and in the pseudepigrapha, Satan, as an evil will apart from God, appears as the single head of the demonic forces (Foerster 1964a; Morosco 1974). This development and organization are important to the New Testament teaching, though the New Testament, like the Old, shows no speculative interest in such matters (Foerster 1971).[16]

[16] For two minor exceptions proving the rule, see 2 Peter 2:4 and Jude 6, both likely taken from material in 1 Enoch; see Newport 1976, 330.

The New Testament

The various New Testament writers, like those of the Old, differ considerably from one another in how they talk about evil spiritual forces. However, they do have a couple of things in common, besides the obvious belief that such spiritual forces exist. For one, by the time of the New Testament, Satan (σατανᾶς), or the Devil (διάβολος)—the terms are used virtually interchangeably, as is sometimes "the Evil One" (πονηρός)—is depicted as a being in absolute antithesis to God, working toward the destruction of humankind.[17] Indeed, the Devil still has all the punishing and accusing functions that he had in Judaism and in that respect is still God's agent. (See 1 Cor. 5:5; 2 Cor. 12:7 [note the divine passive]; 1 Tim. 1:20; see Foerster 1964a; Thornton 1972.) And even in the horror of the last days, not only is the beginning of God's *reign* affirmed amid the great woes (Rev. 11:17), but whatever power Satan has is explicitly given to him by God (Rev. 13; see Foerster and von Rad 1964, 80). The dualism is strictly limited: Satan has no rights of his own over against God. Nonetheless, a dualism there is: evil is attributed to the Enemy and not to God.[18]

Second, the New Testament writers attribute to the Devil broad and organized influence over the world as a whole. The synoptic Gospels (Mark 3:22–27 and parallels) show unequivocally the unity of the kingdom of evil under a single head (Foerster 1971). John speaks of the "ruler of this world" (John 16:11). Paul speaks of the "god of this age" (2 Cor. 4:4) and "the prince of the power of the air" (Eph. 2:2). Because of "the wiles of the devil," we must contend "against the principalities, against the powers, against the world rulers of this present darkness, against the spiritual hosts of wickedness in the heavenly places" (Eph. 6:11–12). John speaks of the Devil's relationship to a person as determinative of the person's whole being, as being like the relationship of a father to a child (1 John 3:10; John 8:44; cf. John 6:70; 13:27; Mark 8:33; note that there is no parallel in Judaism for *Satan* entering a person). Not only is the Devil in the world (1 John 4:4), but "the whole world is in the power of the evil one" (1 John 5:19). Furthermore, he is the power behind magic (Acts 13:10; cf. Acts 19:19, where new believers burn magic books after having confessed their practices); he

[17] See, for example, 1 Peter 5:8; Foerster 1964b; Harder 1968; Wink 1984. It is sometimes difficult to distinguish whether the form πονηρός/πονηρόν is neuter, meaning the evil in the world; or masculine, meaning the Devil (see Matt. 5:37, 39; 6:13; 13:19, 38–39). Thus, "it is, probably, unwise to try to differentiate too sharply between a personal and an impersonal meaning; the evil in the world, and the pressures of the world are so closely connected that it is difficult always to distinguish clearly between them" (Ling 1961, 24). This statement brings out once again the point that the Bible as a whole does not have a unidimensional view of evil. In fact, the Gospels do not even make a clear-cut distinction between natural and satanic ailments (Foerster 1971).

[18] Cf. Amos 3:6: "Does evil befall a city, unless the LORD has done it?"

can enable signs and wonders to be performed (2 Thess. 2:9); and he is able to hinder even believers (1 Thess. 2:18).[19]

Moving from these broad areas of general agreement to more specific differences in how the kingdom of darkness is conceptualized, we note that demons as such are a particular concern of the Synoptics (and to some extent of John's gospel, in which Jesus is accused of having a demon), whereas Paul speaks of "principalities and powers." In the Gospels, a demon (δαιμόνιον; also πνεῦμα ἀκάθαρτον or πνεῦμα πονηρόν; see Mark 3:22 for the virtual equivalence of possession by Satan and by demons) is always an evil-working spirit, and there appear to be an indefinitely large number of them. They work physical evil more often than moral evil and are rarely mentioned except with regard to possession (Foerster 1964a; Langton 1949). Perhaps surprisingly, possession itself is not necessarily seen as a moral disorder—and those denounced most strongly by Jesus for wickedness are not said to be possessed (Langton 1949)—yet in Matthew 12:45 Jesus can speak at least analogically of the "possession" of an entire evil generation.[20] In this way he puts a broad perspective on the problem of the demonic, scarcely limiting it to an individual medical or psychological difficulty (Ling 1961; Michaels 1976). He even addresses a fever (Luke 4:39) and a storm (Mark 4:39) in a fashion almost precisely parallel to his rebuke of demons. Thus we see that evil spiritual power may manifest itself through the created order. Nonetheless, the Synoptics deal primarily with demons in terms of their entering (εἰσέρχομαι) or being present in individuals; and more than one can inhabit a person at a time (Luke 8:2; Mark 5:9). They may come out (ἐξέρχομαι) or be forcibly cast out (ἐκβάλλω) and may enter into other beings, as in the case of the Gerasene swine (see Hastings 1951 [1898]).

Not only do demons appear to be the first to recognize Jesus' divine authority (e.g., Mark 1:24), thus manifesting paranormal knowledge, but their activity in the Gospels always is shown in his presence. (One may speculate whether his presence forces them out of hiding, or whether the gospel writers intend to focus never upon evil itself but on Jesus' triumph over it, or both.) However, the *correctness* of the demons' testimony, whether to Jesus' identity or to that of others (Acts 16:16–18), does not mean that they are good spirits. (See Mark 14:57–59, where testimony against Jesus that is verbally true is nonetheless called

---

[19] Actually, "there are far fewer references to Satan's work outside the [Christian] community than to his battle against it. In the world outside he holds undisputed sway except insofar as the witness of the community contests it" (Foerster 1971, 162; see Acts 26:18). Paul confronted some form of satanic power on each of his missionary journeys (Zuck 1971, 358; see Acts 13; 19; Gal. 5:20).

[20] It is not exegetically entirely accurate to speak of "possession." The biblical phraseology is to be demonized or to have a demon or to be "in" (ἐν) an unclean spirit (reminiscent of being "in Christ"; see Michaels 1976, 42).

false witness; cf. Deut. 13:1–3.) In fact, though the manifestations of possession are many and varied (see chapter 4), the Bible never presents the possibility of possession by some subordinate *good* spirit, any more than it allows for the possibility of simply avoiding the spiritual dimension altogether. One must choose God (the Holy Spirit) or become subject to evil spirits (Matt. 12:43–45; see Wright 1973b).

Whatever power or knowledge demons may have, they are finite (Matt. 8:32; see Schlier 1961). Jesus dealt with them by a simple word of command, as did the disciples in his name (Luke 10:17). It is *not* the case, of course, that the name of Jesus could be used simply magically: witness the fate of the sons of Sceva (Acts 19:13–17), who were overpowered by a demonized man after trying to exorcise him in the name of "Jesus whom Paul preaches." The spirit answered in no uncertain terms, "Jesus I know, and Paul I know; but who are you?" The power of the Lord is not available to those not in relationship with him.[21] Likewise, Jesus and the disciples used no magical means or ritual, much less invocation of other spirits. The approach suggests neither the superstitious nor a terror of evil spirits. It does, however, take seriously the destructiveness of these spirits at both the spiritual and the physical levels.

Paul, who alludes to spiritual powers in each of his writings except the short epistle to Philemon, approaches the matter from another angle. He does not mention individual possession but is concerned with the possession of the cosmos. For example, the "principalities" ($\dot{\alpha}\rho\chi\dot{\eta}$) in Ephesians 6 should be seen as having dominion over the rest of the cosmos, not just over other spirits (in the latter case the word would be $\ddot{\alpha}\rho\chi\omega\nu$; Delling 1964). But—and here is a key point—he does not speak as if the trouble came when an alien force took over an essentially mechanistic universe. Rather, he speaks as if the universe itself has always been pervaded (not just invaded) by spiritual forces; perhaps even, as we shall see below, as if its most fundamental constituents are at least as much spiritual as material. Furthermore, these spiritual powers (and he mentions quite a number of largely interchangeable ones, including authorities, powers, dominions, rulers, world rulers, thrones—$\dot{\epsilon}\xi ov\sigma\dot{\iota}\alpha$, $\delta\dot{\nu}\nu\alpha\mu\iota\varsigma$, $\kappa\nu\rho\iota\dot{o}\tau\eta\varsigma$, $\ddot{\alpha}\rho\chi\omega\nu$, $\kappa o\sigma\mu o\kappa\rho\dot{\alpha}\tau\omega\rho$, $\theta\rho\dot{o}\nu o\varsigma$) seem not to be, at least originally, intrinsically evil (see Eph. 3:10; Col. 1:16).[22] Something has gone wrong. But it is not as if a villain grabbed the controls of a purely material spacecraft; instead, it is as if a spacecraft created to have a spiritual, willful dimension decided to go its own way, like the rebellious robots of contemporary science-fiction horror stories.

---

[21] But see also Matt. 7:22–23, which implies that one may have enough faith in Jesus' name to cast out demons and yet lack *saving* faith manifested through righteousness.

[22] Ling 1961; Schlier 1961. Cf. the law—an "enemy" that also has a basically positive original purpose.

In other words, the whole creation, and not just humankind, is fallen (see Rom. 8:19–22). Things do not work as they were intended to work.[23] Especially striking in this regard is Romans 8:38–39, which speaks of angels, principalities, and powers linked with life itself as forces with the potential for separating us from God: even life, if set up as an end in itself, has "demonic" potential.

Likewise suggestive is the phrase "the elements of the cosmos," or "the elemental spirits of the universe" (RSV; τὰ στοιχεῖα τοῦ κόσμου) mentioned in Galatians 4:3, 9 and Colossians 2:8, 20. The meaning of the phrase has been widely debated: it could refer to physicalistic elements, or basic materials, of the universe; or heathen religious practices; or stellar spirits (a later usage). Any of these usages involves a concept of something less than God to which humankind may come into bondage, but the most obvious sense surely points to some sort of basic component of the world. Especially since the context connects them with heathen practices (see 1 Cor. 10:20 for Paul's statement that demons are associated with idol worship), the question becomes whether such elements are, together with "principalities and powers," part of the spiritual realm. Both the context, which compares them to "guardians and trustees," and the general flow of Paul's thought, which assumes pervasive activity of spiritual powers (see, for example, 1 Cor. 5:5; 15:24; 2 Cor. 12:7; 1 Thess. 2:18), would suggest that they do indeed fit there far better than with impersonal forces.[24]

> [Paul] had no idea of a system of second causes. To his Hebrew mind the force exerted by an unseen spirit in the natural world implied that spirit present and acting, as a blow struck by a man implies a man striking. . . . Bondage to nature is a personal subjection, slavery to the spirits who act in it and shape it. (Hincks 1896, 190–92)[25]

We find no system of "natural law" holding creation in its mindless grasp.

---

[23]Note the effects of the curse in Gen. 3; only after the Fall do pain and struggle become "natural."

[24]For the view that demons are not spiritual but are impersonal forces, see Delling 1971; that the powers in general are not angelic but may be personal or impersonal structures of life and society, see Berkof 1962; that the στοιχεῖα are indeed basic components, or elements (the terms used as variously as we currently use them), but that their "divinity" implied simply their primacy, not any animate or personal quality, see Wink 1984. "Dans un context où les Eléments sont comparés à des 'tuteurs' et à des 'curateurs' auxquels les hommes étaient soumis jusqu'à la venue du Christ (4.1–3), il est évident que les Eléments sont des Puissances personelles, angeliques, dont dependait la vie religieuse de l'humanité avant Jésus-Christ et dont elle depend encore pour ceux qui ne croient pas en Jésus-Christ" (Masson, quoted in Ling 1961, 69; see Schlier 1961).

[25]See Heb. 1:7. In Gal. 4:8, Paul speaks of bondage to *beings* (RSV) that by nature are no gods (the Greek is a little less strong—ἐδουλεύσατε τοῖς φύσει μὴ οὖσιν θεοῖς).

To support this understanding of the created order, we may note the way in which higher powers may be seen at work behind structures such as the state and the fact that sin, flesh, and death, as well as law, are treated semipersonally (Morosco 1974).[26] Whether the forces at work are flesh, law, sin, death, idols, demons, the cosmos, time, space, life or death, politics or philosophy, public opinion or Jewish law, pious traditions or the course of the stars, the important point is that they are seen as somehow more than just themselves (Berkof 1962; Caird 1956; Morosco 1974). There is a unifying theme of spiritual *power* behind them, not simply the natural or mechanical power inherent in structures. In the end, of course, it is Christ, not the powers, in whom all creation coheres ($\sigma\upsilon\nu\acute{\iota}\sigma\tau\eta\mu\iota$, Col. 1:17; see Berkof 1962, 22); he is the head of all rule and authority (Col. 2:10). Paul says not that the powers will be annihilated but rather that they will be defeated, brought to ineffectiveness.[27] In the meantime, Paul's words stand against our tendency to allow the powers to remain concealed in the structures and persons through which they work. He insists that "we are not contending against flesh and blood" (Eph. 6:12)—but it may look very much as if we are.

For Paul, then, nothing about the human struggle, the functioning of temporal orders, or the appearances of nature is spiritually indifferent. Underlying the earthly drama of birth, life, and death, there is a cosmic battle, a spiritual warfare, taking place. And somehow, despite the fact that the Enemy has no final parity with God (as Luther said, the Devil is always God's Devil), the battle matters. The cosmos, in captivity to powers that have gone astray, is out of joint; and we must not align ourselves with the rebellious powers.

Thus we return to a theme common to the New Testament as a whole: the Devil intends to destroy us. Whether we focus primarily upon the possession of persons or upon the possession of the cosmos, we see pain and disruption—evil—as the results of the Devil's work. "Demonized" individuals suffer physical harm or emotional distress. "Demonized" structures produce a so-called natural order in which suffering and wrong become inevitable. And let there be no mistake: Scripture clearly presents the satanic forces as stronger than human beings in themselves (see 2 Tim. 2:26).

Indeed, in some sense persons may give access to Satan's destructive power (see 1 Cor. 7:5; 2 Cor. 2:11; 4:4; Eph. 4:27). However, it does not follow that they can then free themselves from the bondage into which they come, any more than they can free themselves from sin (Foerster and von Rad 1964). In fact, by far the dominant usage of the

---

[26] It is instructive to compare Paul's treatment of $\sigma\tau o\iota\chi\epsilon\hat{\iota}\alpha$ with his treatment of the law: note Gal. 2:19 and Col. 2:20; Gal. 3:23 and Gal. 4:3, 8; Gal. 3:24 and Gal. 4:2; Rom. 8:3 and Gal. 4:9 (Ling 1961).

[27] See Col. 2:15; Eph. 1:20–21; Rom. 8:38–39; Phil. 2:10–11; 1 Cor. 2:6.

word "sin" in the New Testament is with reference to a bondage to
Satan that necessitates rescue, or salvation. (For instance, forty-two out
of forty-five references to sin [ἁμαρτία] in Romans treat it as a
personified, objective force that rules individuals against their will,
Kallas 1966, 64.) The Devil's power may be allowed by God and bound
or limited by Christ (see Matt. 12:29); it may have been unleashed by
the Fall and work through human sin; but it is nonetheless a
supernatural power to be reckoned with and fought against (Eph. 6:11;
James 4:7; 1 Peter 5:7–10).

But if we fight using our own power, we will surely fail. To expect
ourselves or the state or "natural progress" or some other part of the
created order to defeat evil is to try to cast out the Devil by Beelzebul,
for the Enemy has creation in bondage (Rom. 8:21; see Caird 1956).
The thrust of the biblical message is that we must actively depend upon
God if we are to cope successfully with the enemy, whether the enemy
is Satan himself or the demons, principalities, and powers that are
subject to him. All of reality is permeated, not by neutral, indifferent
choices, but by spiritual alternatives.

* * *

Stranger: You really *are* naive! Even more naive than I thought.

Inquirer: Because I believe there is a devil, you mean?

Stranger: Not exactly. It's more the *way* you believe in him—as if there
really were a "him" and not a series of evolving myths (even you
admitted that the story changes) that help to get folks and their God
off the hook or at least to give them some literary handles on their
problems. Actually, your friend William James even said, "The world
is all the richer for having a devil in it, *so long as we keep our foot upon
his neck.*"[28] Whatever he meant by the last phrase, I admire his
tolerance and open-mindedness. He had the honesty to admit that
the world would be a rather dull place without some battles to fight
and opportunities for people to develop virtues such as courage.

Inquirer: It sounds as if you'd like to use the old argument that you can't
have a beautiful painting without shadows, so evil is really good in the
end.

Stranger: Something like that. At least every bit as necessary as good.

Inquirer: I don't like that argument.

Stranger: Since when did your likes and dislikes change the facts?

[28] 1961 [1902], 56.

Inquirer: Your argument tries to get around the horror, the gratui-tousness, of evil. Actually, since the Devil is the personification of destruction and confusion, it's hard to be orderly in dealing with him. I don't think we *ought* to systematize evil as such, using Satan as an explanatory principle, any more than we ought to attribute evil to God.[29] I agree with Brunner: "Only he who understands that sin is inexplicable knows what it is."[30] That statement applies as much to the rebellion of spiritual powers as to human sin. In either case, to "explain" evil is to do away with it. The French have a phrase for it: *Tout comprendre, c'est tout pardonner*—to understand everything is to forgive everything. But we don't experience our *own* wickedness that way: when we sin, we sense that we have a choice, that we *could* do differently. We can more rightfully say about ourselves that to understand everything is to forgive ourselves nothing.[31] Evil is a great mystery, somehow done for its own sake.[32]

Stranger: This discussion is getting more than a little ridiculous. First you argue for the reality of a "devil" as a source of evil. Then you say that evil must not be explained and people must not be relieved of responsibility. Then you speak of "personification" as if the Devil were a myth after all, just as I said in the beginning. I don't think you know *what* you're talking about! This "battle" you're speaking of is fairly obviously a battle with your own shadow—naturally a hard kind to win. And furthermore, talking as if there were absolutes of good and evil when you can't even define them has got to be absurd, not to mention productive of all sorts of unnecessary guilt—but I said that already. (Still, it's a good point, don't you think?)

Inquirer: A good point only if there *are* no absolutes and if, further-more, "myth" implies a lack of organized, personal power in evil; and if, finally, persons, however responsible they may be, are ultimately on their own and responsible only to themselves. No absolute can ever be "defined"; to do so would make it relative to the terms used to define it. We can't even encapsulate something less than ourselves, such as a rose, in a definition. Besides, one hardly needs a complete diagram of an enemy's troop deployments to know that one is in a war, though he may learn a good bit about the opposition from the way it attacks. I haven't finished yet with this enemy and his tactics.

* * *

[29] Berkouwer 1961; cf. 1 John 1:5; James 1:13.
[30] Quoted in Stewart 1951, 292.
[31] Koestler 1967.
[32] Anshen 1972.

INTERPRETING THE BIBLICAL DATA

Symbol and Myth

Many have dismissed the various biblical formulations of evil spiritual power as so much primitive mythology, stories taking whatever particular shape a given culture and heritage provide. Surely, the argument goes, the diversity of the data itself suggests that the biblical writers had no uniform revelation about some actual being called Satan. Rather, they wrestled with the universal experience of evil in nature and in human life, using the symbols and categories they had ready at hand. The conclusion generally runs that to retain in this day and age the idea of a personal, malevolent will as the fountainhead of evil interferes with taking enlightened steps to combat evil. Therefore, we should "demythologize" the scriptural accounts.

Protestations of this general type require several different kinds of response. First, one must ask for evidence that the assumed appropriation by biblical writers of symbols and stories available in a particular society actually took place. To state a hypothesis is not the same thing as to demonstrate its truth. As a matter of fact, the demonstration has been exceedingly hard to come by. For example, it has by no means been established that stories of Jesus' miracles of healing and exorcism were typical of a fund of contemporary stories available to the writers of the Gospels (see especially Brown 1984, chapter 9). Culture may play a role, but in this case it apparently did not provide ready-made miracle stories.

Second, even a superficial reading of the New Testament reveals such a pervasive assumption of the reality of evil spiritual powers that there is no way of tidily separating the offensive "mythical" portions from the inspiring, high-minded, "ethical" portions. Even those disbelieving the existence of demons (e.g., Langton [1949]) are forced to admit that an accommodation theory of Jesus' acceptance of demonology (i.e., that he adapted his teaching on demons to the world view of his hearers) is untenable: he never corrected his own disciples but rather emphasized the reality of demonic forces and gave his disciples authority to cast out demons. Paul, as we have seen, likewise believed in a world of evil spirits vitally related to the human scene. If Jesus and Paul were mistaken here, in teachings interspersed with and intrinsic to their other more credible teachings and profoundly related to our faith and practice, we are indeed in serious trouble if we intend to take Scripture seriously. Those employing a reductionistic program of demythologization will find little of the onion left after all the "surface" layers have been peeled away.[33]

[33] Also, if we demythologize, "we are assuming that the New Testament writers did not

Third, we ought to admit candidly the inadequacy of our understanding of the spiritual reality with which we deal and the insufficiency of our language to encapsulate it. We have already asserted both that language always points beyond itself and that greater realities can never be fully expressed in terms of lesser ones. Thus myths and symbols serve as expressions of what we cannot quite grasp, of what remains beyond the reach of our intellectual tools. Insofar as they are true (that is, point to a reality beyond them), they always and necessarily mean more, not less, than they say. The Bible itself is ever new partly for this very reason.

Within this context I see no objection to terming the idea of the Devil "mythological," meaning not that there is no such being but rather that all of our conceptions of him are inadequate and incomplete. He is not simply a rather ludicrous little man in a red suit (see Lewis 1961) nor the suave, beguiling figure portrayed by Goethe or Milton (though the latter may more approximate his preferred masquerade, while the former corresponds in grotesqueness if not in seriousness to his work in possession). The various scriptural accounts, in my view, indicate various ways that Satan manifests himself and various ways of conceiving the kingdom of darkness. The accounts are not contradictory but complementary, not exhaustive but suggestive, not predetermined by different cultural settings but very probably influenced by them in any number of ways. The "myth" as a whole tells us—which we deny at our peril—that evil involves a personal, organized, active will, external to our wills and wanting to ensnare and destroy us. Rebellion came not from weakness or ignorance but from hatred in the face of knowledge of who God is and what he wants.[34]

Now, to say that evil is "personal" (see biblical references in Penn-Lewis n.d., 27–28) is to say that intellect and will are involved, *not* that evil is always encountered as an individual: "Legion" is both many and one (Schlier 1961; see Mark 5), though Christ was tempted by a seemingly individual, personal being of great wisdom and deep malice. The tendency, of course, is to depersonalize evil, yet the sting of the

themselves make a distinction between myth and fact, whereas they appear to lay great stress on this very distinction (e.g., the Petrine assertion: 'We have not followed cunningly devised fables'—Gk. *mythoi*, 'myths')" (Montgomery 1974b, 24).

[34] "If Love could be loved, Love could be hated. If a single supernatural Will existed, then there could undoubtedly be an extension of *maleficium* against that single Will" (Williams 1959, 38). The postulate Williams here implies—that whatever is posited brings with it the possibility of its opposite—is one way to escape directly attributing the origin of evil to God. According to the classic view of the Atonement, the work of Christ constitutes a continuing, objective victory over the powers of darkness: "Evil is not to be reduced to existential bad intentions" (Kallas 1966, 72). At the same time, the very tyrants overcome are instruments of God's judgment on sin; and the victory is costly to God, who is both Reconciler and Reconciled. This whole theme does not lend itself to a simply consistent, rationalistic understanding (Aulén 1935).

duality between good and evil is scarcely removed in this way; we are brought no closer to an explanation. We are rather further from it: speaking impersonally of "demonic forces" working on humankind from outside wholly neglects the essential and consistent character of the biblical narratives. From the temptation in the Garden to the trials of Job, the temptation of Jesus, and the apocalyptic vision, the representative of evil is presented by Scripture as intelligently, intentionally, and powerfully malicious—*not* as the pawn of inexorable physical or social forces. He is permitted to act upon persons physically and to approach them through their minds. He is shown as having a kingdom, strong and organized (Mark 3:22–27). And he is ultimately envious and ambitious ("the man of lawlessness . . . the son of perdition, who opposes and exalts himself against every so-called god or object of worship, so that he takes his seat in the temple of God, proclaiming himself to be God" [2 Thess. 2:3–4], a passage usually applied to the Antichrist). He desires to dethrone God and take his place. Insofar as this conception of evil is accurate, so-called enlightened steps to defeat it will not suffice— but that is a subject for later chapters.

The Enemy and the Traitor

Clearly, positing a personal devil neither explains evil in any ultimate sense nor makes evident why we succumb to it, even if we attribute to the Devil an organized attempt to perpetrate destruction and confusion. We are still faced, if we are monotheists, with the enigma of the satanic rebellion against God and with the dreadful fact that the spiritual forces of wickedness eventually work *through* and not just *upon* our own will. That our own hearts are traitors to the truth, however, is scarcely evidence that there is no other enemy. To the contrary. Traitors are traitors—and guilty and responsible—precisely because there *is* an enemy with whom they ought not to be allied.

Furthermore, we cannot suppose that, because they ought not to make an alliance, they can break free from such an alliance at will. Thus, as we have seen, Paul speaks even of sin in a personified sense, as something external to humankind, a hostile force (Kallas 1966; see Rom. 5–8). On the other hand, the nature of the armor prescribed in Ephesians 6:11–18 (e.g., truth, righteousness), with specific reference to "the Evil One," would point to internal as well as external struggles (Morosco 1974). The Enemy is *both* within and without. The subjective and objective must not be torn apart or assimilated to each other.[35]

---

[35] "On the one hand the devil is an enemy, a beguiler, a usurper; on the other he has won certain rights over man. The former idea is thoroughly dualistic; it gives us the conflict between God and the representative and embodiment of evil. The second shows the limitations of dualism; for the devil is not a power equal and opposite to God, and insofar as he has power over men, he derives this power ultimately from God, for he

Dostoevsky (1923) illustrates the complex interweaving of the human and the demonic in the famous passage where a distraught Ivan confronts the Devil:

> "Never for one minute have I taken you for reality," Ivan cried with a sort of fury. "You are a lie, you are my illness, you are a phantom. It's only that I don't know how to destroy you and I see I must suffer for a time. You are my hallucination. You are the incarnation of myself, but only of one side of me." (Pp. 688–89)

All the same, Ivan feels as if he does indeed have someone to address, and the Devil says things Ivan does not recognize as his own. One gathers that Ivan's experience includes both the outer and the inner, both an evil separate from him and a personification of the evil in his own soul. Satan gains his power from precisely this ambiguity (see Moeller 1952, xxii).

Parasitic Power

We may speak of Satan's "gaining" or "having" power; yet in so speaking, we lose something of the mystery and the dynamic of his functioning. We all too easily assimilate him to whatever else we perceive as powerful, whether kings or freight trains or oceans. The principalities differ in a fundamental way from all of these: they are invisible. They do not just *have* power—they *are* power (Schlier 1961, 19).[36]

To put the matter this way may seem to contradict our earlier assertion that power requires a union of structure and will, but that is not really the case. The key point is that Satan and his hordes conceal themselves in the structures of the world and human life, making the world and humankind instruments and bearers of their power. In that sense the cosmos is indeed possessed, so that energy and structures meant for good, meant to serve God, are turned against him and his purposes (Schlier 1961, 28–29).[37]

stands, as it were, to execute God's own judgment on sinful and guilty man" (Aulén 1935, 70–71).

[36] Cf. Bass 1976, 369–70: "Demon spirits . . . are not just evil beings who misuse their power, but are frequently presented in Scripture as evil power itself. They do not merely possess power, but they are power. They exist as power (Col. 1:16). Sometimes they are presented as beings who have power; at other times as powers which have being." So too the necessary emphasis on God's power to save us from sin as a power: love alone could not suffice (Kallas 1966, 61–62).

[37] Note Schlier's (1961, 18) intriguing comment, consonant with our understanding of "the nature of everything," that "the invisible is the supreme form of the material; the principalities are phenomena of the invisible in this sense, and, as such, their nature has a double characteristic which seems self-contradictory to us." Thus their power comes from the limit of the natural order—the "heavens"—where it abides (p. 20). The point for us is that the material has a spiritual aspect that is part of created reality and not to be confused with God himself. Wink (1984), in his exhaustive treatment of the powers,

But we must note that it is still *God's creation* that is perverted: the Devil cannot create. Whatever has its own proper reality has that reality from God (Lewis 1961). God can will what is other than himself; thus he makes a universe and human beings with their own sphere of freedom (and thus, too, he can sacrifice himself). The Devil, on the other hand, because he can will only himself, has and is nothing. By denying God, he lost the single Necessity and is therefore insatiable, destroying everything he gets because he no longer is. Thus the Bible pictures the Devil as a devourer (e.g., 1 Peter 5:8; cf. Prov. 27:20). Thus, too, a seventeenth-century engraving showing just a horned head and two cloven feet is entitled "No-body" (Rougemont 1945).[38]

The Devil's power, then, is a purely parasitic power. In that sense— and in that sense only—we may call him a nonentity. Perhaps he can take so many shapes precisely because he can have none that is rightfully his own. But whatever shape he takes, his designs are all anti— antihumankind and anti-God, anticreation and antiredemption (for he can neither create nor redeem)—no matter how much he may appear to be *for* culture, human religions, earth, and the development of life (see Berkouwer 1961). Yet even his perverted will can be antipersonal only out of the same springs that yield the personal.

makes the following relevant points: "These Powers are both heavenly and earthly, divine and human, spiritual and political, invisible and structural" (p. 11). "The Powers are understood to operate as a single front of opposition to God but . . . in any given moment they are discernible only in a particular historical manifestation. . . . The New Testament prefers to speak of the Powers only in their concretions, their structural inertia, their physical embodiments in history" (p. 82). "The synoptic Gospels use the terminology of power almost as frequently as does Paul. . . . This fact has been overlooked simply because the Gospels tend to use the language of power of human or structural, rather than spiritual, entities" (p. 100). Wink's analysis of the data as a whole fully supports the general conclusions in this chapter. His *interpretation* of the data, however—which demythologizes the powers and gives them no separate, spiritual existence (his chap. 5)— differs radically from mine.

[38] Similarly Magny (1952, 432–33): "This wholly null being needs man in order to get a purchase on reality; he subsists only on living spiritual realities which give him 'body' with their positiveness; so that he can only appear where there persists some minimum of faith in his opposite, some grain of belief in a supernatural universe, a belief which he can pervert from its true end and induce to serve his own designs: . . . 'sa haine s'est réservé les saints.' " See also Matt. 12:43–45, where unclean spirits seek a human body. So finally Williams (1959, 310), speaking of witches' seeking evil power: "The thing which is invoked is a thing of a different nature, however it may put on a human appearance or indulge in its servants their human appetites. It is cold, it is hungry, it is violent, it is illusory. The warm blood of children and the intercourse at the Sabbath do not satisfy it. It wants 'obedience,' it wants 'souls,' and yet it pines for matter. It never was, and yet it always is." The demonic will is in the end as self-contradictory and empty as the demonic "body." As G. K. Chesterton (1959 [1908], 39–40) put it, referring to the human will but appropriate also to the demonic will, "All the will-worshippers . . . are really quite empty of volition. They cannot will, they can hardly wish . . . they always talk of will as something that expands and breaks out. But it is quite the opposite. Every act of will is an act of self-limitation. To desire action is to desire limitation. In that sense every act is an act of self-sacrifice." But self-sacrifice is precisely what Satan, in willing only himself, cannot countenance.

To characterize the Devil as essentially "anti" is to say that his intent and procedure is to isolate, to deceive, and to destroy; to break down the integrity of relationships and of mind and body—it matters little which comes first, as any one of them can easily bring the others in its train.[39] If he is finally to succeed, however, he cannot remain a force wholly external to persons but, as we have seen, must snare them as willing followers. Thus we must see his "anti" stance as extending even to his own appearance: he masquerades as good, as an angel of light (2 Cor. 11:14). His very nature is to lie: "He is a liar and the father of lies" (John 8:44; the Greek implies him to be the father of *his own* lies, such that even a standard of truth is denied, which is the most absolute lie possible).[40] He wishes to persuade us that all is relative, that contraries are indifferent, that white is really grey is really black (see Magny 1952). He would represent things to us as he chooses; he would make all appearances lie and make faith itself heretical and godless (Montgomery 1974b, 104; Schlier 1961; 1 Tim. 4:1). To take him seriously is to expect him where we do not expect him (Newport 1976, 332). From his subtlety in the Garden to his signs and lying wonders in the Apocalypse, he presents evil as good. He counterfeits God. Thus human "goodness" or innocence cannot itself prevail.[41]

---

[39] The word "diabolic" has a separating thrust, coming from the Greek διαβάλλω, "to bring charges with hostile intent" (Arndt and Gingrich 1957, 180). May (1969, 135) gives the meaning even more strongly as "tear apart."

[40] See Rougemont 1945. The Greek reads, ὅταν λαλῇ τὸ ψεῦδος, ἐκ τῶν ἰδίων λαλεῖ, ὅτι ψεύστης ἐστὶν καὶ ὁ πατὴρ αὐτοῦ.

[41] The Fallen Angel would say that there is no heaven, no other hope, and therefore no hell; the Prince of this World would say that there is no other world, and therefore no God or Satan; the Tempter, that there is no judge, and hence no offence or Author of Evil; the Liar, that there is no reality, thus no lie or Liar; Legion, that there is no person, so *he* cannot exist; and the Accuser, that there is no pardon (Rougemont 1945; cf. Schlier 1961). Anshen (1972, 125) comments, "It has been proved that it is possible to become evil for scientific purposes without having evil motives. [Witness, for example, the constant, "necessary" sacrifice of means for ends in experiments on animals and people.] It also is true that one can become a prey of the Devil without believing in his existence."

7

Evil as Disruption of Structure or Will

Stranger: I entirely agree with you that innocence won't prevail—whatever its "prevailing" would mean. In fact, I think it shows considerable maturity that folks no longer even consider it enviable.[1] Those who would say that the so-called Fall was really upward, into consciousness and responsibility and autonomy and out of blissful babyhood, have my full support.

Inquirer: But what a price!

Stranger: Price? You mean a bit of conflict and loneliness? That's the only way for people to become self-sufficient, test their wings, conquer opposition. How dull a world of mystical harmony would be—no chance for achievement, for superiority. Surely you wouldn't want to reduce everything to the lowest common denominator, to a sloppy mediocrity? What the world needs is a few more heroes!

Inquirer: Or a few more saints.

Stranger: Have you ever known a well-adjusted, successful saint?[2]

Inquirer: I haven't known many saints.

Stranger: Well *I* have—known them well—and let me tell you, they won't win any prizes for being realistic and well adjusted to the world. In fact, after a while, the more time I spend with them, the less reasonable and tolerant they seem. A very difficult bunch to understand, these saints.

Inquirer: Yes, I imagine so. Actually, it is very hard even to *imagine* beginning to get in touch with the way things were meant to be.

Stranger: Meant to be? Are you trying to imply that there is some sort of *norm* for existence? Nonsense. You can't get a norm out of a moving, evolving process. Unless, of course, you mean a statistical norm, an average taken at a given point—that I understand. Some

---

[1] Anshen 1972, 86–87; cf. May 1972.
[2] See James 1961 (1902).

folks are inferior, some are superior. What is more, either way, if they can learn to function usefully in the world, they can be relatively healthy or normal in the sense of being able to cope. That's another way of looking at it. One hardly needs to invent a mythical, ideal world to discover whether people can get along in this one—in fact, it would clearly just obscure the issue.

Inquirer: Frankly, I disagree. I don't think we *do* have an adequate idea of what health is—or happiness, for that matter. Very successful people are notoriously miserable. Sometimes it seems almost as if the better they learn to make the world work for them, the worse they feel. Something just has to be wrong.

Stranger: Of course. There will always be neurotic, compulsive over-achievers. They're just part of the grab bag.

Inquirer: No, I think the problem is different and deeper than that. I think that misery comes from the violation of norms—of absolutes, if you will—though I don't mean a given person's misery stems wholly from her own wrong choices.

Stranger: If I will? Well what if I won't! It's bad enough to talk about "absolutes" in the abstract, which is in reality nothing more or less than talking about ways in which people have conceptualized forces of good or evil. That's dull, but relatively innocuous. But when you start applying them to the world, you're meddling; and I thoroughly resent it. I believe in tolerance, myself, and I think absolutes are dangerous.

Inquirer: Goodness, I'm sorry; I wasn't trying to violate your feelings. But perhaps in the interest of tolerance, you'll let me present my case?

* * *

EVIL AND STRUCTURE

Brief Overview of Conceptions of Evil

In considering the fundamental nature of evil, how much should we emphasize an internal principle (sin) as over against an external principle (Satan)? Those who give great weight to an external principle (e.g., the early church fathers and contemporary theologians such as Heim and Aulén) concentrate on the objective and active nature of evil. Those who focus on the internal come closer to the Augustinian understanding of sin—evil as turning from a higher to a lower good, or evil as a lack or absence of good (as for Plato) rather than a positive force. In modern times, due in part to the development of institutional life and mass society, many attribute evil (particularly seen as principalities and powers) to structures that become distorted or rigid and deified, structures that foster irresponsibility on the part of the individual and bring in their train irresolvable conflicts of needs and interests so that whatever decision is made will hurt someone (e.g., Berkof 1962; Niebuhr). Indeed, Ambrose Bierce once defined incorporation as "the act of uniting several persons into one fiction called a corporation, in order that they may no longer be responsible for their actions" (quoted in Kelly 1970, 149). But even apart from irresponsibility, one may, simply due to the nature of certain relationships, do evil without the least malice or perversion of intention, just as one may be a victim of structural or other types of evil without guilt.

Nonetheless, evil performed by a moral agent has customarily been differentiated from so-called natural evil: destruction caused by fire, flood, disease, and the like. For several reasons, such a distinction cannot be maintained as tidily as has sometimes been supposed. First, as implied above, being a moral agent does not in fact entail that one could avoid doing evil if only one had sufficient courage or wisdom. Sometimes all the available options involve some sort of evil outcome for someone. Second, "moral" evil and "natural" evil frequently impinge upon one another: lack of food due to a "natural" disaster may induce highly immoral behavior on the part of hungry people; and immoral relationships may spread, say, syphilis through quite natural processes. Third, evil is not even a category on the purely natural level. It is a moral category, referring to what in some sense *ought* not to be; so no natural explanation of it suffices. Even death, biblically speaking, should be considered unnatural: on the one hand, it results from sin (Rom. 5:12–14; 6:23; 1 Cor. 15:56), and on the other hand, it is the tool of the Devil, who uses the fear people have of it to keep them in bondage (Heb. 2:14–15). Insofar as the Devil manifests his destructive designs within the natural order, that order itself is not simply natural.

Similarly, I do not find it helpful to try to bifurcate strictly the roles of sin and Satan. I prefer to emphasize their interrelationship. As we have noted, the corruptible human will, which is inclined to sin, is precisely the will *through* which—not just *upon* which—Satan works. Particular ways in which we make ourselves vulnerable to the Devil's influence comprise the subject of the next chapter. Here I seek to analyze characteristic results of his activity.

We must recall that Satan is a destroyer who cannot create, a will without any proper being of his own, since he denied the Source of all being. Thus all he can be is a great "anti," as his various names imply: Adversary, Liar, Deceiver, Accuser, and the like. As such, he seeks the temporal and eternal misery of humankind—the latter absolutely, the former only insofar as it does not endanger the latter. (That evil must masquerade as good, at least in the sense of providing certain benefits, in order to win its victims is an ironic tribute the Devil must pay to original righteousness, even as he capitalizes on original sin.) Such misery includes everything from the pettiest vice to the most cataclysmic war, from personal loneliness to international intrigue, from a headache to a plague, from an unhappy childhood to an eternity in hell.

All such misery, I suggest, occurs because of *disruptions of structure and/or will*—the Devil spoiling what God has made. Disease is a disruption of structure. So is a flood. So is a totalitarian state (though those who *run* the state may have corrupt wills). Overeating, hatred, and aggression are normally disruptions of will (unless prompted, say, by a brain tumor). Obviously the two categories interact: a disorder may begin in either, and one disorder generally brings multitudinous others in its train. However, power to disrupt does not necessarily entail power to control. The Devil's partial or complete *control* of both structure and will may be said to constitute partial or complete demonic possession. I consider this subject in chapter 9 and here deal only with demonic disruptions.

Disruptions of Structure

The orders, or structures, of creation malfunction.[3] They may be disrupted or depart from the norm in many ways. In chapter 1, for instance, we considered the impact of excessive or insufficient stimulation of the nervous system. Here I speak more broadly of structures in

---

[3] Paul speaks of the whole of creation as subjected to futility, in bondage, groaning in travail, not free to be what it was meant to be (Rom. 8:20–22). Satan is the ruler of this world (John 16:11)—a power somehow allowed to him by God himself. Thus, "To follow nothing more malignant than the mere course of this world . . . is deadly" (Wink 1984, 83). When Satan approaches Jesus and offers him authority over all the kingdoms of the world (Luke 4:5–6), Jesus never hints that Satan has no ability to fulfill his promise (see Wink 1984, 32). When Jesus heals the woman bent over with a "spirit of infirmity," he calls her "a daughter of Abraham whom Satan bound" (Luke 13:16). While the Devil's power is not absolute (else Jesus would not have been able to heal the woman), it is presented as very real. We might think that, if we were truly "spiritual," we would simply rise above such practical matters. Horrendous circumstances do not force us to give up our internal freedom and integrity. Witness Job. It is true, up to a point, that a higher level may compensate for a lower, that a fine carpenter may do a good job with relatively poor tools, that a physically handicapped but highly motivated person may achieve remarkably. However, such an argument clearly holds only up to a point, the absolutely limiting case being death (and God forbade Satan to take Job's life). We noted previously that a lower-level malfunction is quite sufficient to account for the breakdown of an entire set of operations that proper functioning of lower levels cannot by itself produce: just because a plugged-up aorta can prevent blood from circulating as it should does not mean that the blood pumping function is located in the arteries; though conversely, a heart is not much use without arteries. Similarly, people can be quite efficiently prevented from attending to noble, peculiarly human pursuits if they are hungry and threatened on all sides. People's souls and bodies are not mutually independent entities—a truth the Devil has not ignored.

140

general (as defined in chapter 5) and of how they themselves may be aberrant. I would suggest three general categories of abnormality: (1) perversion of an aspect or aspects of the structure (as when parts are wrongly connected or a particular part has undue ascendancy); (2) formlessness (failure of organization or breaking down of natural structures or connections, as by disease); and (3) excessive rigidity. Each of these is characteristically diabolical and, in my view, should be attributed to him who is allowed to govern the structures through the "powers" that connect the visible and the invisible realms (see Berkof 1962).

Before we investigate further the various abnormalities that may distort structures, we must remember that, since the Devil hides, what actually leads to death may present itself as life enhancing. Perversions of structure may show themselves as ends that justify—or at least necessitate—certain means or as "realistic" concentration upon special potentialities or "good ends" or difficulties. Formlessness may masquerade as freedom, autonomy. Rigidity may cloak itself in our self-righteous adherence to moral absolutes or our delighted application of a rigorous, scientific causality. All of these tactics can be remarkably subtle. The first tends to absolutize that which is not True (that is, not reflecting the essential nature of things) or not absolute or no longer true when made absolute. It twists, producing more or less obvious distortions. The second and third are perhaps less visible to modern Western eyes and provide, among other evils, for two of the Devil's nicer ploys, isolation and determinism. Isolation ultimately denies the connection of persons with one another and their God on a human and on a spiritual level; determinism connects persons and everything else in all creation, inexorably, on an inhuman level.

Perversion. To make false connections, emphases, or absolutes is one of the surest ways to turn that which is good to evil and to present that which is evil as good.[4] The clearest example of this point in Scripture is the functioning of the law, which may bring either health or death; others are the state, the cosmos, and the "elements of the universe." Within our definition, all of these items are structures; all were created good and for human good, and all have demonic potential.

Paul is not confused when he says, in one breath, that the law is "by no means" to be overthrown (Rom. 3:31) and that it is by no means sin (Rom. 7:7) and, in another, that by it the trespass is increased (Rom. 5:20) and that by it there is no salvation (Gal. 2:16; 3:11). Rather, he makes the point that what was given for our benefit has been handled amiss. It has been not only perversely connected to newly seen

---

[4] I use the term "perversion" not in a technical psychological sense but in its broad, general meaning.

possibilities for violation of the law but also elevated to an end in itself that presumably can ensure salvation.

Or, consider our contemporary obsession with health. Health, obviously, is a positive good. We would attribute illness, not health, to the Devil. However, obsessive *pursuit* of health (or even worse, of youth or beauty) merely masks our mortality. Good health, while it may give some a longer time in which to come to know God, for many others keeps God far from their thoughts. Poor health, on the other hand, leads easily to virtual worship of physicians and psychologists. In our world, even the most unambiguously good things quickly provide occasion for evil.

Anything at all, however powerful and good, that is absolutized and governs us but cannot save us, belongs practically by definition to the domain of the "principalities and powers, the world rulers of this present darkness," which, though not to be destroyed, must be made subject to Christ. The great problem with the powers is the demonic reversal by which they become gods, still holding the world together, so to speak, but away from God (Berkof 1962; Heuvel 1966). Indeed, any time that which is secondary is treated as if it were a primary necessity, the Devil is the victor.

We may reinforce this point by referring to the common observation that great potentials of all sorts may be used either for good or for ill. A parent of my acquaintance once observed of his very active, determined little daughter, "That kid's going to go far." "Yes," responded her less moonstruck grandfather, "I hope it's in the right direction!" Not only physical and intellectual energy, like that of a precocious child, but also faith or ritual may be turned in various directions: a contemporary witch may rear her daughter as a Roman Catholic, seeing Catholicism as the closest thing to the craft (Nugent 1971). The Devil cannot create but can only corrupt.

Formlessness. I define "formlessness" as a lack of the organization or connections necessary for the proper functioning of a structure. When body cells become disorganized, for instance, they form cancers instead of bone or muscle or organs; and the greater the disorganization, the more virulent the cancer. Likewise, when people decide to "do their own thing," with little reference to its impact on others, they lose their proper connectedness with the rest of the human family. The analogy becomes explicit when Scripture refers to the church as the body of Christ and insists that we are members one of another (1 Cor. 12).

Indeed, the irrevocability of our relationship to our brothers and sisters follows immediately upon the absoluteness of God and our relationship to him. The first question asked by God of the first brother, Cain, was, "Where is Abel your brother?" (Gen. 4:9), in view of which, Cain's response, "Am I my brother's keeper?" is hardly a question with

142

two equally possible answers. Hence the Devil, who through rebellion achieved his own absolute loneliness, works by isolating his victims. The occult practice of drawing a magic circle around one aptly symbolizes this isolation (Anshen 1972, 38–39).[5] And what better way to foster it than to promote exclusive preoccupation with oneself and to deny any positive attitude to other people or even to objects, any attitude not oriented to using them for one's own advantage? An alternative is to lose persons in a mass of anonymity, in "Legion," where every name relates finally to one source, but the source is an ungraspable, faceless composite. The part with no body and the body with no distinguishable parts are equally formless, equally unable to relate in terms of a unique identity that both enables giving and necessitates receiving.[6]

Surely in our society we have lost our way in this department—so thoroughly lost it that we tend to deny any such thing as a way that could be lost. We sever rights from duties, impulses from regulations, desires from roles. We admire high character but scorn discipline. We laud courage but refuse to tolerate pain. We want harmony but will make no sacrifice to achieve it, want peace if (in order that?) our own lifestyle may remain undisturbed, want recognition but flee responsibility. And then we wonder why no one comes through for us in a pinch. That final step completes the isolation, as we become angry, blame the faceless "them" out there, and retreat a step further into our self-centered worlds.

Rigidity. To complete the tasks of pushing God out of the universe and depersonalizing the human creature made in God's image, the Devil needs one more tool: a complete determinism, producing complete rigidity of structures. Then the creation would truly be in bondage. If the sequence of cause and effect could be held absolutely fast by the Devil, then neither creature nor Creator could intervene with an act of freedom transcending (though not necessarily denying) the impact of structure.[7] In that case, we could not differentiate the import of the

---

[5] "Perhaps [the Devil's] boundless pride did not permit him to anticipate that the fate of rebellion by the created against the creator must inevitably be total isolation—even if there is no damnation. Or it may well be that damnation is nothing but absolute loneliness" (Anshen 1972, 7).

[6] So also with forms that are *only* "formal": "The conspicuous moral fact about our generals, scientists, industrial and political leaders is that they are the most obvious and pathetic prisoners of the emerging technological totalitarianism in American society. There is unleashed in this society a kind of relentless, self-proliferating, all-consuming institutional process—institutional life, really—that assaults, dispirits, defeats and destroys human life. It does this even among, *and primarily among* those men in positions of institutional leadership. They are left with titles but without authority, with the condiments of power but without control over the institutions they head. They are in nominal command but bereft of dominion. These same principalities threaten, defy and enslave human beings of other states in multiple ways, but the most poignant victim of this form of totalitarianism is the so-called leader" (Stringfellow 1969, 247).

[7] "The Powers become agents of fate, of necessity, of an inexorability that determines

birth of a worm from that of the birth of Napoleon, for everything would be inexorably connected. Good and evil, poems and chicken eggs, rainbows and wars would be equally necessary, wholly inevitable, and thus morally indifferent. In the darkness of complete determinism, "everything is a cow and all cows are black."[8]

This sort of rigidity of structure, we must emphasize, is not antithetical to formlessness; it is antithetical to *meaningful* forms or relationships. Evil may be ossified; good may not. The reason is that good involves relationship at some level with a being capable of moral choice and actively above structural fixity: good must be done freely to be considered morally good, and the very fact that it may be violated demonstrates its essential aspect of freedom. Evil *may* be done freely, which is evil at its basest, inexplicable core, but it is sufficient that a moral being or matter itself submit to "necessities" for it to flourish.

It is not contradictory to assert that, of two opposite moral categories, acts (or events) belonging to one may be generated deterministically but acts belonging to the other may not. Determinism operates on a level lower than human potential, so human subjection to it is intrinsically evil, even if it produces transient gains. Good, on the other hand, must be sought "upward" because it is clearly not a necessary outcome of structures as we find them. As I have emphasized repeatedly, we may (at least secondarily) look downward for sources of malfunction but must look upward for sources of right functioning. ("So if the Son makes you free, you will be free indeed" [John 8:36].)

While we may distinguish various aberrations of structure for purposes of analysis, they all of course tend to occur together in the end. Examples can be drawn from many realms. Consider the paintings of Bosch and of many modern painters, from the cubists to those whose work is wholly abstract, or formless.[9] Or note the demonic state, in which the "breaking down" of structures is manifested, for instance, in the splitting of family life. For some of the most striking illustrations, consider various manifestations of psychopathology. In this category, I remember particularly a watercolor painting, done by a psychotic young man, that initially appeared to be simply a free, delightful splash of colors. Then I observed a minutely fine ink line circumscribing the

lives without reference to the will of God; in short, of a nonprovidential governance of human life" (Wink 1984, 95).

[8] See Daane 1973, 163. While Daane is arguing against exhaustive rationalism, he explicitly links it to necessity and determinism. See also the article by determinist B. F. Skinner (1972), "On Having a Poem," in which he compares writing a poem with laying an egg.

[9] "Ugliness, plurality, chaos—throughout civilizations most remote from each other in time and in space, these are the characteristics of diabolic art. . . . Satan creates his monsters from shattered remnants of creatures" (Bazin 1952, 352–53).

irregular patches, as if he were making a desperate attempt to impose some sort of control on a chaotic world. The effort was obviously futile, for what he solidified by that fine black line was itself chaos.[10]

In each case, structures—whether of things, institutions, or personalities—become grotesque, hard, and finally meaningless. Disintegration and distortion are calcified and presented as absolute, unalterable facts. And we have become so accustomed to these "facts" that most of us never conceive the possibility that the Devil hides behind them. How he must love it when insurance companies write off disasters as "acts of God"!

Given the perversion of structures in the world and Satan's underlying influence, statements of Scripture that the works of the world are evil (John 7:7) and that those who would be friends of the world make themselves enemies of God (James 4:4) take on added depth. Even the good, unfallen creation could be misused (Gen. 1–3). The fallen, twisted one holds many more snares, especially for the person tempted to deify the world.

* * *

Stranger: Ungrateful, unreasonable, inconsistent, and generally befuddled!

Inquirer: Huh? What?

Stranger: The question isn't *what* but *who*—and the answer, obviously, is you.

Inquirer: I don't understand.

Stranger: Obviously. That's what I just said. And since you're so demanding of some sort of imaginary perfection, you refuse even to appreciate all the indulgences and pleasures the world offers. You just brood obsessively about what you think is wrong or how something a person likes might affect someone else. Neurotic.

Inquirer: But so much is obviously wrong.

Stranger: Of course, and unavoidably so. You can't do anything about it, so you might as well enjoy what you can.

Inquirer: Wait a minute. I don't agree that I'm entirely helpless.

---

[10] Even St. Thomas Aquinas made no facile distinction between so-called naturally based and diabolic mental disorder: "For him, the devils can *only* act upon the human mind through natural, physical, and psychological causes; and conversely all natural physical causes can be instruments of diabolic purposes" (White 1953, 199). I—and White, speaking particularly with regard to paranormal phenomena—would affirm the statement but *omit* the word "only."

Stranger: Hmm. Grandiose, too. No sense of the possible and appropriate. This case begins to look more and more serious. I'll bet you didn't even notice that you can't even keep your categories straight. In all that talk about structure, you kept importing something else: emphasizing, choosing, cutting off—structures don't do that.

Inquirer: Goodness, you're right. I'd better sort that out a little more fully. (But didn't I say already that the categories can't be kept entirely straight?)

* * *

EVIL AND WILL

Disruptions of Will

It is perhaps impossible to speak of "disruptions" of structure without implicitly involving will—if not human will, then the demonic will. At least it is impossible if one is dissatisfied, as we are, with the category "natural evil." If evil is by definition unnatural, then something has impinged on structures that they might manifest the sorts of aberrations we have just categorized and sought to illustrate. They reflect the impact of corrupt wills.

At the same time, distorted structures impinge upon other wills that had nothing to do with the twisting of those particular structures. As a simple example, babies enter a world of economic, political, social, and familial structures that they neither created nor chose. But Satan is the victor if he persuades us that those babies' wills are wholly determined by their circumstances and that they can make no choices between good and evil. Thus we must now look at the problem of evil from the angle of the misdirected will, the will of the person who can resist everything but temptation and knows herself to be the one hopelessly irredeemable sinner (Rom. 7). For the sake of symmetry, I relate the analysis to the same categories used in discussing structure.

Choice of lesser goods (Perversion). To make false connections, emphases, or absolutes is to give some particular good more weight than it can bear. (This point holds even in questions of ends and means: we are often deluded into thinking that certain ends are important enough, or weighty enough goods, to justify faulty means.) Note that good things do not come with their relative values written clearly on their surface. We often do not possess all the information about them that we need (but ignoring the information we do have is another instance of weighing things wrongly—like, for instance, the pressure of our impulses). Note, too, that we necessarily make choices between goods: we cannot devote our careers both to chemistry and to music; we cannot

146

be celibate and be faithful parents as well; we cannot even do something as simple as go to the beach with friends and be at work at the office at the same time—though in most cases there is nothing wrong with any of these things in themselves.

Clearly, the implications of the Augustinian definition of sin as turning from a greater to a lesser good are seldom as plain as they would be if the only choices we faced involved whether to eat a sandwich or to rescue a drowning child. And Satan continually offers us lesser goods in the guise of overwhelmingly great ones. Thus the New Testament presents "flesh" (σάρξ) as having moral import and demonic potential— not because of a Greek body/spirit dualism that holds flesh as such to be evil but because we so easily trust in it to save us; or we use it as an instrument of lust and sin, perverting its functions; or we focus upon it as that which must be preserved at all costs (see Kallas 1966; Morosco 1974). Indeed, without our belief in our right to be kept from hurt or harm, a great many temptations would lose their appeal (see Stinnette 1955, 41).

"Progress" and science may present somewhat different temptations. They have benefited us so greatly that it may appear only reasonable that we sell them our morality and our souls out of our very indebtedness to them. Thus this dialogue written by Chambers (1948):

> "What's wrong with Progress and Science?" asked the pessimist.
> "Absolutely nothing," said the Devil. "Only the most primitive mind would suppose there was. They are, in fact, positively good. That was the nub of my inspiration. Hitherto Hell had tried to destroy man by seducing him to evil. My revolutionary thought was to destroy man by seducing him through good." (P. 82)

The noble, admirable, respectable thing may tempt us much more subtly and effectively than does *raw* perversion.

Or consider smaller things and things that are in themselves indifferent. What behavior can be justified by the desire for success in business or school? (If not cheating, how much neglect of family or friends?) By passionate love? (An affair? A divorce? A fantasy?) By a great artistic or athletic talent? (Sacrifice of one's education in other areas? Acceptance of a life of poverty or excessive wealth for one's family?) At such points of decision, the difference between a God-given gift or responsibility and a satanic temptation may seem very hard to discern—perhaps impossible to discern from the outside.

Neither pragmatism nor desire nor anticipated gaining of power provides a sufficient criterion for following a given path. None of these things can protect one from succumbing to evil in the very pursuit of good. So discovered Adam and Eve in their innocence: the forbidden fruit could be seen as useful food, as a delight to the eyes, as a means to the power of promised wisdom. There it lay, attractively held out by Satan, who sold his wares by breeding doubt of God's goodness and of God's command that the fruit be let alone. One bite and the first couple were hopelessly out of their depth. They knew and gained evil by doing it, knew good by losing it. And the way back to the Garden was barred by a flaming sword. Jesus when tempted did the reverse: he refused to barter righteousness for much-needed bread or to satisfy a worldly desire to awe others or to gain power and authority by which, presumably, he could have enforced great "good" later.

The Tempter continually tries to obscure the relationship of things to one another. He destroys proper balance and proportion, masks what has absolute claim to our allegiance, and hides how we can get from one thing to another without losing track of our goal in the process. He would persuade us to exchange the good for the possible, and thence power becomes god.

Isolation (Formlessness). Especially when the relationship of one thing to another is already tangled, unbalanced, or not producing the desired results, it is tempting to deny the intrinsic importance of the relationship—or of relationships generally.[11] If things are going badly for us, perhaps we should assert our (possibly very real) "potential" and "rights" and work for self-fulfillment. Should not the Devil promote such a program? After all, has he not given us his own example to follow? But he forgets to mention that we would be following his example, that he is the paradigm of the simply self-fulfilled, assertive being, and that the autonomy gained turns very soon, even if subtly, to an autonomy over against God.

After all, if all our earthly wants were fulfilled, what need would we have of God, the Devil may whisper in some deep corner of our minds. And he lures us with the thought that our desires by rights ought to be satisfied, not just that we should be kept from harm. He may pose as the instantaneous gratifier, offering us an "id heaven" (Anshen 1972, 2). And let us remember that he who rules the world can indeed supply these gratifications. The lie is not that they are available. The lie is that they are fulfilling.

The cost of this pursuit of self? Emptiness, and the loss of right relationships with other people. An internal vacuum that finally reduces one's own being to shapelessness. Very often, the using of others simply as means to one's own ends, or the fulfilling of lusts at others' direct expense (see James 4:1–7).

[11] Should willful promotion of disorder seem unlikely, consider this example of the skill of the Devil's tactics: "The present revolt of the younger generation against the machine has made a practice of promoting disorder and randomness" (Carrigan 1970, 9, quoting L. Mumford). The very mode of resistance to the Devil's tool of dehumanizing rigidity is made to serve his purposes.

Not everyone, though, can be lured to pursue self in quite so patent a way, despite all the help given by a lot of popular literature. For the disciplined, apparently self-denying, religious person, the enemy needs a different weapon. He takes up his role of Accuser and tries to get the conscientious one consumed with brooding over his sin. That tactic will produce self-centeredness every bit as effectively as will direct temptation, and it carries the added bonus of getting the victim's eyes off the cosmic nature of the battle with evil.[12] Get a person to believe that his sin not only is the central fact of his being but makes him utterly and eternally unacceptable to God, humanity, and himself, and you have someone not just set apart by a magic circle but a person entirely enclosed in a private sphere of misery. Whenever the will can be twisted so that it swirls and twines like a serpent around the self, it suffocates that self.

Bondage to world views (Rigidity). Finally, we come to the relationship of the will to determinacies. In chapter 1, I argued that we function in the world by observing/imposing structure in/upon the world and necessarily commit ourselves to our paradigms in our every act. In a profound sense, we are determined by what we affirm and imply affirmations in our actions. This is no merely optional determinacy applicable Mondays, Wednesdays, Fridays, and whenever else it seems convenient but is a deeply rooted way of seeing and being that gives the framework for choices and actions. It represents "reality" to us. We do what we know and know only what we do or that to which we relate (the Hebrew יַדַע, "to know," refers equally to intellectual knowledge and sexual intimacy). It is in that sense that he who commits sin is truly a slave to sin (John 8:34). It is in that sense that Paul can say, "Formerly, when you did not know God, you were in bondage to beings that by nature are no gods; but now that you have come to know God, . . . how can you turn back again to the weak and beggarly elemental spirits, whose slaves you want to be once more?" (Gal. 4:8–9).

In a significant way, consciousness "unites" with whatever part of the universe it seizes upon (see LeShan 1974, 44). One cannot simply "get in harmony with the universe"; even attempts to do that are selective. Insight, knowledge—whatever perceptions we might have—can never assure us of a grasp on that illusive thing, "objective reality." In fact, the conviction that we are in touch with the Absolute in such a way that we are absolutely sure of its (his) implications for the world has bred the Crusades, anti-Semitism, and much other horrendous evil done in the name of good—all massive victories for the Devil. Sincerity is no better

---

[12] Thus in *Pilgrim's Progress,* Apollyon's "temptation of Christian is at first an appeal to accept good from the source of evil, to take deliverance, wages and security from the demonic. When Christian refuses, Apollyon counters with a more subtle assault, grounded in truth, as he accuses Christian of spiritual pride and self-righteousness" (Frye 1960, 125).

protection than innocence. Yet to see no order at all is just as bad, and so is to see an order in which we are merely incidental. The Devil, the author of confusion as well as destructive bondage, has us trapped whether we perceive a kaleidoscopic chaos or a single, fixed reality of whatever sort (note that "chaos" is a world view, not the lack of one): these errors each make our "willing" appear meaningless instead of absolute.

Our enemy must hide from us the fact that none of these views is self-evident. They function for us only as our will capitulates to them. We are subject to the structures that we affirm (see "Chosen Connections" in chapter 3). We may live in a reliably deterministic universe if we will; we may live in a chaotic, occult, magical one if we will; or, taking an active stance, we may even try to conform the universe to our designs if we will (remembering that we are subject to our own designs). But the way out is not as easy as the way in: a paradigm once established is hard to break.[13]

The Will and Freedom

There is a complex interplay between the human experience of freedom (or its lack) and the role of the will in human misery. To highlight the role of the will is not necessarily to establish a meaningful preserve for human freedom. Indeed, as I indicated earlier, even to speak of *disruptions* of will is to imply that genuine freedom concerns freedom to will aright, not the ability to will arbitrarily or destructively. Thus one may suggest that the striking recalcitrance of psychopathology, even as compared to many diseases, may be attributed precisely to the fact that *will as well as structure is disordered.*

Furthermore, even apart from a chronically disordered will, outside stimuli can produce a negative impact. Material and physical problems capture our attention, which is the door, so to speak, to the will. Thus even the most exclusively organic complaint impinges on our will, whether we want it to or not. We can have plenty of problems without asking for them!

At the same time, we should reemphasize the common observation that we in a deep sense choose our psychopathology, from the defenses that we employ to the decompensations (ways of failing to cope) to which we succumb (and succumb we do: in dealings with the Devil, the

---

[13] Perhaps we may even throw a little light on the problem of the finality of apostasy by saying that it normally takes a more powerful paradigm to break an old paradigm—not that the new one may not simply obscure the old problems, but it would be the sheerest irrationality to go through radical changes for no benefits. Now if one has known the Truth (as one never does merely scientifically), than which nothing can be more powerful, to reject it demonstrates a spiritual blindness, an inability to distinguish good and evil (see Mark 3:29), that may imply an inability even to recognize the possibility of salvation if it were offered.

step in may be free, but not the succeeding steps).[14] Even the popular talk about the "masks" that normal people wear and the desirability of getting to the "real person" behind the mask, however helpful in one sense, in another sense whitewashes the fact that we choose our masks. Who I "really am" *depends* in part on my choosing a different mask than you choose, and neither you nor I should forget it. The bondage of a will taken in itself is a very deep bondage indeed.

Furthermore, the Devil is not stupid. We must assume that he knows our points of weakness and where to apply pressure. Consider an excerpt from Auden's (1976) poem "New Year Letter":

> The Devil, as is not surprising—
> His business is self-advertising—
> Is a first-rate psychologist
> Who keeps a conscientious list,
> To help him in his ticklish deals,
> Of what each client thinks and feels,
> His school, religion, birth and breeding
> Where he has dined and who he's reading. (P. 171)

The Devil knows our needs and desires. Just because what troubles one person troubles another not at all does not mean that the first could control himself if he only would: if he *could* "control himself" in that area, he would have some other problem instead of the one he has. Precisely where his problem lies, there his will is disordered, in bondage.

Bondage of the will produces predictability; bondage reduces choices. The freedoms that were available, with the uncertainties they bring, are turned into a rigid pattern of responses (which at least eliminates the terror that uncertainty can bring). Psychopathology of all sorts is one way of keeping the will tied to that which is below it, keeping it predictable without a person's conscious consent, and thus reducing that person's essential humanness.[15] Indeed, the healthy person's character contains an element of freshness, spontaneity, creativity, and—very important—*unconcern* foreign to the experience of the disturbed person, who struggles desperately with the deep and terrible significance of everything that crosses his path or mind.

> The last thing that can be said of a lunatic is that his actions are causeless. If any human acts may loosely be called causeless, they are

---

[14] See, for example, Shulman 1968, xi, 73, on the choosing of schizophrenia.

[15] A case in point from a simply physical level is Penfield's (1975) "automaton"—that which may be produced by brain activity alone (as in electric stimulation or epileptic discharge). The automaton has no sense of humor, beauty, love, contentment, happiness, or compassion but only a set of reflexes and skills, inborn and acquired, perhaps including some plans that may serve for a short while.

the minor acts of a healthy man; whistling as he walks; slashing the grass with a stick; kicking his heels or rubbing his hands. It is the happy man who does the useless things; the sick man is not strong enough to be idle. It is exactly such careless and causeless actions that the madman could never understand; for the madman (like the determinist) generally sees too much cause in everything. The madman would read a conspiratorial significance into those empty activities. . . . If the madman could for an instant become careless, he would become sane. (Chesterton 1959 [1908], 18–19)[16]

I am not, of course, arguing that humanness consists in unpredictability. Random behavior leaves human goals at least as far out of reach as an obstructive determinism. To act freely implies a sometimes paradoxical ability to maintain consistent motives, to obey the dictates of conscience, to compel oneself to act in accord with one's ideals and overriding purposes (see Chein 1972, 33; Polanyi 1964, 309). Such behavior we consider "responsible," while the same behavior, produced by force or illness, we would attribute to those causes and not to the person enacting it. Thus, the freedom of the human will depends not on its having no determinants but rather on the locus of the determinants. Those coming from below a person dehumanize him. Those coming from within are arbitrary. Those coming from above may be divine or actively demonic. In the latter case, one may gain an illusion of freedom by obtaining a bit of control over himself and his environment, even gain a whole world, all his own and perfectly private—and lose his soul. But only in the case of devotion to the God who made us and to his ways do we find a determinant for our behavior that sets us free from the world and ourselves and the enemy of our souls.

The Place of the Demonic

To define evil as disruption of structure and/or will does not in itself necessarily entail demonic agency in the disruptions, despite the fact that we have throughout linked them to such agency. The temptation no doubt arises again and again to see that linkage as metaphor. This little section cannot succeed in eliminating that temptation. It simply offers a few reflections related to some problems addressed by the chapter.

First, when we think about the disruptions labeled "psychopathology," does not a hypothesis involving demonic agency seem superfluous? Many have observed that we may have the demon we truly desire and that the names of contemporary demons appear simply to be aspects of human personality (Ebon 1974). Others have noted that cases of multiple personality seem to be explained by a splitting of the psychic structure. Still others remark that "possession" usually entails the

[16]See also May 1969, 36.

exaggeration of some basic attitude common in our own society. Perhaps we would do well to explore more fully our id impulses and unconscious mind, rather than import the Devil as an explanation?[17] Certainly we should do so if those categories are the only ones our paradigms allow. On the other hand, we could also argue that, since Satan cannot create but can produce in us only what is actually or potentially there, we should expect exactly what we see: demonic forces manifesting themselves in and through natural forces (see Martin 1976, 424). Furthermore, we might remember that even Freud eventually abandoned a watertight idea of the unconscious, according to which it held nothing but repressed material "belonging" to the individual's conscious mind. For Jung, "unconscious complexes" are "groups of psychic contents, isolated from consciousness, functioning arbitrarily and autonomously, leading a life of their own in the unconscious, whence they can at any moment hinder or further conscious acts" (quoted in White 1953, 202). Demons, anyone?

Second, when we consider the bondage of human will and the allure of determinism, should we see such bondage as, perhaps, the source of the Devil's knowledge of the future? Does he perhaps have the perfect Laplacean mind, which can carry out to infinity the implications of the positions of structures and wills that are bound to him?[18] There would then be no difficulty in explaining the occasionally amazing accuracy of the crystal-ball gazers or the astrologers: the Devil would simply be allowing them to see in a moment of time the result later in time of a deterministic course of events already in process. Furthermore, there would be no problem with the seeming paradox that a foreseen event, apparently predetermined, may yet be avoided if one becomes aware of its imminence: the rigid structure rests upon the bondage of the will and is utterly destroyed by any change in the will's focus. Hence the usual inaccuracies of prognosticators (usually wills with some degree of freedom impinge upon situations) and the unusual freedom from the Devil's arbitrary determinacies of the Christian whose will is bound to God. (Recall from chapter 4 the horoscope that was no longer true once he who had it cast repented of his sin in doing so.)[19]

[17] See chap. 4, n. 14, for Eeden's view of "unconsciousness."

[18] "The Laplacean mind understands precisely nothing and . . . whatever it knows means precisely nothing" (Polanyi 1964, 141). Polanyi's comment applies dramatically to the Devil. We have already seen that loss of meaning is inherent in attending to lower-level determinants, as surely as a word becomes nonsensical when only its vocalization is attended to. In a similar and suggestive vein, Barrett Wendell of Harvard commented in 1891, "I am much disposed to think that necromancers, witches, mediums—what not,— actually do perceive in the infinite realities about us things that are imperceptible to normal human beings; but that they perceive them only at a sacrifice of their higher faculties—mental and moral—not inaptly symbolized in the old tales of those who sell their souls" (quoted in Kehl 1976, 124).

[19] Thus, the accuracy of a given prognostication is emphatically not to be confused with

Third, as we look at the temptation narrative, we might suggest that internal dynamics would surely seem adequate to explain Jesus' experience. An entirely realistic stress or threat may easily put disproportionate focus on one aspect of a person's being: Jesus was obviously tempted to make bread because he was hungry (Matt. 4:3). One cannot live by bread alone—but neither can one live *without* bread. Or perhaps a need for love turns one to hatred; to an irrational concentration on other pursuits, intellectual or sensual; to a chasing after security or fame; or to demands that love be manifested in particular ways: did Jesus wrestle with the idea that, if God really loved him, he would guard him even from the harm risked by pursuing that love substitute, the awe of others (Matt. 4:6)? Or perhaps a sense of impotence with regard to one's own personal life or with regard to the evil in the world leads one to become obsessed with power, magical or mechanical; to institute compulsive rituals or manipulations in hopes of somehow curbing chaos: so Jesus contemplated having control over all the kingdoms of the world. Perfectly natural temptations. But *only* natural? Or is it the case that,

> what in fact is always at stake in every moment of temptation is not a higher self or a lower self, personal integrity or dishonour—that is the least of it: what is at stake is the strengthening or (please God) the weakening of the spirit forces of evil that are out to destroy the kingdom of Christ. (Stewart 1951, 293)

Evil, then, is structures that are distorted, perverted, broken down, or rigidified, structures given a different shape, direction, or status than that established by God's perfect will. (In thus suggesting that there *is* a norm, I do not claim that we can exhaustively know it.) Evil is will that is misdirected, absolutized, or denied. Trouble is instigated by him who destructively and deceptively controls structures, by him who temptingly weasels his way through the chinks of weakness in our wills so that, first freely and ever afterward as slaves, we do *his* will. Thus what may begin as an attempt to gain dominance or any number of perceived "goods" leaves a person in increasing bondage. Or begin from the other side: any disruption of structure or will as we have understood them leads to an area of powerlessness, since one of the essential components of power has been put out of commission. Is not, then, the natural solution to seek more power?

some sort of "truth" in horoscopes and the like: I argue that that very accuracy is grounded in the profound untruth that all is determined. If the Devil controls the world and is a liar, there may be many connections in the world that are not True and are not valid or accurate for one who has been set free by the Truth (see John 8:31–36).

8

Power Seeking as a Response to Powerlessness

Stranger: Seek power? Obviously. If one has a lack, he must supply what is lacking. He who has no power, needs power. Obviously. You have a habit of posing unconscionably foolish questions as if they were profound. Do you suppose anyone but the most heartless and greedy of the powerful would want to deny resources to the ill and underprivileged? Well, perhaps so, but not for very noble reasons. In my opinion—and I know humankind a lot better than most people do—those who extol the virtues of weak, humble distress and poverty are simply trying to allay their guilt feelings over being healthy and well heeled. Since when have the *powerless* deemed their state a blessing?

Inquirer: You're absolutely right. They would do anything to change it.

Stranger: And in the face of all that terrible need, "religious" sorts suggest that earthly bread ought to be foregone for the sake of the heavenly. Have they no pity? What of those who haven't the strength? The only gift of "religion" to them is guilt piled on top of their misery, a conscience rubbed raw. Cruelty, I call it.

Inquirer: You mean like jumping on the person who's down because he can't or won't keep our rules? Moralism, if not greed—I guess we manage to hurt each other one way or another . . . but I gather you'd like to propose a solution.

Stranger: Indeed; one I remember reading somewhere and approving. Listen to this:

> I maintain that nothing need be destroyed, that we only need to destroy the idea of God in man, that's how we have to set to work. . . . As soon as men have all of them denied God . . . the old conception of the universe will fall of itself without cannibalism and what's more the old morality, and everything will begin anew. Men will unite to take from life all it can give, but only for joy and happiness in the present world. Man will be lifted up with a spirit of divine Titanic pride and the man-god will appear. From hour to hour extending his conquest of

nature infinitely by his will and his science, man will feel such lofty joy from hour to hour in doing it that it will make up for all his old dreams of the joys of heaven. Every one will know that he is mortal and will accept death proudly and serenely like a god. His pride will teach him that it's useless for him to repine at life's being a moment, and he will love his brother without need of reward. Love will be sufficient only for a moment of life, but the very consciousness of its momentariness will intensify its fire, which now is dissipated in dreams of eternal love beyond the grave.[1]

Isn't that great?

Inquirer: It's quite a vision—one that a lot of people have shared, I suppose, though you may see it more clearly than most. I think most people just catch a glimpse that keeps them always looking for more. What puts the picture out of focus for them, though, is death—they don't seem able to manage such a positive view of it as you hold. But then, they can usually refrain from thinking about death except to try to avoid it for the moment. It's true that present needs are generally much more pressing than dreams of heaven.

Stranger: Precisely. Most people entertain the latter simply because they're so miserable now. And ironically, those very dreams interfere with their adjusting and succeeding in the present. I'm absolutely committed to health and self-fulfillment here and now.

Inquirer: A strong statement for one who doesn't like absolutes—but an appealing one, I must admit. Not many seem to disagree with you.

* * *

THE SEARCH FOR POWER AND
THE PRODUCTION OF IMPOTENCE

Power: the ability to produce desired, intended effects in the world. Even more fundamentally, the assurance that one *is*, one's existence being manifested and made concrete by the effects one produces. What, then, could be a more natural aim, a more necessary goal, than to search for power? Utterly to lack power, to produce no effects, or to make no difference anywhere or to anyone is not to exist. To *feel* impotent is to encounter *fear* of nonexistence, fear that nothing matters, fear that everything is utterly meaningless and hopeless because one is helpless. Says Nietzsche, "Where I found the living, there I found the will to power" (Kaufmann 1954, 226). May (1972) reports that virtually all of

[1] Dostoevsky 1923, 701–2.

156

his clients for psychotherapy come to him because they feel in one way or another powerless and experience the anxiety that is both cause and effect of the felt lack of power. Adler considered the basic dynamic of all human life—as well as of all psychopathology—to be a striving from a felt "minus" to a felt "plus" (Ansbacher and Ansbacher 1956). Steiner (1975, 64) suggests that *Oedipus Rex*—and the Oedipus complex—are so moving because they send the message of human impotence in the face of fate. And so human beings have developed numerous strategies for seeing themselves as having some impact on—or at least some proper place in—their recalcitrant world. They have sought to subdue it through science or to manipulate it through magic. They have lashed out against it in violence. And they have sought to redefine their experience in order to count everything that happens, whether good or evil, as simply "natural" and hence no threat to them or to the overall cosmic harmony.

Science, Magic, and Violence

Science and magic both promise control over the world, and naturally enough, they share many of the same roots (James 1961 [1902]; Lewis 1947). Not the Middle Ages but the Renaissance was the golden age of the occult (Nugent 1971). Both science and magic set aside the classical problem of cultivating virtue in favor of concentrating on techniques that produce power. And both freely violate conventional piety and sensibilities by doing such things as digging up and mutilating the dead (Lewis 1947, 88). Presumably, science has flourished simply because it works—works far more reliably than magic.

Scarcely anyone would deny that science works, even if its power is gained by a magician's bargain that entails giving up our souls piece by piece. We learn to treat what we have conquered as mere object, to regard it quantitatively rather than qualitatively. After all, who could cut a tree he regarded as a friend into beams? So we gain a house—and lose a friend.[2] This bargain may be all very fine in terms of "progress," particularly when we avoid adding ourselves to the list of conquests. Fine, that is, for the "healthy" ones among us.

However, in a culture governed by such views of the value of control and technique, the person who finds her own life rather unmanageable

[2] "We reduce things to mere Nature *in order that* we may 'conquer' them. We are always conquering Nature, because 'Nature' is the name for what we have, to some extent, conquered. The price of conquest is to treat a thing as mere Nature. . . . The wresting of powers *from* Nature is also the surrendering of things *to* Nature. . . . But as soon as we take the final step of reducing our own species to the level of mere Nature . . . the being who stood to gain and the being who has been sacrificed are one and the same" (Lewis 1947, 82–83). So also Walsh (1971, 25): "Ultimate computer men, clean-cut and wholesome, set foot on the moon, robbing it from poets, lovers, and science-fiction writers."

may easily be tempted to treat herself, too, as mere object, or to put herself in the hands of someone else who will treat her that way. If thoughts and actions are seen as essentially material, mechanical, and entirely necessary events, how does one manage them?[3] By a tight behavioral reinforcement schedule? Or does one use them to manage the world by enacting complex rituals that will presumably forestall great harm? The closer this latter (i.e., obsessive-compulsive) solution comes to paranoid psychosis, the more the magical quality of such tactics comes into focus, particularly in the complex delusional systems that are so often mechanical in nature. In each case, though, rigidity buys a certain sort of gain or safety. And in each case the path linking desire for scientific control with magical control—a path forged by the human need for safety and gratification—is a two-way road, a fact obscured only by our evaluation of the relative mental health of the practitioners of each tactic.[4]

However, even for "normal" people there comes a point—and the point has surely come for many in our day—when conquest becomes banal and the counting of the spoils, boring. Or worse, the battle losses become evident, the sense of a lack of control over burgeoning technocracy increases, and a mechanical world provides nothing to which it seems worth committing one's mechanical self—if a mechanical self could indeed commit itself to anything. Neither rationalistic science nor rationalistic religion combats the spiritual starvation of such a society. Without any integrating spiritual resources to draw upon, the will that is supposedly captured and caged by the progress of science may simply revolt, seeking a power different from the overly confining power of structures and "natural laws" that leaves persons serving their supposed tools.

One mode of revolt against dehumanizing structures that turn us into

---

[3] A variation on this theme is the "helpless" role, whereby one both exonerates himself—since he has been victimized by heredity or environment in a way completely beyond his control—and also obtains very effective manipulative power, attention, and similar secondary gains. Whatever the degree of truth in the person's protestations or demonstrations of helplessness and however many benefits eventuate from the role, submitting to it (or welcoming it) obviously entails heavy costs in terms of one's sense of personhood.

[4] This point is graphically illustrated by the "scientific" psychological principle of "reinforcement"—defined as anything that will increase response frequency—as a determinant of behavior. The focus here is on the terms "safety" (negative reinforcement) and "gratification" (positive reinforcement). The "science" comes with the observation that reinforcers may transcend specific situations, so the definition is not entirely circular, and that reinforcers may reliably be applied to produce intended effects. The "magic" enters with the occult assumption that events later in time (reinforcers) can determine events earlier in time (i.e., "stamp in" neural connections leading to behavioral sequences). Both science and magic would assume that, if desired effects are *not* forthcoming, the potion must have been mixed or applied incorrectly. And both science and magic point to effects *produced* as obvious demonstration that their explanations of the effects are valid.

inconsequential automatons is violence. "At the heart of our violence, in act or in feeling, lies the wish to show ourselves men with a will" (May 1972, 165, quoting Bronowski). Determinism violates our sense of ourselves as *willing* beings and therefore, however powerfully it serves us, makes us feel impotent in our inner selves. In this sense as well as in a sociological one, felt powerlessness leads to violence, and violence is a desperate expression of impotence (May 1972, 23). How like the Devil's impotence it is, destruction (reducing things or persons to nonbeing) done to increase one's sense of being! In the impulse and in the act, it is a way of unifying the self that omits rationality, a way that can seem compellingly necessary when rational approaches have failed.[5]

Another mode of revolt is the open pursuit of the occult, which either rejects rationality outright or else seeks a higher, private rationality. It flies in the face of the very science with which it shares a common heritage and promises a special knowledge, producing a special sort of power that is somehow "different" and "superior." Unlike aggression, which does establish a sort of contact with others, the occult isolates, making a person concentrate on himself (Bauer 1967). But like aggression, it makes a devil's bargain by seeking to combat absolutized structures with an absolutized will.

Absolutization of the individual will is tantamount to setting oneself up as God. "The cry for recognition becomes the central psychological cry: I must be able to say *I am,* to affirm myself in a world into which, by my capacity to assert myself, I put meaning, I *create* meaning" (May 1972, 20)—precisely the Devil's declaration of independence.[6] Such an affirmation sends one skidding down the double spiral of loneliness plus the need to be more than human, the one component exacerbating the other.

Loneliness and grandiosity are both characteristics of psychopathology. The "striving from a felt minus situation towards a felt plus situation" becomes an "exaggerated, uncooperative goal of personal superiority" (Ansbacher and Ansbacher 1956, 1–2), and in that striving, "the more we become superman, the more we become inhuman" (Frye 1960, 51, quoting A. Schweitzer). Thus, "the loftiest goals are to be found in the most pathological cases—that is, in the psychoses" (Shulman 1968, 170, quoting Adler). In fact, "reality" can hardly be devalued enough for one to escape its constraints unless the personal aim becomes everything. The schizophrenic may, for example, even increase his level of aspiration after failure, thus demonstrating that possibilities are viewed as relative to his intent: the importance of his

[5] Cf. Frye 1960, 33: "Satan's reliance on power represents an exclusion of reason as well as love, or, perhaps more accurately, one cannot be excluded without the other."

[6] May is making a descriptive, existential comment and would doubtless deny the value judgment entailed by the context in which I have placed his words.

personal goal outweighs the importance of all rational considerations (Shulman 1968, 12). More painful yet, the personal goal at issue is not as much a specific achievement as the desire to remedy felt deficiencies or a sense of threat by attaining some sort of impregnable perfection. Hence any failure, however minor, becomes intolerable (p. 9). The psychotic person implicitly denies his finitude, denies the limits imposed by structure. He therefore demonstrates *par excellence* that a person,

> by surrendering to extensive infinity, imperils the core of his being, which is finite and demands limitations and measure. The flight into infinity breeds vain ambition, disappointment, and disintegration— conditions which permit easy entrance for the power of evil under manifold disguises. (Anshen 1972, 99)

In this sense magic goes hand in hand with madness. On the one side, magic has the same aim (omnipotence) and the same result (isolation).[7] On the other, it is the technique and recourse of those who find themselves powerless, a covert means of self-assertion (May 1972, 94–95). It can even be said that the schizophrenic is a magician who fails (Roheim 1955, 166); and yet the very failure makes the magic more necessary.

Is the magician who fails in more trouble than the magician who succeeds, who sees results from his spells, who becomes a shaman or a witch?[8] The totally self-centered aim of the magician's ritual is to intensify his power (Williams 1959); the symbolism of witchery is to do so by becoming one with that which confines, limits, and masters humankind.

> Witches are so given over to their own reality, in the popular conception, that they are "obsessed" with evil, they are "compelled" to do evil, it is even "involuntary" with them: it is this very *piety* which so dehumanizes them that they loose [*sic*] contact with mankind and so can no longer be argued with, but must simply be either avoided or killed. (Zuesse 1971, 225)

[7] In psychoanalytic terms, Roheim (1955) notes that both psychosis and magic are regressive and narcissistic, rooted in infantile omnipotence. He also comments that many taboos are directed against mirrors because of their regressive, narcissistic aspect (p. 191). The relationship to the occult use of mirrors and crystal balls ("spirits" often seem to be associated with mirrors) is intriguing, another suggestion, in this context, of the demonic nature of self-centeredness. That is to say, self-centeredness, whether under the guise of magic or madness, has at least two links to the Devil: first, the breaking down of mutuality and relatedness with others and with the world; second, the possibility of making contact with demonic forces directly. It would seem that mirrors as such both symbolize and facilitate focus on the self. (It is indeed interesting how many psychiatric patients are frankly preoccupied with mirrors.)

[8] That is, a shaman of the sort I. M. Lewis (1971) would classify as "peripheral," one having uncooperative, personal goals.

It is not necessary, though, that the "piety" of doing evil be paramount; it is sufficient that reciprocity be broken down and that all good be defined with regard to an isolated self. Such aloneness is the "shape" of the pursuit of power and is the reason that its enticements can render a person both a willful follower and a helpless victim of evil (see Anshen 1972, 1). Indeed, the very nature of a pact with the Devil is the assumption and promise that superhuman power can be made available here and now. If the here and now is what counts—and if human ties have proved unreliable and vain—why not accept (p. 139)? And just because such a commitment reduces all, including the beyond, to the here and now, its paradoxical result is that witchery does not finally transcend the finite but rather capitulates absolutely to the finite. Everything becomes a tool for the preservation of the self and the furthering of one's own agenda.[9] Perhaps, then, the demonic nature of witchery may be found precisely in this reduction, this hope to exploit the superhuman for merely human, temporal ends (see Zuesse 1971, 238).

A fine state of affairs! He who would remedy his powerlessness by unconditionally embracing science or by rigidly programing his own behavior is forever on the brink of turning himself into an automaton that is locked facelessly into an infrahuman world or into a psychotic or neurotic frozen in his pathology. He who resorts to violence breaks free at the cost of setting himself against others, destroying them and his own rational transcendence at each blow. He who embraces magic wins the absolute individuality—and consequent unrelatedness—of madness or witchery. Surely there must be another way besides the demonic forms of reductionism, whether reduction of human beings to nature (seeking power by absolutizing structure) or reduction of the beyond to human purposes (seeking power by absolutizing will).

Art, Genius, and Mysticism

In the effort to escape the thought of unsettling encroachments from beyond the human realm and the risks of a reductionistic mechanism or voluntarism, some have sought to define all that persons can be or experience as simply "natural." Their goal is not to contrast—or encompass—categories such as "finite" versus "infinite" but rather to see everything as providing, at least potentially, opportunity for positive, creative expression.

From this stance one may speak, perhaps, of "the dark side of human *nature*" but hardly of a foe that must be vanquished. After all, cutting

---

[9] Ironically, the person most concerned with preserving himself consistently sees the human ties that could protect him from the isolation of magic as threatening instead of gratifying (see Laing 1969, 44).

out the dark side would leave humans no longer human. The battle cry, then, is to integrate the demonic into life rather than to succumb to it or pursue it. Those who follow such an agenda may speak of integrating the *daimonic* into life, by this spelling intending to avoid any connotation of an evil power that is not merely natural. Every lovely painting must have its deeper tones, properly distributed, of course. This integration is, in fact, often the role or result of art, of genius, and of mysticism, those most noble and yet perhaps most ambiguous possibilities for mortals— for some mortals. The artist, genius, or mystic may seem to be the antithesis of the powerless person: rather than seek power, she appears to channel and express it.

Stepping back from the extreme case of true genius, one may define the daimonic as "any natural function which has the power to take over the whole person. . . . The daimonic is the urge in every being to affirm itself, assert itself, perpetuate and increase itself" (May 1969, 123). It is the power of life or of nature, beyond good and evil, that may be creative or destructive.[10] Repress it, and apathy plus "eruptions" results.

Thus one might say that a person feels powerless, with respect to the world or herself, when her daimon is denied expression and integration with her personality. The apparent solution to the difficulty, or at least the aim, would then be simply to be and to accept oneself. Several problems, however, present themselves. First, we appear "naturally" to increase and assert ourselves at others' expense. Second, the "power of life," grounded as it is in the transrational, is mysterious. It is beyond our control and produces uncanny feelings that do not integrate easily and harmoniously. Thus, third, we see evils arise in our various relationships, cannot fully comprehend our own impulses, and become afraid even of ourselves, a prime form of impotence.

It is by no means surprising, then, that while *daimōn* had for centuries a meaning interchangeable with *theos* ("god"), it gradually assumed in popular usage the sense of an evil spirit hostile to humankind (Zucker 1969). Accepting and expressing "natural" power is by no means a simple matter. There is no obvious way to do it freely as soon as more than one being exists. If there were, perhaps this whole discussion would be unnecessary because there would be no problem of evil. Perhaps the very difficulty of expressing natural power is the reason those who do so most potently are often close to madness.[11] And perhaps we see again that power is never wholly natural.

[10] "For the rational philosopher in an age of demythologization, the demonic appears as a benevolent helper toward his self-realization, consenting to man's autonomy as long as he does not lose himself to his passions ($\dot{\epsilon}\pi\theta\nu\mu\dot{\iota}\alpha$) or contentiousness ($\phi\iota\lambda o\nu\iota\kappa\dot{\iota}\alpha$). The Latin interpreters showed a perfect understanding of what Plato had in mind when they translated the word [$\delta\alpha\dot{\iota}\mu\omega\nu$] as 'genius' " (Zucker 1969, 39).

[11] Starting from the opposite direction, one researcher found that schizophrenic

For the creative person, the more-than-natural implications of her art or genius reside in at least two areas. Consider first the ambiguous nature of problem solving and conflict resolution, for certainly most art and genius have their point of application or their source in internal and external problems and conflicts. There may indeed be relatively pure expressions of, say, delight in beauty (though even masterpieces of this sort lift us by contrast to the pain and ugliness of which we are all too aware), but for the most part the creative act is a struggle, *a striving for resolution*. The fruit of the resolution may be scientific or technological advance, the two-sidedness of which we have discussed, or it may be "beauty"—an expression of problems however great or of material however dreadful in a form that is aesthetically satisfying. Hardly is there a "solution" to life in great art; solutions strike us as cheap and tawdry, as calendar art, as naive romanticism. The very beauty of the expression, however, not only is emotionally cathartic but also gives an illusion of control and harmony: pleasing form has been given to that which was chaotic and perhaps unsettling.

In this sense, "it is understandable that the poets should be 'of the devil's party.' . . . The ultimate end of poetry is to offer us the mirage of a world at last reduced to unity, and this by every means, from metaphor to sheer sleight-of-hand" (Magny 1952, 439–40). While on the one hand we must have creativity in order to deal with our material and emotional problems and conflicts—surely a better tool than violence, for which art may even be said to be a substitute (May 1972, 233)—yet on the other hand there is a tendency to get the order mixed up and laud the conflicts because of the excellence of the product produced.[12] We may tend to take Romans 8:28 simply as "all things work together for good" (KJV)—and forget the rest of the verse. If we do, evil is not bound but masked and loosed.

Second, creative artists (e.g., Keats, Blake, Mozart, Tennyson, Morgan Robertson) strikingly often report that material is given them that seems to come from another source, even against their will. Wagner and Coleridge both described inspiration as coming when they were in a different state of consciousness; Browning engaged in automatic writing;

children increased their IQ scores twenty or more points beyond their healthy norm, or their score after recovery, in the period just preceding a psychotic break. Another researcher has linked genes fostering schizophrenia to potential for special giftedness or creativity via increased arousal level of the brain (Ferguson 1975, 204).

[12] On the personal level this error is often made in attempts to comfort people struggling with the problem of suffering: after all, there are few great human beings who have not suffered greatly. We would insist, however, that one can use that argument *only in her own case*. As soon as it is applied generally, she who does so violates the mutual vulnerability of our shared humanity and destroys rather than heals. Said differently, suffering may be an *occasion* but not a *cause* of growth; it produces criminals and madmen as well as saints. To confuse occasions and causes breeds continual mislabeling of evil as good.

Brahms got mental images from "vibrations," following contemplation on oneness with God; and Richard Bach (author of *Jonathan Livingston Seagull,* a book that many Christians who know nothing of its history consider deeply anti-Christian) got his story in a vivid waking dream (Ferguson 1975, 323–24; Moss 1974, 227–29). Robert Louis Stevenson wrote, "The whole of my published fiction should be the single-handed product of some unseen collaborator"; and George Sand, "It is the *other* who sings as he likes, well or ill, and . . . I am nothing, nothing at all" (quoted in Moss 1974, 230).[13]

In a similar vein, at the end of the eighteenth century many artists belonged to an antirational cult of genius that held the daimonic to be a force comparable to an élan vital stemming from neither God nor the Devil; for Dostoevsky, however, the daimonic was the crystallization point for evil (Zucker 1969). I do not—let it be clear—identify the creative muse with the Devil. Neither do I deny the value of transcendent creative achievement. Nonetheless, surely something of Dostoevsky's instinct is right. While in some sense the daimonic is "natural" (it is certainly naturally channeled), yet we remember Schlier's fascinating contention (see chap. 6, n. 34) that the power of the principalities (which we gave active, spiritual status) derives precisely from the limit of the natural order. The line may well be extremely fine between the daimonic and the openly demonic. So fine that Rilke, rejecting psychotherapy, could write, "If my devils are to leave me, I am afraid my angels will take flight as well" (quoted in May 1969, 122). Or changing the figure somewhat, if "the saint and the criminal stand back to back on either side of the demonic" (Kehl 1976, 115, quoting Thomas Mann), facing opposite directions, perhaps some artists are straddling the line and staring straight along it. Particularly questionable are those materials seeming to come full-blown from "beyond," with the recipient in a state of passivity. In such a state, it is very difficult to tell from which side of the line the input is coming, especially when sheep's clothing garbs lamb and wolf alike.

For the mystic, too, danger may lie in her state of passivity, though that is not her only link with the "inspired" artist or genius. Like them, the mystic has an investment in beauty and harmony, though she more

---

[13] Cf. Jung 1963, 356–57: "There was a daimon in me, and in the end its presence proved decisive. It overpowered me, and if I was at times ruthless it was because I was in the grip of the daimon. I could never stop at anything once attained. . . . A creative person has little control over his own life. He is not free. He is captive and driven by his daimon. . . . When the daimon is at work, one is always too close and too far. Only when it is silent can one achieve moderation." Jung did experiment with the occult, considered the clash of opposites necessary for consciousness raising, and held that, as with Faust, evil may play a mysterious role in *relieving* people of darkness and suffering. This sort of harmonization might well evoke great caution in those who take the power of evil and its deceptive nature seriously.

perceives and receives it than wrests and molds it actively from raw experience. It is far from the case that all mystics have been quietists. Nonetheless, an experience of oneness, completeness, and "rightness," so intense that all questions of "evil" as opposed to "good" are dissolved, certainly has quietistic—not to mention solipsistic—potential when it is applied beyond one's own personal reconciliation with the cosmos and God or when it is so enchanting and ensnaring that one's sister is lost from sight.[14] Indeed, another similarity between mystic and creative artist is the aloneness of the peak moment, even if the *feeling* is that of unity. If feelings of unity become substitutes for reunion, the Devil is the victor.

Returning to the issue of passivity, we may note that, while mystical states (as also the daimon) are absolutely authoritative over the individual, yet they lack any specific intellectual content (James 1961 [1902], 333).[15] However, the sense of the loss of personal boundaries is usually accompanied, at least in those at all advanced in contemplative disciplines, by an increase in paranormal cognitions, whether clairvoyant, precognitive, "messages from God or the gods," or whatever (Deikman 1973b). In fact, it rather appears that the experiencing of paranormal phenomena may virtually *require* the development of a passive, receptive mode. If critical faculties and perceptions of good and evil are thereby put on the shelf, while communications received have a ring of absolute authority, the problems are obvious. Furthermore, passivity as a regular practice has its personal perils: when persons who have regularly engaged in it suffer a severe emotional trauma, they may become totally unable to act. Instead, a rush of receptive-mode thoughts and perceptions overwhelms them, and they may respond with a delusional reordering of their experience. That is, they suffer an acute mystical psychosis (Deikman 1973a, 80).[16] Not every mystic has a

[14] In more theological terminology, turning a personal revelation of God into a theodicy verges upon the obscene. Reconciliation with others cannot be made a rational necessity or an abstract, cosmic principle. It is intensely personal and individual. To apply one's own experience as a universal law is to dehumanize others and utterly to cut oneself off from them and their pain as individuals. It is positively indecent, to extend my comment in n. 12, to accept the bliss of one's own harmony with all things as right and just when the agony of others is in view: to do so is to build one's castle on the shifting, grainy sand of human misery. Paradoxically, if the mystic's sense of being herself beyond the reach of impinging goods and evils fails to increase her sensitivity to her sister's need and the evil and injustice of the everyday world, it would appear that the god to which she has fled is sprouting horns and a tail.

[15] Laski (1962) finds no essential difference, except in interpretation, or "overbelief," in ecstasies experienced by believers, infidels, literary geniuses, and the man on the street.

[16] Similarly, James (1961 [1902], 334) speaks of paranoid states as a sort of "diabolical mysticism": "The same sense of ineffable importance in the smallest events, the same texts and words coming with new meanings, the same voices and visions and leadings and missions, the same controlling by extraneous powers; only this time the emotion is pessimistic; instead of consolations we have desolations; the meanings are dreadful; and

psychotic break, of course, any more than does every artist. Nor do they all become complete recluses, though solitude is certainly the norm. Nor, perhaps, do all succumb to messages from the limit of the natural, though virtually all seem to receive them. It would appear, however, that mysticism per se, unadulterated by community norms and human fellowship, fosters all of these. Its power as soon destroys as saves.

* * *

Stranger: Wonderful. Most impressive.

Inquirer: Huh? What do you mean?

Stranger: Why, your little analysis of how to get into trouble, of course. Where do you think I've been?

Inquirer: You liked it?

Stranger: Liked it? Well, I can hardly deny that it was thorough.

Inquirer: Why, thank you.

Stranger: In fact, so thorough that it looks as if you've deprived people of anything they could possibly do, ever. Science and innocent magic, violence and self-assertion and the occult, the inspiration of art and genius and mysticism, even attempts to resolve conflicts so that they can be a bit more comfortable—every form of power a helpless person might seek after, you deny. No wonder you started out by talking about death: that's apparently the *only* way the person you've hamstrung can stay out of trouble!

Inquirer: You don't listen very well. You *never* heard me say that a person was likely to keep out of trouble by being dead! And . . .

Stranger: Oh, pardon *me;* I was being insensitive to your mythology, wasn't I? So sorry. But let me tell you that I've had more than enough of these arguments implying that, just because a thing can be pushed to extremes, there's something wrong with it. It's like saying milk is obviously bad for babies since they'll drown if you throw them in a swimming pool full of it!

Inquirer: Quite right. I'd have said just that if you hadn't interrupted me. I can positively affirm science, art, genius, conflict resolution, and up to a point, mysticism; though I admit I'm not so excited about violence and the occult.

the powers are enemies to life." Noting that physiological data on schizophrenics are ambiguous, Deikman (1973a) interprets them as possibly indicating a shift to the receptive mode, leading to a desire to regain control.

Stranger: There goes your narrow-minded prejudice into orbit again. And your positively befuddling unwillingness to stick with a position. Now I don't befuddle easily, but you are explicitly negativistic about everything people do to fulfill themselves, and then you back down as soon as someone confronts you head-on.

Inquirer: No, I'm not negative about human achievements. I'm negative about power seeking.

Stranger: So you want people to be impotent. That means dead, just as I said. Just as you said yourself, even.

Inquirer: You are deliberately misinterpreting me.

Stranger: You are an absolute obscurantist. I haven't the slightest notion of why you're so paranoid about power, of your objections to it.

Inquirer: Then let me try to make myself perfectly clear.

* * *

SNARES IN THE SEARCH FOR POWER

One may easily argue that the trouble with power is simply that people cannot use it wisely. We all know the slogans and epigrams: "Power corrupts; and absolute power corrupts absolutely" (Lord Acton). "I am very doubtful whether history shows us one example of a man who, having stepped outside traditional morality and attained power, has used that power benevolently" (Lewis 1947, 78). "There are few Christians who can carry a full cup with a steady hand" (Harper 1970, 58, quoting Bishop Ryle). Simple observation surely supports these statements. Furthermore, I have argued that, because it is empty—meaningless—in itself, power does not satisfy but creates a need for more, more, more of it. And if it is true that the more power people get, the worse they handle it, we are obviously in trouble.

Should we, then, promote impotence as a sort of safeguard? On the contrary. We have already identified impotence with pathology, clearly something to be combated. The problem is that, seemingly paradoxically, the search for power does not cure but rather increases our overall impotence. In the preceding section I argued that our ways of *actively* seeking power distort or unbalance the elements (structure and will) constituting power, undermining its foundations. *Passively* seeking power or considering oneself merely a channel of natural power leaves one with no criteria for separating good from evil. Power seeking does not resolve persons' pathology, even if they do gain the ability to produce certain sorts of effects in the world. Things remain out of joint unless both structure and will are properly and harmoniously fulfilled.

However, power seeking generates dangers perhaps deeper even than the paradoxical production of impotence. The perils we shall discuss are still rooted in our understanding of the nature of power itself, but we are now explicitly pushing the issues into the area of values. The first danger is the adoption of pragmatism, standards of intensity, and "self-fulfillment" as yardsticks to measure value.[17] The second is the opening of the self—voluntarily or unintentionally—to evil spiritual power. The former usually provides both the instigation and the justification for the latter.

Pragmatism, Standards of Intensity, and Self-Fulfillment

Power, defined as the ability to produce desired effects, easily leads to pragmatism, or the justification of means by ends. Pragmatism asks, Does it *work?* and the "work" implies the effective channeling of power. Such a question can be answered only after first asking another one, namely, What is it supposed to do? The achievement of the goal or desired effect is in fact the only criterion to which power is subject. That fact creates problems. For one, effects are not discrete. We *never* on this earth fully know the results of any application of power. We never have "the" outcome. Further consequences keep showing themselves.[18] For another, any effect chosen as the single goal to which all subsidiary effects point and are subject is quite simply an idol. (Actually, we could define an idol as an absolute that is reachable or appeasable by power of one sort or another. Modern persons try to *attain* their deities of prosperity, happiness, or whatever by the power of science and money; primitive persons try to *placate* and *manipulate* theirs by the power of sacrifice and magic.) And finally, the fact that some ends (such as love) cannot be produced by means of power begins to escape one. There is a

---

[17] Zilboorg and Henry (1941, 144), critical of medieval religious faith and superstition as leading to the lumping together of magicians, sorcerers, heretics, and psychotics, comment, "The physician of the time reasoned in a manner betraying deep apprehension that his preoccupation with clinical matters might be mistaken for indifference to the questions of sin and virtue." Whatever errors these persons made—and I do not wish to whitewash the errors—I would argue that, far from being irrelevant to clinical matters, "questions of sin and virtue" are close to their core. The solution to errors, in my view, is hardly to discredit the entire world view within which they occur: we do not throw out trigonometry because someone's miscalculation led to the collapse of a bridge, even if a number of people on the bridge tragically plunged to their death.

[18] This same problem applies to situational ethics, which, by focusing wholly on temporal effects, really creates an ethics of power, not of pure "love" as Fletcher intends. To argue as Fletcher (1966, 144) does that we must refute the old rubric, "Do what is right and let the chips fall where they may" on the grounds that "whether what you are doing is right or not depends precisely upon where the chips fall" appears rather presumptuous. We should not ignore the data we have, but how dare we assume that we can see the only relevant chips and can predict and evaluate their landing point?

tendency to slide into the patent the logical fallacy of assuming that, if power is the ability to produce desired effects, then should not all desired effects be attainable by power? Thus people try to buy or take by force what can only be freely given.

The aim, the idol, of psychology is "health." Health (which is, not so incidentally, a vaguely defined excellence of physical and psychological *structure*) is the end toward which all means must lead. And is not health "good adjustment," hopefully with some happiness and prosperity mixed in? Suffering must be reduced—a noble enough intent, in it-self.[19] But to what does one "adjust" and to what lengths of immorality will one go to increase comfort? Is he healthy who is adjusted to a sick society or to a world ruled by the Evil One? How do we decide when the price of health, comfort, and security is too great? Or when might we sacrifice it for another? He who has nothing he would die for has, oh, so little to live for. Power, pragmatism, and effectiveness give no guidelines: they produce goods but fail to show us when and how to give them up. They produce an illusion of control, an illusion of security in an uncertain world, but in doing so absolutize that world.[20]

> I find it easy to imagine the Devil as a universal insurance agent. He understands human vulgarity and prides himself on being able to reduce us to it. He will tell you what is good for you! . . . He ends up promising you that pure nothingness of the soul, health, happiness and prosperity. (Rougemont 1945, 79)

While we measure the objective impact of power by using some sort of pragmatic analysis, we discuss its subjective impact in terms of categories such as intensity and self-fulfillment. Both of these categories may, of course, be linked to a more objective calculus, for "intensity" may be measured in mechanical units as well as poeticized in experiential ones; and the dividing line between self-repair (leading to objective "health") and self-realization is not sharp (Koestler 1967, 177). Nonetheless, because the categories focus on individual experience, they particularly implicate the individual will. Intensity of emotion (positive or negative, and whether viewed as a reaction or as an intrinsic motivator), for instance, can justify almost anything, as can a person's "right" to self-fulfillment.[21] We have rubber-stamped—or rather, made

[19] In a less flattering light, "humanitarianism has increased together with the consciousness of responsibility, both perhaps corresponding to a growing incapacity to bear suffering, our own as well as that of others" (Anshen 1972, 87).

[20] Consider James 4:4. "In contrast to the principle of retribution that insists you can measure a man's piety by looking at the blessings he has accumulated, Jesus thunders in Luke 6:20f. that the exact opposite is true. If you live in a world under the power of Satan, the only way you can prosper is by identifying with Satan" (Kallas 1975, 67).

[21] This statement is too strong to be entirely fair to those who hold that, while they affirm self-fulfillment as a goal, they do not sanction infringements of the rights of others.

normative—the right of every sufficiently great potential to realize itself. I mentioned earlier that power presses toward its own realization. Far be it from us to interfere. He who cannot be driven by passion or anger is obviously inhibited—how dreadfully unhealthy!

Passion and likewise one's "rights" tend to be considered personal and private. Thus, when a society highly values passion and rights to self-fulfillment, it is hardly surprising that psychology would justify— even laud—self-assertion. Now certainly a reasonable assertiveness is in some sense superior to aggression or to a stance that says, "I'm a doormat; step on me." However, assertiveness is in the same camp with these other tactics in the sense that it emphasizes separateness from others rather than mutuality. Whether or not assertiveness is closer to being a bridge to mutuality may be an open question: increased ability to "be oneself" without punitive consequences and to obtain what one wants from others may produce not true community but a certain independent isolation sustained by successfully garnered gratifications. Thus we have the irony that expressivity so sanctioned and fulfillment so pursued may eventuate in shallow, vacuous emotionality or even emotional frigidity instead of the deeper, quieter passions of profound relationship.

In summary, then, directing our power or search for power toward health as such quickly puts us in the domain of the principalities and powers. Granting free rein to emotions and rights puts us in league with the Tempter (and thence under the thumb of the Accuser). The "necessary" becomes ipso facto permissible, and values are dissolved. As Rougemont (1945) says so well,

> Our period has put in the place of criteria of truth, standards of intensity, and in place of respect for the good, respect for "life." To what appears to be sufficiently intense, standards of truth and falsehood cease forthwith to be relevant. It is accepted, nowadays, that passion and even emotion and hysteria place you by right above good and evil. . . . Our respect for passion and "life" are signs of decadence in those passions themselves, and of true vitality. (Pp. 117–18)

Openness to Evil Spiritual Power

In discussing the opening of the self to evil spiritual power, we may mention only in passing the occult per se. It is fairly clear that to invoke the aid of the Devil or inferior spirits is to presuppose that current needs and desires are pressing enough to justify the endeavor, that there are "deep things of Satan" (Rev. 2:24) as worthy of being known as the

---

The theory is good, but it fails to consider adequately that *everything* one does impinges on others and is impinged upon by others. One's "rights" are not independent entities any more than one's fulfillment is: both are interwoven with, not juxtaposed to, other persons' rights and fulfillment.

"deep things of God" (1 Cor. 2:10 KJV; see Langton 1949, 214), that what God has provided is insufficient, and that what he has denied—such as knowledge of the future (Acts 1:7)—is really good and necessary (see Barnhouse 1965; Harper 1970). It is hardly surprising that the Devil would answer a direct invitation, and the annals of the occultists provide no small indication that he does. I am more concerned, however, with where he may pop up in disguise rather than appear in full regalia; the person who wants to meet him in any case doubtless will, but so may some of us who would rather not.

I have repeatedly commented on association of assorted paranormal phenomena with receptive passivity, suspension of critical faculties, and altered states of consciousness—generally with what may be summarized as a right-brain modality. (Whether the modality is actually so localized and precisely how right-brain functioning corresponds to and differs from a generally receptive rather than active stance is a question very worthy of exploration but irrelevant to the present discussion, which rests only upon the fairly consistent effects of a shift away from the verbal-linear, action-decision mode.) As we have seen, occult, mystical, and parapsychological activities very often rely heavily upon a receptive style of functioning induced either by intentional passivity such as meditation or by forms of stimulation that yield similar brain states. Techniques used in some forms of psychotherapy may do the same thing. Drugs can alter one's state of consciousness. Hypnotism is based upon inducing uncritical suggestibility. Biofeedback requires suspension of deliberate, conscious effort. Yoga and TM, advocated to produce relaxation, do so by helping one slip into the receptive mode (see Ferguson 1975). And in sexual intercourse—an activity emphasized by religion, occultists, and psychological sciences alike—one's capacity for satisfaction depends heavily on one's ability to relinquish control and share in a mutual regulation (Deikman 1973a).[22]

One may certainly argue that the association of sexual disorders with occult activities and possession states, as well as with psychopathology, derives from the association of sex with great sin (see Ebon 1974). However, it is quite intriguing to consider the possibility that the receptive mode, however induced, leaves one peculiarly vulnerable and that misuse of it opens one to influences beyond one's control, whether those influences are interpersonal or demonic. If so, techniques and activities promoting this mode must be employed with the greatest caution.[23]

[22] See James 1961 [1902], 28–29, for a strong argument against the hypothesis that religion is simply perverted sexuality.

[23] It has at the very least been found that "the breaking apart of ego and the conviction that consciousness has inhabited a strange body are curious components of the altered states" (Ferguson 1975, 112). Perhaps the generally verbal mode of psychotherapy

I do not say that the techniques and procedures just mentioned are in themselves occult or demonic. As one writer put it, "Aerodynamics [does not] become an occult science because a contemporary witch rides to a Sabbath on a jet-liner" (Woods 1971, 29). Likewise I am not saying that sex is evil or occult because it ties one into a receptive mode. However, I *am* saying that, *any time will and decision are relinquished, the nature and quality of relationship in which the relinquishment occurs are of critical importance.* This observation perhaps helps to explain why the Bible is so restrictive about the sex act and why Christian prayer and meditation are not, biblically speaking, states of vague, blank openness. Jesus and Paul both associated prayer not with sleep or dreaminess but with watchfulness: "Watch and pray that you may not enter into temptation" (Matt. 26:41); "Continue steadfastly in prayer, being watchful in it with thanksgiving" (Col. 4:2).[24] Prayer must *not* be confused with assorted relaxation techniques; let those who use it as such beware.

Indeed, some people believe that, apart from sin, passivity is the prime condition for the working of evil spirits, which, unlike God, work against human freedom.[25] For this very reason, knowledge and insight may offer less that is truly critical for our human enterprise than do will and decision (see Anshen 1972, 3). The Devil can offer plenty of the former—mingled with his specialty, confusion—but none of the latter. In other words, the intentional focusing of the will (an active, left-brain sort of procedure) cannot in the end rest upon perfect, rational assurance of the correctness of the focus. No such perfect assurance can

contains in itself an extremely important safeguard against capitulation to a passive-receptive brain state. (Classical psychoanalysis, however, despite being verbal, may provoke a certain passivity and need for structure leading to suggestibility [see Sargant 1974].) In fact, Rollo May (1972) considers action therapies dangerous precisely because they by-pass language. He reasons that distrust of language and aggression both arise from a broken communion among people that leads to the omission of rationality and that reestablishing rational contact with others is essential. It may or may not be incidental that psychodrama and encounter groups are mocked by Satanist Anton LaVey, who associates them with the Black Mass (Woods 1971, 137).

[24] See Bauer 1967. It is most instructive to check the biblical references to ἀγρυπνέω ("to watch, keep guard, be wakeful") and γρηγορέω ("to watch, be awake, vigilant"): see Matt. 24:42–43; 25:13; 26:38, 40–41; Mark 13:33–35, 37; 14:34, 37–38; Luke 12:37, 39; 21:36; Acts 20:31; 1 Cor. 16:13; Eph. 6:18; Col. 4:2; 1 Thess. 5:6; 1 Peter 5:8; Rev. 3:2–3; 16:15. The emphasis on vigilant alertness as over against passivity runs throughout the New Testament. It is true that there is also a strong strand of "waiting" on the Lord in the Old Testament that, interestingly, is not in view in the New and that in any case we have no reason to believe—and every reason not to believe—entails lack of watchfulness. The two are by no means mutually exclusive (see Penn-Lewis n.d., 45–47).

[25] "In brief, the powers of darkness aim at obtaining a passive slave or captive to their will; whilst God desires a regenerated man, intelligently and actively will-ing and choosing, and doing His will in liberation of spirit, soul and body from slavery. The powers of darkness would make a man a machine, a tool, an automaton; the God of holiness and love desires to make him a free, intelligent sovereign in his own sphere" (Penn-Lewis n.d., 51).

be obtained. Every choice of focus involves an act of commitment and trust, just as does a marriage. The validity of the commitment—unlike the validity of science or magic or the physiological sex act—cannot be demonstrated or consummated in mere "effects." The commitment goes beyond any observable effects. It also imposes its own limits. By contrast, a pseudological, pseudoscientific "openness" to whatever effects may accrue from experiments with passivity may be directly analogous to pseudoenlightened openness to sexual experimentation: whether minds or bodies be penetrated, more may be lost—and more evil gained—than can logically be foreseen.

In the light of the similar brain states involved, it is doubly significant that the Old Testament imposes the most severe penalties for sexual and occult sins. (The occult sins embrace idolatry as well.) On one level, one can interpret these heavy sanctions by saying that the great dangers are immorality and by-passing God's laws of communication (Harper 1970). On another level, one may suggest that the two are the same in that they involve substituting another image for God, whether in body or in soul (Williams 1959). We might suppose that the Devil takes advantage of both levels combined: whenever another image in heart or mind is substituted for God, particularly if one is in a passive stance oneself, the Devil may use it to work in and through both immorality and paranormal communication. The two are by no means discontinuous: sex is obviously a form of communication, and the perversion of sex is common to the occult and to idolatry. Furthermore, perverted sexual relationships signify the breakdown of the most intimate sort of communion among persons, while the occult and idolatry break down the communion between persons and their God: both produce deep isolation. It is hardly surprising, then, that these sins should be the Devil's key tools and prime contributors to psychopathology.

In chapter 5, I raised the question of why psi phenomena were relatively so rare if the "nature of everything" is as I have suggested. In particular, why does not passivity or openness produce more consistent paranormal experiences than it seems to? I speculate as follows: as part of the bondage of creation, mind is generally—if not absolutely—confined by matter, and will is generally, though not absolutely, confined by structure. Thus the natural connections of mind and mind are restricted, just as is the natural continuity of mind and matter. Thus the floods cannot clap their hands (Ps. 98:8), nor the hills skip like lambs (Ps. 114:4). This restriction is a consequence of sin and hence a tool of the Devil; but due to sin and evil it is also a gift of God. Were others' thoughts always loving, the future always bright, and our intentions incorruptible, complete knowledge would be bliss. As it is, such knowledge is most often destructive. (In fact, as we have seen, most psi communications are of negative, terrifying events or, if not, still induce considerable discomfort in the recipient.)

The "freedom" of the mental dimension perhaps can only be spiritually produced, by action of God or of the Devil. We gain access to the paranormal through God or through the Devil—which one depends not upon any such endowment as intelligence but solely on the focus of our will.[26] And because the meaning of the manifestations depends on their source rather than on their outward form, it is not surprising that the Devil's miracles may be mistaken for God's when one is applying empirical standards of observation and evaluation. (Some believe that Satan may particularly imitate the "gifts of the Holy Spirit" [1 Cor. 12]. Contrast the *fruit* of the Spirit [Gal. 5:22–23], which does not appear as a decisively obvious intervention in the natural order and which the Devil appears unable to counterfeit—or uninterested in promoting!)

Given that the Creation is fallen and that psi phenomena are both ambiguous and tempting, we can see a reason for the rather startling fact that the only ancient group among whom magic and the exploitation of psi were consistently forbidden was God's chosen people, the Jews (Haynes 1961, 101). Though they could recognize and deal with unsought experiences, yet God continually led them out of more advanced cultures where the way of life distracted them, particularly in these ways, from him. Still, where an undeveloped society comes into continuous contact with a developed one, it naturally tends to assimilate to the latter's values, customs, and assumptions. Indeed Israel did— *except* with regard to magic and psi (p. 102), which simply could not be harmonized with worship of the biblical God.[27]

The occult, the magical, and psi phenomena are dangerous not primarily because they are unreliable, capricious, and often illusory in their effects, though they are indeed all of these. They are, rather, dangerous because of the real power behind them and the lure that a few unsought experiences—as may result, for example, from TM or biofeedback techniques—may be to the unsuspecting. They promise previously unimagined realms of knowledge and power—and hide the price tag.

---

[26] I have given already an argument for the Devil's own paranormal knowledge, positing for him a sort of Laplacean mind plus governance of structures. This focus of the will is emphatically not to be confused with "good intentions," which are pragmatically based and a prime place for the master deceiver to substitute evil for good or lower goods for higher ones. It has to do with an actively responsive relationship, a topic I consider further in chapter 12.

[27] Mallory (1976) summarizes the basic biblical prohibitions in these areas as any mechanism to predict the future, the casting of spells, and the consulting of spirits—which we might extrapolate to the buying into determinism, the exerting of the psychological influence of one's own will upon and over against another's, and the direct intent to utilize the spiritual world on our own terms.

To seek power as a remedy for impotence—whether through science or self-assertion or psi, whether in materialism or "me-first" autonomy or magic, whether justified by pragmatism, passion, or passive receptivity—is a sure way to get into trouble. God has so ordained it. Humankind shall overcome "not by might, nor by power, but by my Spirit, says the LORD of hosts" (Zech. 4:6; cf. Acts 1:8).

9

The Possibility of Bondage
to Demonic Powers

Stranger: This is ridiculous. By *your* standards, *everybody* is in some sort of lovely—I mean, awful—bind.

Inquirer: On one level, that's quite true, and maybe not only by my standards. Lots of psychotherapists seem to presuppose that everyone needs therapy.

Stranger: But for *growth,* not because everybody is sick. Fine lot of good a definition of pathology is that doesn't leave anybody out. And furthermore, I'm tired of this business of "levels." The one we have to deal with is the one we've got. I'm for promoting health and happiness *now.*

Inquirer: All right, all right; I hear you. I agree that, by our definition of "trouble" and how to get into it, we've included virtually everyone to some degree . . .

Stranger: And without a single constructive word on how to get out of it!

Inquirer: *Will* you be a bit patient? As I was saying, we've already been fairly inclusive, so further discussion would seem rather unnecessary.

Stranger: Right, for once. But doubtless that won't stop you, if past performance is any indication.

Inquirer: The point is that we haven't yet dealt specifically enough with the Devil's direct attacks. They're important, even if he does have subtler ploys.

Stranger: Oh no, "possession" again? I thought we'd been through that once before. This is where I came in!

Inquirer: Yes, possession again.

* * *

DEMONIC POSSESSION RECONSIDERED

Let me state clearly at this point in the discussion that I consider it both useful and proper to speak of the possibility of demonic possession. I ground this intellectual commitment both in the data of Scripture and, secondarily, in the experience of persons of all times and nations, including my own limited observations.[1] I consider "evil" to be the depersonalized name for the demonic and the complicity of the human will. I thus strongly disagree with the formulation whereby "devil" is construed as differing from "evil" only by the addition of a letter to the beginning of the word, the former being considered a personification and projection of evil.

However, since the personal is a larger and more comprehensive category than the impersonal (and not simply an alternative to the impersonal), evil naturally finds expression in lower, impersonal categories as well as in personal ones. Thus the only objection I offer to "alternative explanations" or "demythologized" versions of the material in this and the preceding chapters is that they are not true alternatives. In my view they consider only manifestations of the basic problem and, however useful in keeping weeds from overgrowing the whole field, fail entirely to deal with the root. Let the reader, then, use whatever categories he chooses to handle the phenomena we are considering, but without assuming that I "really mean" to say something less or other or subtler or more respectable than I "really am" saying, namely, that persons may be subject to an evil will other than their own.

Reprise on Openings in Structure and Will

This chapter is linked to chapters 4 and 8, particularly by the hypothesis that certain passive-receptive states of consciousness or certain brain states may leave one vulnerable to demonic attack. Such brain states are fostered by occult activities, sexual intercourse, and pagan religions (the latter involving, in the East, meditative techniques); in many primitive areas, by assorted rhythmic stimuli; and in many cultures, including ours, by drugs. Lest there be misunderstanding, I do

---

[1] So Nevius (1893, 255): "It thus appears that the hypothesis of demon-possession may claim a divine sanction, as well as the common consent of all nations and ages. The question of such events being repeated in the world's history is simply a matter of evidence." Likewise a contemporary missionary in Madagascar: "It has occurred to us that spirit possession (or obsession) and angel visitation are probably as prevalent in the West as in Africa. But our sense of human freedom prevents us from conscious, interdimensional relationships between the sensible and the supersensible. We think that a medical term solves the mystery" (quoted in Hoffman 1970, 47). Therefore even in our reading of the Gospels, we tend to minimize in practice—whether or not we accept in principle— implications of the dynamic, ongoing involvement of supersensible reality in all daily life. See the "Addendum" below for summaries of three cases of possession not found in the literature but known to the author. See also Peck 1983 for a recent treatment.

not suppose the brain state per se to be "wrong" or "evil": the mystical experience and the sexual experience can be very great goods. The problem stems rather from the access an *empty* house (Matt. 12:43–45) may provide for the Evil One. Few are so pure and filled with God's Spirit that they are immune from attack—surely the saints have not been. "Emptiness" may give a structural opening (although not a necessary and sufficient cause) for possession.

Structural openings may also be provided by congenital or environmentally imposed weakness of body or mind.[2] Epilepsy is a possible case in point. Many peoples have associated fits with possession; epileptics are often psychically sensitive; and more epileptics than chance occurrences would predict develop schizophrenia-like psychoses (Small 1973; Wright 1973b). Certainly we should not retreat to a facile identification of any recognized illness with direct demonic activity. Perhaps, though, we also should not suppose that we have in every case exhausted the possible explanations for a malady by applying a medical label. What if certain medical conditions produce brain states leading to spiritual vulnerability? Such a connection would mean not that an epileptic, or anyone else, *must* be demonized but only that a risk may exist, just as a person with a deficient immune system is at risk for various physical illnesses.

Or consider the catch-all character of the label "schizophrenia." The label hardly constrains us to affirm that all schizophrenics are simply "pseudo" demoniacs, even if many are. Even milder disorders of the hysterical sort, with their attendant psychic splitting, could provide an entry point for the Devil. In fact, some observers feel that any psychic splits, because of the way that they violate basic human unity, give particularly effective footholds for demons (see especially Koch 1965). Koch associates such splitting with mobilization of the subconscious. This hypothesis has plausibility in the light of the data we have noted relating dissociative states that become involuntary to experimentation with altered states of consciousness.[3] Koch's forty years of experience

[2]See Jackson 1976; James 1961 (1902). It seems likely that physical and psychological pathology does foster easier influence of the spiritual level, almost as if breakdowns in lower levels can sometimes allow higher ones to shine (or glower) through, as well as make higher levels dysfunctional. Note that this argument could apply both for the Devil and for the Holy Spirit, though the Devil has, humanly speaking, an edge, in that breakdown is his special domain and, as we have seen, techniques "naturally" used to remedy it tend oftentimes to feed into his system.

[3]Further note Jung's comment (1963, 322, emphasis added): "In most cases when a split-off complex manifests itself it does so *in the form of a personality, as if the complex had a consciousness of itself.* . . . We might, if we wish, adduce these complexes as evidence for a continuity of consciousness. Likewise in favor of such an assumption are certain astonishing observations in cases of profound syncope after acute injuries to the brain and in severe states of collapse. In both situations, total loss of consciousness can be accompanied by perceptions of the outside world and vivid dream experiences. Since the

lead him to believe that even being the recipient of occult healing practices (in Europe, charming and the use of a pendulum for diagnosis, e.g., are more common than here; but we too have a raft of psychic healers, such as those who work on the patient's "astral body") can eventuate in a malignant subjection through the healer's impact on the subconscious.[4]

In certain cases of demonic oppression, however, one finds no evidence of consciousness-altering experimentation or patent pathology or occult hocus-pocus. Sometimes just a trauma resulting in extreme fear or despair may give the needed opening (see Basham 1972 and "Addendum" below). Here we again see inklings of the close interaction between structure and will. Who is to say what momentary capitulation may result from a traumatic incident?

Clearer openings in will may come from any "root of bitterness" or indulgence of immorality (Heb. 12:15–16), any wrong attitude or act (Eph. 4:25–27; 2 Cor. 2:10–11), any "sin." Not that these sins are themselves demonic; rather, like structural weaknesses, they provide occasions for demonic encroachment. Thus any temptation or trial becomes a test of one's readiness to commit himself wholly to God (Seesemann 1968).

Though misdirected will may not be a sufficient cause of possession (except in the case of a deliberate pact with the Devil, though, even so, his sealing of it is necessary), probably some turning of the will toward evil, some yielding of it, some breach of faith, even if due to ignorance or weakness, however slight, is necessary to possession.[5] Though the physical world is caught in bondage, persons have the possibility of being truly free in Christ (John 8:31–32). Even if without him they always do evil, yet it is not wholly unwillingly that they do so. (Actually,

cerebral cortex, the seat of consciousness, is not functioning at these times, there is as yet no explanation for these phenomena."

[4] Koch (1965, 64) says that, after occult healing practices, "in which the sub-c of the patient is actively influenced or passively tapped, decisive changes in the psychic constitution of the patient takes [*sic*] place. A psychic torpor results which not only shows in the melancholic temper, but above all paralyzes a joyful dispatch in daily, small decisions, and outright blocks any faith decisions in religious life." Considering that many of the mind-control movements seem to be going into the occult-healing business, we should not lack subjects to confirm this observation.

[5] A pact with the Devil need not be dramatic. A woman who finally obtained release at age thirty-four through a simple exorcistic prayer relates that her first contact with the Devil came as a child. An abusive father had spawned in her doubt of the goodness of God and awareness of evil as a power. When the girl was next mistreated, she appealed for the aid of the powers of darkness and felt just a momentary, fleeting presence, accompanied by calm but not peace. Returning to the house, she faced her angry father, silently asking help from the powers. For the first time ever, she saw him turn away from her in fear. She paid little attention to the "pact" but was increasingly drawn to occult literature and activities and a self-gratifying lifestyle, ending up in bad relationships and continual dissatisfaction (Robenson n.d.).

the *struggle* against doing evil is more apparent in the mature Christian than in the unbeliever, whose sense of sin is less acute. Thus Rougemont [1945] notes Théodore de Bèze's thought that the only unequivocal human progress is to recognize our faults more and more.) Furthermore, the greater our persistence in sinning, the more sin will manifest itself involuntarily in our lives (Montgomery 1976). We must be liberated from our bondage to sin and the inclination of our will to sin. To make that point, however, is not to equate sin with possession.

Finally, it is scarcely surprising that actual possession should be most highly correlated with activities that combine promotion of psychic passivity and a turning of the will away from God—namely, the occult. It is sobering to contemplate the possibility that some dangers attend even recreationally or medically used techniques that promote these brain states and that at the same time foster dependence upon the techniques as a sort of temporal salvation.

Definition of Possession

To affirm the possibility of demonic possession and to identify states, actions, or inclinations that may promote it are not to define the term. I define "possession" as *demonic control of both structure and will in part or all of a person's life.* This definition leaves room for many degrees of demonic power over an individual. Thus a person might have, say, a demon of lust or fear, with the effect that, when attacked, he absolutely cannot govern his thoughts or actions in that particular area. Or a person might be quite fully possessed, having really "sold his soul to the Devil," such that all areas of his life are subject to demonic control.

By this definition, I intend to differentiate having a demon of lust from engaging in sinful, passionate, lustful thoughts and behavior per se (though the latter may provide opening for demonization). I do not intend to use names of demons merely as reifications of psychological compulsions and obsessions. The latter are unlikely to be relieved by a word of command, even if a person believes earnestly that he wants release; affliction due to the former may be relieved if the person gives the slightest assent of his will to accepting release, and sometimes even without his knowledge (McAll 1976). The point is that, while all pathology, like all of life, has a spiritual component, and all beliefs and actions have spiritual repercussions, some pathology may be combated with comparative effectiveness, at least in secular terms, by repairing damage (e.g., performing an operation, giving dependency gratification, and mobilizing a person's resources) or standing against temptation. One may appropriately cope with attack at the point of attack.[6] With

6To reemphasize this point, perhaps the huge majority of lustful desires and the like are properly dealt with through self-discipline, repentance, and refusal to capitulate to demonization, the point of attack is different, however similar the appearance, and repair work at a lower level will not suffice. Such is the testimony of those who have run the gamut of psychiatrists before attaining release through exorcism (see chapter 4). The challenge is to take this matter seriously without succumbing to disproportionate fear, uncritical hysteria, or irresponsible quietism—or, for that matter, enthusiastic designation of every stubborn difficulty as demonic possession.

In some strange sense, the meaning of possession seems to be that, in their own emptiness and nothingness, demons can find rest and some sort of gratification only through other selves, by incorporating and destroying them (Frye 1960; Nevius 1893; Williams 1959; Matt. 12:43–45). They appear actually to use the body of those whom they indwell to express themselves (Peck 1983), which they may do in actions, in facial expression, and in words, usually in a voice strikingly different from that of the individual himself, and usually only when confronted directly: the Devil hides, rather than advertises his presence. It is chilling and quite indescribable to look into the face of a person whom one knows and see something quite alien staring back.

A possessed person is usually not aware of the nature of his problem, though he may be puzzled by some intractable evil in his life: it is emphatically not one who is preoccupied with demons who is most likely to suffer from possession. In the Gospel accounts, the demonized manifest assorted symptomatology but are not portrayed as raving about demons.[7] Again, the Devil hides. Iatrogenic symptoms, splits experienced and then labeled, contagion, hallucination, and guilt plus autosuggestion may all produce a sort of hysteria (of which, of course, the Devil may choose to take advantage) that only indirectly, if at all, relates to true possession (Oesterreich 1974). In fact, though there may be paroxysmal attacks of various sorts at any stage, often the most striking, grotesque aspects of possession appear during exorcism, when a demon is resisting leaving his home, not while he is comfortably situated. In the Gospels, as we have noted, the demons spoke out only in the presence of Jesus, but hardly in a way indicating response to some psychological manipulation or pressure: often they spoke and resisted him before he said a word. I intend here only to repeat my caution both against identifying all cognitions concerning spirits with their direct

impulses. Scripture would not lead us to assume that basic self-control is easy or that exorcism is an alternative for it.

[7] Even if we use this observation as a cautionary device, we do well to avoid making *any* rigid rules behind which Satan can hide. We should certainly not take it as a foregone conclusion that he who raves about demons can be no more and no less than "crazy," even if that generally might be the case.

activity and against assimilating all symptomatology to the iatrogenic and hysterical.

Possession and Psychopathology

It would be convenient if we could say that bondage, whether extensive or relatively circumscribed, could be neatly distinguished from psychopathological phenomena on the basis of the general psychological health of the afflicted person. To limit consideration of possession to cases meeting that criterion is clearly the conservative, cautious approach. It has its distinct advantages. For one, it promotes careful observation that may enable us to locate symptoms not in accord with what psychology would lead us to predict either from a known personality structure or from recognized psychopathological states; and it may foster alertness when multiple diagnoses have been given hospitalized patients or maybe even when drugs yield results that are opposite to their normal effects (Jackson 1976; McAll 1976). For another, it filters out some of the persons (such as severe borderline patients) most likely to be badly confused or traumatized by the thought that they might "have a demon." When bondage is not the problem, the inept suggestion that it is can provide a very destructive stress or a false and equally destructive assumption that relief is just around the corner.

Having made and appreciated these points, we must nonetheless demur from that approach. Not only is there very considerable overlap of demonic and psychopathological symptomatology, but also we have not the slightest reason to believe that the psychotic or neurotic is somehow immune from any further attacks of the Devil. Strictly "differential" diagnosis may be a futile and even a counterproductive dream, since we are dealing with an enemy whose very nature is to hide, deceive, confuse, and appear to be what he is not. The observable data are always ambiguous: we can prove Satan's influence no more than we can prove God's. Yet in another sense, on another level, any intervention leading to true wholeness attacks the Devil's influence.

Looking at the ambiguity of the symptomatology, we may note that periods or areas of lack of control, lability, and changes in consciousness are shared by the demonized and mentally ill. Hostile or fearful reaction to the things of God and speaking in another voice or language are thought to be more specific to demonic influence (White 1976b).[8] Such need not be the case, however. A person who speaks in another voice may suffer from a multiple personality disorder (see Peck 1983, 192).

---

[8] Koch (1973) uses particularly these latter two symptoms as an argument that the symptoms of possession do not fit those of ordinary mental illness. He goes on to say, however, that many so-called schizophrenics are actually oppressed and admits that we cannot offer proofs, as if we could make either God or the Devil the subject of our experiments.

One who manifests access to another language or who reacts to the presence of religious objects of which he is consciously unaware or to the prayers of a person in another room could have very well-developed psi capacities. If the reactions are unaccountably violent, an answer is to adduce some hysteria. Particularly if a person has been confronted directly with Scripture or prayer, one may invoke any number of guilt and anxiety hypotheses to account for "demonic" manifestations. Or consider the report of one missionary (cited in Collins 1976) that reading Scripture to the demonized may result in trance, confused or false understanding, sudden headaches, belching, hearing voices, extreme anxiety, and rapid breathing: how many of the symptoms may stem from the last, as a result of hyperventilation?

On the other hand, some cases diagnosed as hysteria or particularly as multiple personality meet the gamut of criteria for possession; and who is to say how much depression and assorted evil behavior may be due to direct satanic influence (see Wilson 1976)? Atypical back-ward patients have sometimes been fully cured by exorcism, and "true schizophrenics" have reportedly been relieved of some symptoms such as hallucinations and delusions (McAll 1976). One psychiatrist, by no means ignorant himself of demonology, cites a case in which exorcism by a rather poorly educated exorcist succeeded in relieving one of his patients of multiple symptoms he had assumed to be psychotic.[9] The most reasonable hypothesis appears to be that demonic and psychopathological phenomena are frequently intertwined in a complex manner. Such a conclusion follows readily from the entire preceding discussion of the Devil's nature, tactics, and range of functioning.

* * *

Stranger: Well, I can't say I'm exactly impressed. By what you've said, there's no way of telling whether there are half a dozen or half a billion demonized people. This devil you've improvised does a tremendous job of hiding, if I do say so myself. If, of course, there is anything to hide.

Inquirer: Just from experience, I imagine there are a lot more people in some sort of bondage than most pastors or psychologists would like to admit—and a lot fewer than the fanatics assume who look under their own beds before going to sleep.

Stranger: You "imagine" from "experience." Lovely way to reach conclusions. Supposing I imagined from the experience of not seeing

---

[9] Interestingly, several previous exorcists engaged by this patient had failed to achieve lasting results (White 1976b). McAll, another psychiatrist, takes his examples from a file of 150 documented cases in which exorcism was used.

many elephants on the street that I was keeping them away by burying marbles?

Inquirer: Right, right; but still, how can we deal with demonic subjection if we simply presuppose that it doesn't exist? Besides, if the Devil hides, maybe we ought to expect him where we normally don't.

Stranger: You never fail to amaze me. How, do tell, do you propose to "deal with" what you can't even identify? You led me to believe that you think it unwise to exorcise everyone in sight, and there's not a whole lot you can do with what is out of sight.

Inquirer: Ah, but that is where you are wrong.

* * *

But the natural [$\psi \upsilon \chi \iota \kappa \grave{o} \varsigma$] man receiveth not the things of the Spirit of God: for they are foolishness unto him: neither can he know them, because they are spiritually discerned. (1 Cor. 2:14 KJV)

DISCERNING AND DEALING WITH DEMONIC POSSESSION

Before proceeding, I must emphasize a few cautions. First, I have taken considerable pains to insist that possession is far from the Devil's only tactic; it is far from his cleverest and, perhaps in the end, far from his most important one. In fact, when concern about possession gains such fad status as it has in some circles today, it may serve partly as a diversionary tactic: the Devil astutely turns our attention from his broader activities and sends us cowering to supposedly secure corners of churches, where we leave him as safe from us as we think we are from him (see Kallas 1975, 109).[10] For this reason I have discussed his range of activities first and will conclude this study with a general rather than a

[10] "First: too many Christians confine the sphere of the demonic too exclusively to the Occult. They fail to realize that we can be more easily deceived and enchanted by the Devil's input in the New York Times, the schools, the government, and some parts of the church than we can by some human iodine bottle representing the Process or the Church of Satan. Second: some Christians have a fear of being attacked or contaminated by the Occult which is positively superstitious. They take for granted that a Christian who encounters a warlock or researcher in the Occult is up against an insuperably dangerous force. And of course this is true to the presumptuous, the curious, and the carnal. But the Christian who faces Satan with superstitious terror is like the trainer who enters the lion-cage smelling of fear. After all, we serve the Hero who crushed the serpent with his heel. And we must not forget that he said to us, 'I give *you* power to tread on serpents and scorpions without suffering harm.' And, as Paul adds, 'The God of Peace shall shortly bruise Satan under *your* feet.' Jesus said of the church that 'The gates of Hell will not prevail against it' " (from an earlier draft of Lovelace 1976, obtained from the author).

tightly circumscribed theological response to that range of activities; I cannot emphasize too strongly that we *must* recognize the breadth of the battlefront. Second, the preceding paragraphs could easily make even the problem of direct demonic attack seem far too individualistic a matter. I must reemphasize Koch's observation, noted in chapter 4, that evil effects of occult experimentation may reach down several generations, quite in accord with the principle that the sins of the parents may indeed be visited upon the children (Exod. 20:5). In any event, we all suffer the effects of a fallen world. Third, and consequent to the first two comments, possession is not necessarily discrete from other pathology, an "all or nothing" affair or one that necessarily occurs in a moment of time. I do, however, differentiate it at least phenomenologically from some kinds of demonic "attack" (physical, psychological, through temptation, or whatever) that may lead to feelings of oppression at an emotional level.

Symptomatology

There is no reason to suppose—and I have never intended to suggest—that the spiritual nature of evil can be neatly read from its physical and psychological consequences in the world.[11] Furthermore, the Bible gives us no checklist by which to determine whether a person is possessed, a rather surprising lack if the criteria *could* be included in such a list. The only "test" of spirits given in Scripture (1 John 4:1–3) is doctrinal and addressed to the historical situation of encroaching Gnostic heresy. Not that this test is thereby rendered inconsequential, but it would appear that today we have spirits interested in promulgating other heresies and other evils. (In addition, the demons in the Gospels seemed to have no trouble confessing the identity of Jesus; and the veridicality of their confession scarcely prevented Jesus from casting them out.) Anything said about "symptoms" of possession, then, must be taken as tentative, highly provisional, and tending to highlight the superficial and outward rather than the essential and inward. Nonetheless, I at least mention certain phenomena often seen as clues of possible spiritual bondage.

Perhaps because of its fairly clear and dramatic nature, presentation of a new personality is a phenomenon very often cited as linked, at least

---

[11] For a curious case in which the evil was identified *before* there were even any consequences to evaluate, consider Michael Cassidy's (1975) story of a friend lecturing on the occult at Essex. Unknown to the speaker at the time, a girl had been sent from a spiritist circle to disrupt the meeting. The speaker sensed something in her, prayed while lecturing that any spirit would be bound, and proceeded to lecture as planned. Afterward, the girl came up and asked what spell had been cast on her, as she had been unable to move or speak. Later, another friend called the speaker and asked how the lecture series had gone. He, many miles away at the time, had had a vision of the meeting and the girl and had prayed for the binding of the evil spirits.

in some cases, to possession. As mentioned before, persons suffering from multiple personality disorder also present one or more different personalities, complete with different voices, expressions, physical manifestations, and spheres of knowledge. (I know a young woman, for instance, who says that she can drive a stick-shift automobile only when some, but not others, of her personalities are "in control.") However, particularly when a new personality has an evil character, manifests paranormal knowledge, and shows aversion to the things of Christ, one may at least question whether evil spiritual forces play a role in the problem.

Strangely enough, it has been observed that afflicted persons may not only have a family history of difficulty, but may even fall in a particular pattern on the family tree. For instance, they may be the oldest or youngest male in each of several generations (McAll 1976, 276). And again, occult practices within a family or by an individual correlate consistently with apparent demonic oppression.[12]

Possessed persons also show a striking lack of what can only be called "humanness"—as if they had been somehow disconnected from all the springs of empathy. For that reason, they have an empty, barren, boring quality, a deadening sameness, despite superficial differences. While this judgment may seem excessively subjective, yet it has a ring of truth to those having had occasion to recognize the presence of an evil spirit (see Martin 1976; Peck 1983).

Whatever the most easily labeled clues to possession may be, however, many believe that reaching a state of so-called perfect possession usually takes many years and is by no means an instantaneous matter. Different writers describe the process they have discerned or observed somewhat differently. Nevius (1893, 285–86), drawing upon his experiences in nineteenth-century China, suggests an outline beginning with what he calls "obsession"—a sort of attack from the outside that is hard to distinguish in many cases from mental deficiency, psychosis, or epilepsy. The significant point, though, is that these characteristics do not persist as one would expect them to. A transition phase follows, wherein the afflicted person is involuntarily possessed.[13]

[12] Considering the apparent genetic (familial) factors in schizophrenia, it is doubly interesting that the textbook *Psychiatry for Students* by Skottowe includes involvement in occult practices as a factor in differential diagnosis of schizophrenia (McAll 1976). Skottowe, then, must believe that such practices may yield symptoms mimicking, but not to be identified with, schizophrenia.

[13] It is an interesting question to what extent the phenomena of obsession could perhaps be *either* a preliminary point of attack *or* a result of actual, developed possession. It is not immediately clear whether a demonized psychotic or epileptic would be more or less "perfectly possessed" than a more Faustian character. The one represents graphically the Devil's nature as destroyer; the other, his nature as deceiver. In any event, it may be that the preliminary stage of "obsession" may be seen in all sorts of temptations and attacks that work on a person's will and not just in clear and rather violent manifestations. I have

Then comes a stage, which may last for many years, in which the subject appears normal (though is allegedly in a state of subjection and subserviency), only occasionally suffering a paroxysm. This stage develops at last into a state of voluntary subservience wherein the subject may, perhaps, become a medium with special capacities.

Another writer, drawing upon observations of twentieth-century America, describes the process thus (and also presumes that the whole process may take years): first, an entry point (such as those I suggested above), whereby a demon or demons are given access; second, a stage of erroneous judgment in vital matters; third, voluntary yielding of control to a force or presence felt to be alien, resulting in a loss of control over will, decisions, and actions. In the final stage, the possibility of perfect possession, there may even be a great gain in human efficiency, no symptoms discernible in psychological tests, and perhaps special protection granted for life and limb (Martin 1976).

While these outlines differ considerably in detail, both emphasize increasing assent to an alien influence and a superficially symptom-free final state. Of course, in neither case is the final state really final, for possession degenerates the personality, particularly with respect to human relationships. Both writers also report extreme antagonism on the part of the possessed to all things Christian and immediate healing of true possession by exorcism. (Such immediate relief is striking indeed when one takes seriously the length of the "gestation period" in many cases.)

The above outlines seem to imply that, though the process of possession may be arrested at any given stage, it is essentially progressive and tends to become all-consuming. However, "perfect possession" is not necessarily the final outcome; rather, sometimes the Devil may gain control in quite circumscribed *areas* of a person's life, as well as (or instead of) manifesting himself by rather complete domination at limited *times*. That is, evil spirits do not show themselves solely by forcing persons into an altered state of consciousness for which they have no memory. Thus, when Jesus cast out a "spirit of infirmity" (Luke 13:11, 16), he did not imply that the afflicted woman had fits or that anything was necessary beyond a specific healing. Similarly today, persons may report irrational and unmanageable attacks of fear or despair, perhaps of long duration, from which they gain lasting relief through exorcism.[14]

suggested that, however "unwilling" a person to be possessed, there must yet be some breach of faith for possession to occur. I was, however, speaking from a Christian context, whereas Nevius is referring to a pagan culture. It is certainly possible that the unbeliever is *not* defended even provisionally against possession and thus may indeed suffer it truly involuntarily. Unbelief itself may be a sufficient point of access.

[14] See Basham 1972 and "Addendum" below. The role of naming demons, or

It may thus be extremely unwise to decide that only in certain ways or areas can the Devil gain control. Even use of the word "possession" may be unwise, both because it induces fear and because it conjures up images inappropriate to the more usual and limited sorts of bondage (in addition, the usage is technically foreign to the New Testament). It is different whether an enemy captures an outlying town or overruns the whole country. In the latter instance, there is potential for both more destruction and more calm; we would expect the greatest battles, possibly the most personal struggle, to take place in the middle ranges of encroachment. Nonetheless, in each case there is an enemy who has gained certain rights over certain territory. If terms such as "infestation," "obsession," "bondage," or "oppression" evoke fewer hysterical reactions than "possession," we should by all means use them (see Bennett 1976).

I do not agree with those who, though ministering deliverance in any case, rely upon comforting distinctions between presumably outer attack and inner control, precisely because I hold generally to the complicity of the human will to one degree or another, by act or by default.[15] I hold, in fact, that it is precisely the bondage of the will (plus whatever physical manifestations follow upon the enemy's presence) that may be undone by exorcism. (By this comment I do not gainsay the appropriateness of rebuking storms or fevers or retract my earlier statement that possession in the New Testament is not seen primarily as

demanding that demons name themselves, in the process of exorcism is fascinating and widely debated. Some hold it to be essential; others consider it optional or entirely unnecessary, as Jesus did not seem to make a regular practice of it. Obviously, it has associations with word-magic and the ancient belief that to know something's name gives one power over it. The same principle operates in psychology when, in some instances, identifying the enemy disarms it. One could argue that naming demons allows a person to reject or henceforth repress the troublesome feelings, but on at least two counts that argument is not too persuasive. First, very few psychiatrists can banish, say, lust by identifying it. Second, a person may be exorcised of a dozen or more demons within a day or so, gaining freedom in a large number of areas; if he were to repress his reactions in all of those realms, it would seem more likely that he would experience apathy or a whole raft of symptoms rather than the peace, freedom, and joy usually reported. As one interesting example of an effective "naming," consider the following case: "Recently in a meeting a woman was being shaken terribly by a spirit which refused to give its name. Suddenly a child on the other side of the room told us he could see a word in big capital letters imprinted on his mind (often the way they appear), but he did not know how to pronounce it or what it meant! We urged him to spell it aloud for us, which he did—'L-U-S-T.' It left at once, with violent coughing, on the first command to come out" (Brooks 1971, 61). Without discrediting specific reports, I nonetheless repeat my caution against overgeneralizing them in such a way as to make inconsequential the human responsibility to resist temptation.

[15] I do not consider here whether or "how much" Christians may be possessed, or what term is more appropriate for the troubles from which they need deliverance. Empirical evidence leads us to believe that, whatever labels we apply or whatever our convictions about their ultimate salvation, Christians may get into states of bondage from which deliverance appears necessary.

a moral offense. A town may fall more because it is weak than because it is wicked; and its very fall will persuade it all the more of its weakness. He who would liberate it must both stop the enemy from ravaging it and restore its ability to make necessary choices; genuine choices were not an option while it was occupied.)

Discernment

Given the wide range of types and depth of spiritual bondage under which one may fall and the empirical difficulty of distinguishing some cases of bondage from physical or emotional pathology, one might be tempted to throw up his hands and declare that, even if genuine possession states exist, picking them out from the array of other human ills is simply impossible. Such might indeed be the case if we had nothing but empirical data to work with. Scriptural teachings, however, point to another tool.

Discernment, or "the ability to distinguish between spirits" (1 Cor. 12:10), the Bible counts as one of the (supernatural) gifts of the Holy Spirit, by implication not something automatically within the range of any observant, competent Ph.D. Also by implication, then, we should not be too surprised at the difficulty we encountered at the objective level, if spiritual matters can in the end be rightly weighed only by spiritual means.[16] Lest such a gift seem too uncanny, we might use musical talents as an analogy: a person with perfect pitch may immediately hear that something is wrong, even when a singer has the general shape of the tune right. Likewise, one with true discernment may know that something is amiss spiritually, even when words and behavior are superficially unexceptionable.

In rebuttal one may correctly point out that what is not sharable is simply not science, that science does not deal in special gifts. Not every reality important to human well-being, however, can be reduced to science. And a science that rightly understands itself will recognize its limits. Particularly in psychology, of all disciplines, the scientist unable or unwilling to face the transcendent aspect of human life is simply not equipped even to be aware of the roots of many manifest problems. (Not that ministers who simply assimilate psychosis to sin may not do

[16] We have likewise noted the failure of pragmatism and sheer reasonableness to protect us in our own choices. Note the words of St. Teresa, describing her reaction to approaches by the Devil: "This disquiet is such that I know not whence it comes: only the soul seems to resist, is troubled and distressed, without knowing why; for the words of Satan are good and not evil. I ask myself whether this may not be so because one spirit is conscious of the presence of another" (Lépée 1952, 99). In other words, she was unable to distinguish good from evil by logic and appearances alone. One could say that she should have—that there was nothing beyond the appearances and that her malaise was simply an anxiety attack— or that her spiritual perception was precisely accurate, despite the resistance of her everyday rationality.

just as much damage by stepping out of their proper calling. Our present task, however, is not to deal with ministers.) If even a handful of institutionalized patients or a small fraction of those paying high prices in plush offices actually do suffer from some sort of demonic possession or oppression, only a humanly callous scientist will profess no concern for the problem, even if his own tools will not resolve it.

I thus suggest that one may sometimes be rather sure that a given person is under the influence of an evil spirit, just as one may be rather sure that one loves another person or recognizes her voice, without that relative certainty making the mode of apprehension transferable.[17] Arguing with those who deny any possibility of such discernment is not fruitful. I further affirm that those who genuinely need a gift of discernment of spirits (for something other than a parlor toy or points in a game of spiritual one-upmanship) and will receive it on God's terms need not doubt that they will have it, if and when it serves God's glory. It cannot be purchased (see a parallel case in Acts 8:19–24), nor is it a correlate of intelligence. However, practice in using it may indeed be a factor (see Heb. 5:14). And if one has no such gift oneself but must deal regularly with troubled people, locating a responsible, spiritually sensitive consultant might well be a priority.

Exorcism: Promise and Limits

Even granting our hypothesis that all evil has spiritual roots, and even taking the possibility of possession seriously, we do not have instant guidelines for when we should deal with evil by prayer alone, when by resisting temptation, when by repairing damage already wrought, and when by exorcism. Overzealousness in seeking to deal with spiritual evil has without doubt produced more evil than it has conquered—not a small triumph for the Devil. Modern Hollywood versions of exorcisms as grueling ordeals may cater to unbalanced tastes, not to mention misrepresent the simple services of deliverance sufficient in many cases.[18] Furthermore, there is no office of "exorcist" in the New Testament. Exorcism may even be a bad specialty, in that too much contact with evil is not healthy (Harper 1970).

Still, the Lord has instructed us to deal with demons (Luke 9:1–2;

---

[17] Even by this statement I do not mean to imply that responsible persons never proceed to exorcism without that personal assurance. Sometimes, perhaps, circumstantial evidence may be taken as sufficient. Sometimes a powerful assurance may occur only during the exorcism. However, the person not actively seeking the guidance of the Holy Spirit and not making every effort to avoid sensationalism and hysteria has no business engaging in this sort of ministry. (Also, I am aware of the dangers of private certainties and approach that problem in chapter 10.)

[18] That simple, matter-of-fact services do often suffice goes against the theory that would attribute any successful outcome to implosion or to extremely powerful and repeated use of suggestion.

10:19), though we find no injunction to seek them out. Even today, many persons do report striking results from exorcism. For instance, one author cites cases of exorcism that led to relief from suicidal and homicidal desires, listlessness and withdrawal in a child already under psychiatric care, depression, hay fever with a thirty-five-year history, and rheumatoid arthritis (Brooks 1971; see "Addendum"). While these ailments all have psychological or psychosomatic components, the instant relief obtained is impressive. Not "just any" suggestive technique has been found so effective. Yet more dramatic may be the release of persons with more bizarre manifestations (such as a strange personality), though I do not assume that the spectacularity of phenomena necessarily corresponds to the depth of a person's bondage. More important, those who have suffered for years seem to be released instantly—not a likely occurrence by normal standards.

Exorcism is not magic but may be the right and duty of any Christian faced with an appropriate occasion. Indeed, in the early church, Origen observed the effectiveness of uncomplicated ministry by the most uneducated lay people (Brown 1984, 337, n. 82). Unlike discernment, exorcism is not a special gift but may be carried out even by the humblest or youngest believer through the power of Christ: "If Christ is not known, nor his victory and authority, understanding exorcism would be like trying to understand—without any knowledge of the law and the authority of those who represent it—how there are some people who can halt a thousand cars by raising one hand!" (Richards 1974, 18).[19] That is the sense in which it is not magic.

Exorcism is not a panacea, not only because the Devil works in more ways than by possession, but also because of complications even when spirit activity is direct. For one thing, although there is considerable

[19] One of the better Christian statements on exorcism is the following one by Richards (1974, 161): "The casting out of demons is the work of God through his Church and a sign of the coming of his Kingdom, the doing of his will, and the deliverance from evil for which every member so faithfully prays; it is God's action, not ours, because the Kingdom, the Power and the Glory belong to him not to us. It is not a fight-to-the-death between the natural and the spiritual, nor is it, as Canon Pearce-Higgins has maintained, 'the gift of some spiritually and psychically gifted clergy.' It is not a contest of psychic powers or wills described in Freudian terms of demonic archetype, nor is it, in Christian terms, an externalised battle between the new nature and the Old Adam. Christian exorcism is not the externalisation of basic drives and impulses in order that they may be recognised and renounced, however much Christ would bless such a process, nor is it an accommodation to the delusions of the mentally ill by supplying them with a therapeutic ritual. It is not the action of a diminishing Church to publicise the reality of a diminishing God—a God-of-the-Gaps in medicine and psychology. Christian exorcism is not a deliberate return to earlier Christian practices on the naive assumption that the Church should, or can, return to the Apostolic era, or a retreat from the challenge of evolving a Space Age spirituality. Nor is it, as some have maintained, '*part*. . . of a revival of a magical world-view.' It is not a defence against spiritual armies which are about to overrun us. It is instead a demonstration in power and love of the Lordship of Christ over his world."

evidence, as we have said, that persons can be released even without their knowing that anything has been done in their behalf, it also appears that those who actively want to "keep" a spirit, familiar or otherwise, are generally not successfully exorcised. Thus, similarly, some poltergeist phenomena that stem from family tensions or adolescent rebellion are thought to be more satisfactorily handled by addressing the family situation rather than a spirit: bringing in authoritarian resources may exacerbate the tensions, though prayer does sometimes relieve the disturbances (Ebon 1974; Richards 1974; actually, I do not identify poltergeist phenomena with possession as such, though they do seem to be some sort of spiritual activity mediated through an individual, as we have seen). Those who will to remain bound may do so.

A stickier question is whether some psychopathological states in themselves make even the best-justified (spiritually speaking) exorcistic procedures either unwise or ineffective. To conclude that they were unwise would mean that so severe a psychological reaction could be produced that the net result was countertherapeutic. To say that they were rendered ineffective (supposing that the patient was not actively unwilling to be helped) would be to make an analogy on the psychological level to the observation respecting physical healing that persons do not regrow amputated limbs. Without relinquishing the basic conviction that, whatever God wants done, he is quite able to accomplish, we may still find the answers here to be less than completely obvious. It is highly dangerous to assume that they *are* obvious, so that one either becomes afraid to offer help to the severely afflicted or charges in to "do the Lord's work" whether he wants it done or not. We seek to stand between unbelief and presumption, capitulating to neither. If a demon should manifest himself—unlikely unless there is some spiritual stimulus—our duty is obvious. Should we simply have run out of therapeutic ideas in a difficult case, our duty is equally obvious—and opposite (unless, of course, we are led through prayer or discernment to suspect an unforeseen source of the patient's problem). Exorcism is not just one more technique that one might as well try: witness the similar error of the sons of Sceva (Acts 19:13–16).[20]

Finally, an exorcism is the beginning and not the end of a ministry of healing. It may give a person a brand-new freedom and brand-new possibilities for willing and acting, but it does not automatically solve all past, present, and future problems. The one delivered still needs

[20]Nonetheless, I have admitted that there may be non-Christian exorcisms (see Ebon 1974; Gasson 1966; Richards 1974), sometimes seeming to involve the invoking of other spirits and sometimes employing physical means. My comment is simply that exorcism in the name of Jesus was distinguished in the ancient world as being both astoundingly effective and lasting, yet employing no ritualistic manipulation.

fellowship, guidance, and support in his faith if he is to remain free of difficulty; and it is by no means unlikely that therapy may yet be helpful for a time. Creation of possibilities does not necessarily bring with it a blueprint for living or provide the tools of which years of bondage have deprived one. All the same, any who have seen a bound one freed will not doubt that something momentous has indeed been accomplished.

How does all of this discussion relate to the theme of power? Ontologically, if possession is genuine, it entails the Devil's having power that may bind individuals. Exorcism entails that that power is not ultimate. Psychologically, lesser forms of bondage may arise from weakness, powerlessness per se, or ancestral influences, that leave one vulnerable; but the more virulent forms seem usually to stem from attempting to combat one's weakness by power seeking.[21] Why be surprised that one often meets the Devil that way? I have said that he not only *has* but *is* power. So the seemingly obvious route to health and strength does not end where one expects. There must be a better way; there must be another path toward wholeness.

ADDENDUM

The following three unpublished cases come from personal contacts and experience. The first two were related by a friend, a well-educated pastor in a main-line denomination. (I have met the subject of the first account several times but do not have all the details of the story.) I personally observed the third case.

A young woman of Jewish background in her late twenties or early thirties had been suffering from depression and withdrawal verging on psychotic proportions. Specifically, she had remained in her room at home, alone and thoroughly disheveled, for fully two years, refusing to come out or to communicate with anyone. Naturally, friends and family were in despair but did not want to hospitalize her. Pastor F heard about the case and came to visit, entering the room with his usual boisterous good cheer, rather startling the girl with his evident and unshaken joy. Discerning that the difficulty had demonic roots, he later got permission to perform an exorcism. At that time, he identified and cast out seven spirits, securing an abrupt and complete change of personality and

---

[21] For a clear statement with respect to shamanism in this regard, note Lewis 1971, 204: "Yet it is difficult to avoid the suspicion that for all its confident optimism, shamanism protests a little too much. For if, as I am arguing, possession is essentially a philosophy of power it also seems tinged with a kind of Nietzschian desperation. If this is a valid inference, it seems again to confirm the high threshold of adversity to which shamanism appears to respond." This statement—particularly the "Nietzschian desperation"—seems to apply *a fortiori* to occult pursuits.

behavior in the young woman. She became a Christian, has been "clothed and in her right mind" (see Mark 5:15) for a number of years, and recently married.

The second case occurred at a conference in 1974. A girl in her late teens who had never known her real parents came to the prayer room for ministry. Pastor F's wife had a vision of a silo and milk buckets, with a girl smiling and happy. This vision sparked the girl's response that she had hated milk ever since an oppressive school experience in fifth grade. Her fearfulness suggested demonic activity to Pastor F, and the girl accepted the suggestion that he minister exorcism. A demon identified as Fear came out readily, but the girl said there were more. Those ministering to her expelled some of them, but they then began to notice some unlikely testimony. They hypothesized that a demon of deceit was giving false names. Having cast out Deceit, they recognized Confusion as the big one; but they were unable to cast it out right away and dealt with still others first. Each demon spoke with a voice different from the girl's. During the process, it took four people to restrain this small, frail girl; she went to the floor in her struggles at least four times.

One woman noticed that the girl kept dropping her head and closing her eyes. Pastor F assumed she was simply tired, as the exorcism took four and a half hours. The woman, however, recognized an attempt to escape, commanded the demon to look her in the face, and saw abject terror staring back out of the girl's eyes. After commanding her attention, they finally got rid of Confusion, with much coughing and choking. The last demon was Hate—she said for her mother. Pastor F reminded her that she had never known her mother. The demon answered back that the mother had tried to abort her. After Hate was exorcised, the girl was evidently free; she became relaxed, almost limp.

One could doubtless "psychologize" this episode, though its correspondence to classical descriptions in terms of great strength, different voices and personalities of demons, and paranormal knowledge (i.e., of the attempted abortion) is striking. (I assume, of course, that someone had not at some forgotten time suggested the attempted abortion to the girl or that she had not imagined it. In any case, relief was obtained.)

In the third case, an attractive, middle-aged woman had suffered for about six years from severe depression and almost-continuous suicidal ideation, following upon a period of very real stress and trauma. During a visit out of state, a girl at a (nonreligious) meeting she was attending saw a vision of demons around her head, a fact later communicated through a mutual friend. Back home and somewhat later, a rather prominent Christian leader (known both to the author and to the subject), who knew nothing of the first incident, was awakened from sleep one night with the conviction that the subject was demonically oppressed, which conviction this leader shared with the author.

This leader happened to be acquainted with exorcist Don Basham, who was ministering in the area at that time, and suggested that we might make use of this contact. The author and subject attended a meeting he was conducting and stayed afterward for ministry. No sooner did he request the troublesome spirit's name than "Despair" came out of the subject's mouth with an eerie wail. He commanded it to come out, which it did with a minimum of coughing. Basham suggested that there were more demons left, but he did not wish to deal with them that evening.

Following the deliverance, the subject reported that she still felt despair (no simple denial or repression here; there were objective reasons for some despair), *but the feeling of unbearable torment was gone;* no longer did she awake in the mornings feeling incomprehensibly and unmanageably oppressed and harassed. Incidentally, there doubtless were other attacking demons, from which the subject was not freed until a thoroughly glorious moment about a year later. At that time the job was completed and so transformed her that the change was immediately apparent to anyone who knew her.

Part 4

Paradox

My thoughts are not your thoughts, neither are your ways my ways, says the LORD. For as the heavens are higher than the earth, so are my ways higher than your ways and my thoughts than your thoughts.
—Isaiah 55:8–9

10

A Paradoxical Way:
Word and Weakness—Renewal

Inquirer: There must be another path. There just *has* to be a better way.

Stranger: You said that before.

Inquirer: There has to be a better way. Better than power seeking. More than exorcism—that can't be more than a starting point, even if necessary in some cases. There must be a way to real health, available to everybody.

Stranger: Health? If I remember correctly—and I do; I'm especially skilled at remembering people's errors—you, unlike me, weren't very interested in health.

Inquirer: Oh, but you're wrong. We wouldn't be going through all of this if I weren't. The question is what "health" means. What we mean by it and the way we reach it—those are really the same thing.

Stranger: Since when? Besides, you can bet people by now are on to whatever ways *work;* after all, they've had several thousand years. As I said, any doors in that corner you painted yourself into are strictly illusory.

Inquirer: Yes, the Door. It's been said that the way hasn't been tried and found wanting but been found difficult and not tried . . .

Stranger: Difficult! You would propose something *difficult?* I thought you were against catering to power. How about a little consistency— or is that against your pet principles, too?

Inquirer: Yes, difficult. But difficult especially for the powerful, the wise, the well born and well educated. Maybe they seldom find the Way because they have so many alternative ways? Much less difficult for the weak and poor and burdened.

Stranger: Slave mentality. Absolutely counter to basic evolutionary principles.

Inquirer: If I may be naive for a moment, . . .

Stranger: For a *moment?* Would that it were only for a *moment!* Some people seem incorrigibly naive, absolutely incapable of learning from the hard facts of experience. I had hope for you for a while, but I'm fast losing it.

Inquirer: I'd like to talk about a vision of health that has never been popular—probably never will be. It isn't a new one; it's two thousand years old. It isn't especially attractive on the face of it (maybe that's why you didn't see the door?). It doesn't promise to relieve people of all their psychological quirks, much as it envisions their wholeness. And so it does not clearly differentiate healer and patient. Are we not, all of us, called to be both?

* * *

A Tisket
A Tasket
The computer blew its gasket.
A Tisket
A Tasket
What is there to ask it?
I wrote a letter to my life
And on the way I lost it.
(Walsh 1971, 14, from the movie *2001*)

Would it help to replace the gasket?

WORD

The Elusiveness of "Health"

Psychotherapy patients, it is said, have problems in *being* and are often beset with the mythological assumption that something is wrong in the very way that they are made. Any intervention, even medication, may amount to a confirmation of this mythology. Thus, for healing to take place, it is not enough for a healer to discern pathology. Healer, and patient too, must also have at least an inkling of what health would be like (Linthorst 1973, 360). Only thus can one know what to ask, where to address the letter, what it is that is lost so that one might recognize it when found—or what may be found only in the losing.

And theology makes the assumption, *not* intended to be merely mythological, that humankind, though not ill made, is fallen. True humanity is not simply that which we know and experience as human, because all living persons are in fact flawed—by sin. Health cannot be discerned by looking at them more closely. Health cannot be restored merely by mending and reclothing minds and bodies. Sin, evil, and the Devil make humankind impotent; but giving fallen humanity power only magnifies their potential for wickedness.

Power will not suffice. An army cannot capture what it cannot recognize—and employing an army may prevent one even from looking in the right places. Power will not suffice. Might and magnificence can turn the will no further than to bow in awe before them. Power will not suffice. The increase in our military and technological force leaves us fearful and dehumanized as a result of the very achievements that promise to make us secure and comfortable.[1] When structures have become tyrannical and wills self-serving, they can yield only a power that destroys. When structures are flawed and wills weak, the mirage of power lures and deceives. When structures are ambiguous and wills uncertain, power tempts and seals the temptation. Power draws everything imperfect into itself and devours it, endlessly promising what it cannot deliver.

The question before us, then, is twofold. First, how does one discern "health" when one cannot define it in terms of the world as it currently exists? How does one determine the norm (not the average but the proper standard) for structures and wills under these circumstances? Second, if power seeking is only an illusory remedy for human omnipotence, what alternative way of uniting structure and will can be found—a way that fits while they are yet imperfect and wavering as well as makes possible their ultimate coherence? The answer is single: Word.[2]

The Mystery of Word

In speaking of "Word," I mean several things that are yet one: God's original creative word; the living Word, Jesus Christ; the written Word

---

[1] "We see around us on every hand the decay of the institutions and instruments of power. On every hand intimations of empires falling to pieces, money in total disarray, dictators and parliamentarians alike nonplussed by the confusion and conflicts which encompass them, and the weaponry at their disposal so monstrous in its destructiveness as to be unusable except to blow our very earth and all its creatures to smithereens. Confronting this scene, it is sometimes difficult to resist the conclusion that Western man has decided to abolish himself; creating his own boredom out of his own affluence, his own vulnerability out of his own strength, his own impotence out of his own erotomania; himself blowing the trumpet that brings the walls of his own city tumbling down, and, having convinced himself that he is too numerous, laboring with pill and scalpel and syringe to make himself fewer, until at last, having educated himself into stupefaction, he keels over, a weary, battered old brontosaurus, and becomes extinct" (Muggeridge 1974).

[2] Actually, in the absolute sense, Power and Word are one and the same; only power's rebellion and humankind's weakness make power an enemy now. As Buber wrote, "I do not know what would remain to us / Were love not transfigured power / And power not straying love" (quoted in May 1972, 251). If power devours the imperfect, love completes and restores it. The former is a false, consummatory love or reunion; the latter, a self-sacrificial manifestation of creativity, the only ultimate power.

of Scripture; and even in part, insofar as they are an expression of the *imago Dei,* human words. God expressed his will through structures by the word of creation and gave his creation the benediction "good": what he made was normal, in no way lacking. He proclaimed his structures to people in the words of his Book, even as he spoke them in history. And in the person of his Son, God lived visibly what he meant.

The divine Word normatively creates, orders (in both senses), and reveals, shaping and expressing at the same time, with the result that act and fact, will and structure, motion and stability, come together as equally True. In the original wholeness of God's creation, that which is spoken, simply is. The things that are seen are made out of things that do not appear (Heb. 11:3). Thus, truly creative power can be measured not against anything, but only against nothing.

We have lost that wholeness, as shown in the fact that our willing always involves the wish that things might be different than they are. Such was the first temptation, to seek an imagined good condemned by Reality (Rougemont 1945, 25; cf. Williams [1942] 1984, 21); and never since have we been able to disentangle the imagined good and the real.[3] Indeed, the search for power is in some sense the desire to be able to force whatever good is imagined to *be* real. The imagined even comes to be preferred, for what can be imagined can be conceived to be in our power, whereas that which is real never was and never will be.[4] Thus the truth itself is now a threat, for every attempt to utter the truth in some sense destabilizes the complex edifice of little self-deceptions we build to make life seem more manageable (see Rougemont 1945, x). And thus it is naive to suppose that people simply love the good: the good makes demands on us, and the demands involve sacrifice of what we have sacrificed all to gain—omnipotent fantasies and fantasies of impotence (see May 1972, 207). So,

---

[3] As an example *par excellence,* consider the story of the Prodigal Son (Luke 15:11–32). The tragedy of the story in the midst of the triumph is less that the Prodigal would squander his inheritance on an imagined good that he nonetheless assumed he had a right to pursue than that the elder brother apparently assumed that the Father was withholding goods arbitrarily from him. To put it crudely, the story teaches us not only that God forgives us but also that he is not a cosmic wet blanket: here, as in Eden, nothing that is for human good—and the party honoring the Prodigal's return would lead us to believe that joy and celebration are part of that good—is held back. Note John 15:10–11: "If you keep my commandments, you will abide in my love. . . . These things I have spoken to you, that my *joy* may be in you, and that your joy may be full" (emphasis added).

[4] "The insoluble contradiction between divine and demoniacal formation of power is the fiery sword of the cherub which prohibits to the thought of fallen mankind the entry to the ultimate mystery of history" (Heim 1961b, 39). That is, we can never resolve how Satan's power at once belongs to God and is yet fought to the death by God; hence the dynamic of life and history is inscrutable to us and beyond our manipulation. The path to understanding (or to entirely rational programs to restore Eden or bring in the kingdom) is barred by apparent contradiction.

the real reason why people reject God is not that the message concerning Him is distorted by dubious witnesses, fanatical prophets, and mendacious priests and is compromised through intermixture with antiquated economic ordinances. On the contrary, these things are no more than a very welcome pretext. . . . It is a serious error if we believe that people would turn to God in masses, if all offenses were removed. . . . On the contrary, the purer and the more unselfish the witness to the truth, the more the hatred of God flares up. When Jesus went through the country helping and healing, the demons everywhere broke forth against Him and uttered blasphemies. Him particularly who did not seek anything for Himself, the world could not bear. (Heim 1961a, 97)

We in our wickedness prefer darkness to light (John 3:19).

Insofar as we neither can nor wish to hear and perceive Truth, insofar as we would preserve what we consider to be ourselves by defending against anything threatening that self-conception (self-conceit? self-deceit?), we twist word back against itself. We use our God-given rationality to define ourselves apart from God or to attack the created order. In the first instance, we take our words as providing an airtight, rational formulation of reality and thus lock ourselves into the paradigm the words define—while those outside the paradigm would perceive that its supposed absolutes merely seem to be necessary truths. In the second instance, we use words irrationally, whether emotively as in cursing or superstitiously. Used in these ways, words are merely powerful (or impotent); they are tools bent to serve our purposes. They are related to Truth only insofar as any power tapped may express God's intent for wills and structures and not just the perverted possibilities for them. We have covered this ground already.

At this point, though, we should acknowledge that there does appear to be a limited range of secondary creativity granted to the words that persons choose to speak: the animals were brought to Adam that he might name them (Gen. 2:19) and afterward know them according to the names that he gave them. On this level, the very discipline of science is grounded in God's own act. But the word persons may speak is not limited merely to naming; they may also bless and curse. Scripture implies that it *matters* which is done, not just because of the emotional effect on the persons involved, but because somehow a deeper reality is tapped. In some mysterious way, good or evil wishes verbally expressed, or perhaps even thought, reverberate through us and our universe (see James 3). *Our words count for good or evil, not just for fact or error.*[5] So too

---

[5] Though certainly, error chosen or untruth chosen is a great victory for evil: "Because speech was given us in order to expound the truth, to extend it, and to bear witness to it, it is clear that the great satanic ambition must be to distort the word in our very mouths, to corrupt our evidence at its source. And that is why the Bible states so categorically that

must our witness to the truth and our confession of our sin be verbal and public (Rom. 10:9; James 5:16).

Through his emphasis on the words we speak, perhaps God is saying to us that, particularly by speech, we affirm—and hence secure as reality to ourselves—the nature and interrelatedness of the world. To speak is to share as well as to structure a reality. Even (or perhaps especially) our individual faith and our individual sin are necessarily part of a shared existence; for in them above all else we confront the issue of what reality is and what violates it. We have already considered the point that we do not particularly desire God's reality; we would much rather have our own. Hence, our very rationality becomes rationalism or irrationality.[6]

The question, then, is how our rationality, our words, may become one with God's purpose; how we may affirm in our science and law and philosophy, not structures just as we find them, but God's intent for those structures and how we may affirm for ourselves, not our imaginings, but what God wants us to be. How can one identify one's will with God's without doing so by identifying God's will with one's own?

> For the will to be regenerated much more is needed than an infusion of new power (perhaps from a new power source), or the furnishing of more suitable objects, or a better and wiser law, or any process of molding or curbing. What is required is the replacement of the "me" as an action center. For even if I will the good, even if I will God, the seducing power of the "I" who wills so lofty a thing remains. The trouble with the ideas of self-realization and self-actualization . . . is that they are self-propelled activities emanating from a center called "I" or "Self." (Pruyser 1969, 65)

The Hope of Repentance

How can we get beyond the seduction of the self, beyond the struggle of a self seeking to transcend itself? Quite simply, we cannot. We cannot jump out of our skins to evaluate the presuppositions by which we make our evaluations. We cannot see ourselves as others see us or know as we are known. We cannot fix our corrupt selves by means of our corrupt selves. The possibility of *radical* change can come only from outside ourselves—from what the Christian calls *grace*.

The movement enabled by grace must be both one of hearing and one of repentance. In saying that we may hear a word from beyond us, I imply that rationality is transrationally grounded, but more, that what is beyond us can change us. Indeed, when we hear such a word, the change

when we lie it is the Devil himself who puts his tongue into our mouth" (Rougemont 1945, 31).

[6] "To live in the plain light of binary reason is to cut off the source, not just of salvation, but of reason itself" (Walsh 1971, 108).

has already begun, for it is God who gives us ears to hear and ordains that by hearing we may be made different.

Now God leaves plenty of room for the doubter. His word, like his work, is not coercive in the ordinary, mundane sense of the term. Human freedom has its allotted scope. But to be free to disbelieve is a different and much smaller thing than to be free to believe: the one is the natural result of our bondage to our paradigms; the other is God's creation of an entirely new possibility, a possibility that is not "sensible." The Word not only *forms,* or brings into being, but also *transforms.* Thus those who are enabled to hear what God speaks are no longer bound by mere fact but have opened to them the infinite and perfect possibilities of God's omnipotence and grace. Nothing that merely "is" *has* to be; in fact, all that merely "is" must be sacrificed to what it is meant to be. For this reason, hearing promotes and demands repentance.

To repent is to be willing to will what God wills and so to recognize (by hearing) the wrong one actually does will—recognize it with sorrow and a profound desire to change. So is the mind renewed and the life changed.

> For those who live according to the flesh set their minds on the things of the flesh, but those who live according to the Spirit set their minds on the things of the Spirit. . . . The mind that is set on the flesh is hostile to God; it does not submit to God's law, indeed it cannot. (Rom. 8:5, 7)

> Do not be conformed to this world but be transformed by the renewal of your mind, that you may prove what is the will of God, what is good and acceptable and perfect. (Rom. 12:2)

Now Scripture presents the mind as *either* renewed by God *or* darkened by Satan (2 Cor. 4:4); and our deception is certain if the mind is not renewed (Jer. 17:9; Isa. 44:20; Titus 3:3; Heb. 3:13; see Penn-Lewis n.d., chap. 1). Because appearances deceive and because true repentance entails relinquishment both of appearances and of the paths we follow to obtain the world's goods, repentance is absolutely crucial to discernment and authority in dealing with Satan (see Harper 1970). We cannot even see his working unless we are willing to give up the biasing spectacles he provides for us. (We also need to repent because we confront the Devil in God's authority and not ours alone, so we had better have our wills freely aligned with God's!)

A curious but theologically appropriate result of this view of hearing, repentance, and renewal is that one cannot measure it strictly by observing evils eschewed and good accomplished, an important consideration for ethics as well as piety. On the one hand, the deceptiveness of appearances renders our tidy judgments of persons in this regard, as well as in others, inept (see 1 Cor. 4:2–5), a matter we shall take up again. On the other, concentration on presumed goods and evils easily seduces us to Pharisaism (Luke 18:10–14). In a psychologist's language,

> trying to be good all the time will make one not into an ethical giant but into a prig. . . . No longer shall we feel that virtues are to be gained merely by leaving behind vices; the distance up the ladder ethically is not to be defined in terms of what we have left behind. Otherwise goodness is no longer good but self-righteous pride in one's own character. (May 1972, 238, 259)

That is not to say that renewal does not change behavior—indeed it does and must—but part of its very transcendence is that behavior as judged by one's own or others' standards cannot serve as an ultimate.

The thought of having no worldly absolutes by which to measure one's acts and accomplishments can be enormously anxiety provoking, for then one has no means of gaining firm control and predictability for one's life. Those who begin to leap to the thought that "everything is permitted" in an antinomian sense have not begun to understand that it is precisely the will "to do one's own thing" that is given up. The legalists' problem may be even greater, though, for they may feel that they are being required to sacrifice a good that is higher than themselves.

Truly to love the good, then, we must count lightly the cost; and the cost is light if and only if it is so counted. The cost? There will be unpredictable demands—demands that we change. There will be reshaping of our ideas about the possible and the impossible and about how to attain the former; there will be sacrifice of our private control over our lives and of our self-righteousness.[7] Old things must pass away

---

[7] As an instance of the impossible being spoken into existence at the violent expense of nature and reason alike, consider this poem (Slotten 1971, 317):

> The rosy body of a girl
> inclines in the twilight
> at her spinning
> before the marauding visitor from heaven.
> Reassured by gentle, brawny words,
> she gives consent
> in a virgin's Gethsemane prayer
> to be pierced
> by the everlasting joker
> in the maidenhead of the ear,
> while Joseph stands around and
> Italian peasants make merry on
> St. Cuckold's Marchy day
> in the laughing salvation of
> a conceiving name, the
> punch-line of creation.

It may be important to repeat that the demand to relinquish control can be one of the most threatening that can be made; for virtually everything we normally do, we do to

in order that all things may become new (2 Cor. 5:17). Is anything left? No, and yes; nothing, and everything. What is left is the living, speaking God who wants to make known his intent for his creation. Those who are renewed and being renewed listen.

They listen and then act and speak, for such is the path of renewal: the great plan is somehow channeled through believers who obey what they hear. How dare anyone be so bold? How can one avoid corrupting what he has heard and making even God's word serve his own purposes? To steer clear of these hazards would demand a commitment and assurance so deep and secure as to be absolutely unshakable. A person would have to know God more surely than a mortal can—so surely that, if everyone else on earth disbelieved, yet he would sense God's presence. Only with that kind of assurance would a person consistently be able to avoid using his witness and actions as a way of attempting to expiate his own guilt or of bolstering his own belief system. Only with such knowledge would he be able to avoid succumbing to works and manipulation and be able to focus upon another's needs rather than his own. We can scarcely give freely what we are still trying to prove or earn for ourselves. Furthermore, we will scarcely bother to give freely unless we know that we cannot keep what we have without giving it away, even if the giving brings suffering, and unless we realize that *nothing* else is of equal importance or value. Absolutely unshakable commitment and assurance: impossible? Of course. We walk by faith and not sight, and the darkness spawns doubt.

*   *   *

Stranger: And furthermore, anybody that sure of anything is a positive hazard. Haven't you ever looked at the history of "true believers"? Not that I'd want to put down my friends, but the more certain they are, the more reckless their behavior gets. A bit of doubt is excellent seasoning for "virtue." In fact, the more doubt, the less likely virtue is to get entirely out of hand. As Bertrand Russell[8] put it, especially if a person or organization "has ideal ends, and therefore an excuse for

maintain control in one way or another (see Frank 1974, 236). But "to be master of one's own destiny is a pre-Christian ambition, it has missed the distinctively Christian paradox that there is greater security in committing one's future to a heavenly Father than there is in trying to manipulate it oneself " (Richards 1974, 24). To relinquish one's will to the God who speaks is, however, a very different matter from the passivity against which we have cautioned. A repentant turning to God involves an active focus and the attuning of all one's faculties in order that one may hear. Thus it may be by no means incidental that submitting to Word entails use of our critical intelligence at the same time that it refuses to absolutize it. The whole mind (and brain) is involved; nothing is put in neutral. Thus it would be more accurate to say not that will itself is set aside but that *self-centered* will, self-determination, self-righteousness, and self-definition are laid on the line.

[8] 1938, 72.

love of power, a reputation for superior virtue is dangerous, and is sure, in the long run, to produce a superiority only in unscrupulous ruthlessness." Not that I'm against power, as you know, or even virtues, so my caution here should be given due weight.

Inquirer: That's exactly what I've been saying, that any "virtue" made absolute can justify anything. Witch trials, for instance. Perfectly sincere, absolutely dedicated people presumed that they had both the duty and the ability to make absolute judgments. And being sincere and dedicated, how were they to know how much of the evil they were fighting was really in themselves rather than in others; how much they were motivated, at bottom, by cruelty merely masquerading as devotion to righteousness? "The tale of witchcraft is a tale of the deception of virtue by itself";[9] to achieve *that* has got to be one of the Devil's handiest feats.

Stranger: I must admit that it's quite a clever thought—and most effective, I've noticed. The surer of some "truth" people are, the less they can resist establishing it by force. After all, how else can you establish anything?

Inquirer: Ah, yes, that is the question, the *big* question. How do we keep our personal certainties from judging and destroying other people or at least seeking to mold them in our image? Partly, maybe, by knowing that the God who has touched us is quite able to touch others and quite able to maintain control of his world. That's why I'd submit that another necessity for right acting and speaking is that we never presume to know God in such a way that we can precisely predict or prescribe how he will meet or deal with another individual. Even when we are sure about our own experience, we also know it to be incomplete. Our witness to our own encounter with God and our following what he asks of us are merely illustrative, not normative; they are a testimony to God's power rather than a road map to salvation. In short, we may not have a "true believer" mentality exactly because we know so assuredly that it was God who found us and not the reverse. But perfect humility is every bit as elusive as perfect certainty. You know, paradoxically enough, I think we'd do better at being humble if we were more certain, not less—if we were more deeply secure in what we believe. As it is, we're afraid really to believe that God's Word is sufficient and that we can't either control it or force anyone else to hear it. Only God gives ears. Only God renews. We'd much rather bolster our confidence by getting credit for bringing in our image of the kingdom.

[9]Williams 1959, 305.

Stranger: Speak for yourself—but obviously that's what you've been doing, and at exorbitant length. If you're done with the oratory, what would you propose? That you sit on your hands and do nothing? That you believe something and have it make no difference? I don't see any particular evidence that God is doing much in the world, and I think people should grow up and take responsibility for themselves. You think *Word* changes anything? Only by mobilizing *power*. Power, pragmatism, and skepticism make a very healthy combination. I recommend it.

* * *

WEAKNESS

On the practical level, putting Word in the place of power as the proper source of healing for structure and will and putting the possible in the place of the actual as the point where structure and will can finally be perfectly unified entail more than relinquishing the absoluteness of our own ethics, piety, witness, and ideas of health. Our repentance and renewal are not just from all of these human ideals but to an entirely new way of seeing and being. The power that can no longer be seen as a source of righteousness or an end in itself is deprived with the same stroke of its validity as a means. We come to the paradox that our lives can be saved only by losing them (Matt. 16:25), that God's folly is wiser than our wisdom, that our weakness rather than our might puts the strong to shame, that what is low or despised or even not yet existent may render what merely "is" to be nothing rather than everything (1 Cor. 1:25–29); and all of this overturning of our perspective in order that not we but God might be everything. Any end we can attain "on our own," we may safely assume to be at variance with God's purpose, for the simple reason that God does not purpose that we do anything "on our own," without reference to him. And there is another reason as well: we *are* weak and limited, and it is in this very weakness and limitation that God has chosen to manifest his own power and glory (see Grundmann 1964; Zizioulas 1975).

Freedom and the Illusion of the "Necessary"

Consider the dilemma of "freedom." To be meaningful rather than simply nihilistic, freedom must have direction; but if the terminus is finite and hence at least theoretically attainable, all meanings are relative, possibly conflicting, and ultimately empty. If the terminus is beyond time and space, the present takes on both a greater significance and an entirely different framework for interpretation. Since the end is

209

not visible, one has a sanction neither for self-satisfaction nor for despair but can only commit oneself to the Director and the Director's ability to bring about his end.

The freedom of the believer is thus a curious thing, different from independence or autonomy. The latter is the ability to do, within a limited range of possibilities, what we want. The former is the opportunity, not bound by the limits of ways and means, freely to assent to become what God wants, in the assurance that what he wants is what we would want for ourselves if we could see as he sees. When we belong to God, no ultimate victory or disaster is signaled by any of our temporal triumphs or failures. We may simply listen and believe and obey, knowing that the forces of evil obtain their power through our unbelief (see Schlier 1961, 58) and that, with respect to dealing with the Devil in particular, we must not seek to go beyond what simple belief would lead us to do (Berkof 1962, 43). These two statements mean the same thing practically speaking: to "go beyond" belief is to *disbelieve* that God's ways are sufficient and to consider it necessary to utilize the Devil's means against the Devil, power against power.[10]

Insofar as we capitulate to the Devil's means, we become subject to him. That is what happens in every persecution and "holy" war. We take upon ourselves the responsibility to do that which God has said that he would do; and the only arms we have are the Devil's. God has chosen not to give us worldly weapons (2 Cor. 10:4), and all the might and wisdom of the world (1 Cor. 1:27; 3:18–20) will not suffice to accomplish his purposes. Thus the New Testament mentions two kinds of victory, corresponding to the aims of those who seek their goals in the world as it stands and the aims of those who look beyond this world. The first sort are the physical and evident, yet provisional and ultimately illusory, victories granted to the Enemy (Rev. 11:7; 13:7); the second kind are the decisive but unrecognized ones of Christ, of the martyr, of faith (Matt. 12:29; John 16:33; 1 John 5:4–5; Rev. 12:11). "Only faith can appreciate Christ's power on earth, for the beast is master here" (Schlier 1961, 82; see also Bauernfeind 1964; Ling 1961).

The beast is master here. For this reason, temporal victory is illusory, and the apparent "necessity" of using power against power, only apparent—really a lie perpetrated by the Enemy. When an individual capitulates to that temptation or even when one sins, one believes that lie instead of God. By accepting the Devil's interpretation of what is real

---

[10] "Even with a long spoon, we must not accept the invitation to sup with the devil, for he only wants us to borrow his own weapons. However hostile a dialogue may seem at first, the very fact that it is a dialogue tends to destroy the notion of the Adversary and turn him first into an interlocutor, and then into a partner, and the duel into a match; finally he becomes an accomplice, and we ourselves are transformed into our old enemy. We must not want to vie in cunning with Satan" (Magny 1952, 455).

and what is necessary, one reinforces the Devil's hold on one's life and on the world (Schlier 1961, 60–61).[11] The sort of world in which power wins and sin profits is a fantasy of the Devil, made actual because we accept the picture he paints. And so made actual because, as I have said, he has an ally in us (2 Cor. 2:10–11; Eph. 4:26–27; 1 Tim. 3:6; 1 John 3:8). Consider this telling excerpt from Auden's "Thanksgiving for a Habitat" (1976, 524-25) :

> Time has taught you
>   how much inspiration
> your vices brought you,
>   what imagination
> can owe temptation
>   yielded to,
> that many a fine
>   expressive line
> would not have existed,
>   had you resisted:
> as a poet, you
>   know this is true,
> and though in Kirk
>   you sometimes pray
> to feel contrite,
>   it doesn't work.
> *Felix Culpa,* you say:
>   perhaps you're right.
> You hope, yes,
>   your books will excuse you,
> save you from hell:
>   nevertheless,
> without looking sad,
>   without in any way
> seeming to blame
>   (He doesn't need to,
> knowing well
>   what a lover of art
> like yourself pays heed to),
>   God may reduce you
> on Judgment Day
>   to tears of shame,
> reciting by heart
>   the poems you would
> have written, had
>   your life been good.

[11] At this point I am speaking most particularly from the standpoint of an individual's handling of his own case. For modifications of this position, painful but important when the suffering of one's brothers and sisters is in view, see chapter 11.

How easy it is to become slaves of the necessary—or even the useful or desirable—and to doubt that there is anything else! We are free only if we are free to sacrifice exactly those. They tie us to what we are and to what the world is; and to be free is to be enabled to move beyond those.

Thus the New Testament promises of life and blessedness go to all the "wrong people"—those not having the good things of this world. Furthermore, the New Testament means of establishing God's kingdom go flatly against any means that we might devise: it shall not come by good behavior, for salvation is by grace alone; nor by strict justice, for we are to forgive those who wrong us; nor by wisdom, for ours is foolishness to God; nor by strength, for God uses instead our weakness. We serve a God who is not dependent on the world he has spoken into existence. To know that truth is to know surely that one is perfectly safe within the fiery furnace *whether or not* he perishes there. One will not be touched unless God allows it. Sin, not death, means defeat.

Weakness, Freedom, and the Present Order

Now it is easy to say that we have conjured a strictly illusory freedom, a freedom even more illusory than the temporal victories of the beast. At least those victories do take place. Could we not conclude that the conviction of victories not manifested here and now is a fantasy of the dispossessed, instead of concluding that the apparent necessities and the carnal pleasures of this world are a fantasy of the Devil? Surely the former conclusion would be more sensible.

We can find, however, at least two additional reasons for the persistence of belief in heavenly rewards, beyond the obvious one that such belief conveniently reduces stress on the socioeconomic status quo. The first additional reason stems from the empirically validated principle that, from a psychological standpoint, any sort of surrender to an external power reduces stress and may thus promote health (Rose 1971, 124). Speaking pragmatically, we can thus say that a certain amount of passivity sometimes helps. The notably successful Alcoholics Anonymous and similar "twelve-step" recovery and support programs, for instance, insist that their adherents affirm some sort of higher power, or "God as one understands him." Things work better, physically and psychologically, when one is not trying to carry the whole world on one's own back but believes it will be carried in spite of one. Things sometimes change when one stops struggling, just as for biofeedback to succeed, one must not try too hard. We may thus simply observe as a fact of life that it is useful sometimes to give in to our incapacities. Nothing requires us to turn that worldly observation into a cosmic principle that gives acceptance of incapacity a special, venerable status.

A second reason stems from an active and "existential" approach: by struggling for a worthy cause without regard for outward success, for example, we may discover—or define—our own character (see May 1972, 252). We may persuade ourselves that we are creatures of will and not just mechanisms programed by large-scale M & M's if we pursue a goal without a victory in sight. So we may conclude that our desire to show ourselves not merely determined by the tangible may sometimes (not too often, of course) make ignoring success more rewarding than attaining it. This behavior, too, is useful. It balances the sheer exploitation of others as a means of getting rewards; so altruism is sanctioned by society. Nothing would require us to say that our will is altered or given over to God when we act in this way; it is rather given a sort of dominion.

Notice that these two types of examples rest upon this-worldly determinants and yet yield behavior that may be similar to that engendered by a rejection of the usual this-worldly standards. The question then becomes whether the supposedly paradoxical suggestions of the New Testament are not really paradoxical at all but simply useful correctives that occasionally have practical results.

The answer to that question must be twofold. First, insofar as these directives simply work—whether followed for right or wrong motivation, whether from obedience and repentance or from pragmatism and pride—we must remember that God, after all, put the world together. There is no reason to suppose that the Devil should be unwilling to let vestiges of that original order show through, especially when God will get no credit for the results. However, the New Testament message is most emphatically not, Follow these suggestions for a sure path to the good life. Instead, it assures us that the servant will be treated no better than the Master (John 15:20), that those not of the world will be hated and rejected by it (John 17:14), indeed, that "all who desire to live a godly life in Christ Jesus will be persecuted" (2 Tim. 3:12). To the eye of the pragmatist, the contingencies are strictly lose-lose: "obey, or you'll go to hell" and "obey, and you'll have your hell of suffering here on earth." As we noted earlier, the purer the good, the surer the rejection. Only the occasional, the incidental, or the wrongly motivated good escapes unscathed.[12] The good that is gained is not necessarily of

[12] This point is a possible explanation for the fact that "virtue" often seems more easily realized by the Stoic or humanitarian than by the Christian: virtue that glorifies the self is no ultimate threat to evil. Scripture links suffering not to the good that can be accomplished by accepting and utilizing to advantage the world's resources but to refusing to accept them as adequate (being "not of the world") and to resisting the Devil (1 Peter 5:8–9). Those who "realize the highest human potential" are honored; those who are more interested simply in obeying God are counted mad or fools or subverters of the current order—and they certainly are at least the latter. As we shall consider in the next chapter, suffering can have *more* ultimate power over evil than can mere good: Christ demonstrated power over the Devil when he traveled the countryside healing and casting out demons, but he *defeated* him on the cross (Heb. 2:14).

the same order as the "good" that is given up. In fact, nothing has *been* given up if it is released with the thought that, by letting it go, one will receive it back. The Bible's prescriptions are not presented as means to *our* ends.

But on the other hand, that which truly is potentially good of what one has given up may indeed be given back, freely and to overflowing, when it is no longer an end: "Seek first his kingdom and his righteousness, and all these things shall be yours as well" (Matt. 6:33; see also Mark 10:29–30). We are not even supposed to be blind and passive regarding our desires but to *ask* in order that we may receive (James 4:2–3; 1 John 3:22; 5:14–15); and insofar as what we ask is rightly motivated and in accord with God's will, we shall receive it—but presumably not *without* asking. God did not design us as puppets.

Furthermore, all of those acts and characteristics that can never be the root of salvation and the kingdom yet *must* be its fruit: the righteousness of the believer must exceed that of the Pharisee (Matt. 5:20; Jesus here compliments more than rebukes the Pharisees: by all the standards of the law they were supremely righteous; see Phil. 3:5–6); the doing of justice, especially with regard to the underprivileged, becomes a mark of the genuineness of one's faith (James 2:9–10); the mature are to be endued with a wisdom that comes from God (1 Cor. 2:6–7); and yes, even the mighty strength of God's Spirit empowers the believer (Eph. 3:16; Acts 1:8). Giving up one's own ends results in one's becoming more, not less, than one was before; and giving up one's own strength puts one in a position in which more, not less, will be demanded, because by God's strength all things are possible. Indeed, one cannot speak meaningfully of what it is to be human and to be free without speaking also of God, for one is free not when one is self-determined (that is futility) nor when one is determined from below (that is dehumanizing) but only when one can move toward that which is greater than one currently is.

To say that weakness leads to freedom may be truly paradoxical from a worldly standpoint, at least if one speaks of freedom in terms of capacity (ability as well as purposed direction) and not just in terms of emotional detachment from that which most people value. For instance, for the pragmatist, as I said, either "the only ends ('goods') worth working for" are denied or else "the only possible means" to desirable ends are passed by. But for those who know that God has greater goods and surer means, to experience which one must quite obviously let go of one's own cherished goods and means, there is no paradox at all.[13]

---

[13] It is nonetheless an interesting question (more than just interesting to the ethicist, for whom it is central) how we establish as "good" that which does not necessarily have measurable, pragmatic results, such as the preservation of life. The alternative is generally considered to be some absolute law or laws, whether derived from universal verities of

Returning momentarily to those who find themselves in a fiery furnace, recall my comment that they are safe whether they live or die there. The latter eventuality is no problem to imagine; and there are goods, such as honor, for which even those believing death to be ultimate will yet die. Still, Word is a powerful thing if it can engender the free sacrifice of life. Powerful, but not powerful enough. Unless it can also make possible life in such a furnace (and not only "can" but at least once, analogically but in a greater way, *has,* 1 Cor. 15:12–19), everything I have said is pious rhetoric. Rhetoric is powerful, but not over flame or flood—or death or the irrational evil in our hearts. If God cannot do more than persuade us according to our own paradigms, without changing the paradigm so that we can hear something new; if God is so subservient to the rules of the universe he has constructed— and the Devil has twisted—that he cannot deliver us from the inexorable march of cause leading inevitably to effect; then his Word is a dead language, his Book is more deceptive than Satan ever thought of being, and we are wasting our time (though in that case we might as well waste it this way as some other way, since it is all the same in the end). Word for us would then be *only* powerful, powerful in a way comparable to any other power that can produce but not create, destroy but not renew.

I must also offer a closing word about weakness and its companion incapacities. In this chapter, I did not explicitly differentiate the weakness resulting from our finitude and the impotence stemming from our guilt. The one gives occasion for celebration because it is the channel through which God works; the other gives occasion for profound repentance because it is displeasing to God (there is no room for "sinning that grace may abound" [Rom. 6:1]). The one is an intent of the Creator; the other is the design of the Deceiver. The one is the continual means to good; the other should come to be less and less in evidence.

This conclusion about impotence actually follows directly from our discussion in chapter 7, where we saw that one loses power whenever

human nature, revealed truth, or some other source. "Good," though, has a component that is more than merely cognitive, an element that is recognizable before consulting the rule books or making the pragmatic calculus, something to which our being resonates and which it affirms. Otherwise, if the good were merely "laws," we would not be so incensed by the very possibility posited by some that "good" as defined by God might be so strange and alien that we could not even recognize it as good. Thus the good higher and greater than the goods people ordinarily seek is not, according to a chorus of saints and martyrs and more ordinary, less-sung mortals, merely a painful duty to which the only motivation is guilt or responsibility, but rather a joyful, *experienced* good. Now experience is not sharable, and a private vision generally gets the label "hallucination." But a vision that is invisible offers no more than a canvas painted black. The number of persons who have looked in the same direction and brought back similar reports could lead us to suspect that there is something to be seen—for those who have eyes.

structure or will is warped or distorted because of the combined efforts of our enemies without and within. Obviously, then, not power per se but rather impotence is bad. Impotence is merely a symptom and not a cause, however, so we saw in chapter 8 that trying to remedy impotence with power simply escalates the problem. Here we have come full circle: radical renunciation of power and exclusive longing for forgiveness—affirming God's purpose for structure and will—yield power![14] Our real power depends strictly upon our acknowledged weakness. And so we are made new not only once for all by the Word of God but also in a living, growing realization of our wholeness as individuals.

Renewal is the way of Word and weakness: a new mind, over against all deception.

[14]It is instructive to compare the views of a theologian and a psychologist on the issue of impotence, which both consider to be evil. Heim (1961b, 35) says, "The whole Biblical view of the world rests on this original relation between innocence and power, guilt and impotence." May (1972), on the other hand, looks at impotence, whether sociological or psychological, basically as environmentally imposed, which makes it a source more than a result of personal evil; and he considers innocence usually to be blind and naive, tending to lead the helpless to a passivity that compounds their problems. He speaks particularly of "pseudo-innocence," our failure to recognize our complicity with evil and our making a virtue out of powerlessness—clearly not the sort of innocence that Heim intends; but the fact remains that he does not conceive a sort of innocence that could be genuinely enabling. May's treatment provides some profound insights for "how things really work in the world." Heim's treatment provides an entirely different vision of sources of our problems and resources for dealing with them.

11

A Paradoxical Way:

Fellowship and Forgiveness—Reunion

Stranger: I've come to a conclusion.

Inquirer: You have?

Stranger: Yes, I have. You're crazy. The alternative is that you're stupid, but I thought I'd give you the benefit of the doubt.

Inquirer: What do you mean?

Stranger: You don't know what I mean? That proves it. You're crazy. And probably stupid to boot. I despise craziness and stupidity and people who try to get others hooked into such nonsense.

Inquirer: At least be so good—or bad, if you prefer—as to explain yourself.

Stranger: You are probably too obtuse to understand. And if I explained *myself,* I'd say I am what I am and have every right to be exactly that.

Inquirer: Oh.

Stranger: There is no reason why I should want to be anything different, as if I could jump out of my own skin; there is no reason why I should put up with any sort of misery that I can possibly avoid; and there is certainly no reason why I should set my mind on "God" or other people when it won't do me any good.

Inquirer: You react as if I were attacking you personally.

Stranger: You were, you idiot, and everyone else with an ounce of pride and self-respect. You'd breed a race of groveling, slavish, dependent earthworms and persuade them to like being walked over. Then every time one managed to miss being stepped on, you'd call it a "miracle." You wouldn't know a coincidence if one bit you.

Inquirer: As I remember, we discussed in another context the possibility that coincidences might not be so coincidental; but I never

217

suggested they were miraculous either. Coincidences have something to do with the interconnectedness of creation (though one might better call it providence, to speak theologically). Miracles have to do with the dynamic, living Word of the Creator.

Stranger: Word, words, words. Somebody remarked that, when all is said and done, there's a lot more said than done. You think "Word" does something? *I* say whatever you perceive is coincidence. Besides, "Word" or "words," as you choose, mean exactly what a group of people decides that they mean; and that's bad enough, that they should so sacrifice their individuality that they communicate with one another. Getting something transcendent out of words is a piece of legerdemain. Worse, it can con people into giving up their present welfare, as you were trying to do. Fine humanitarian you are!

Inquirer: I never claimed to be first and foremost a humanitarian. That is strictly secondary. You are quite right, though, about the fact that Word and community are related. Word creates community.

Stranger: That is *not* what I said. I said community creates words.

Inquirer: I know. *I* said that Word creates community.

* * *

The Christian religion, on the whole, tends to discourage self-interest and self-importance; against that discouragement there are two methods of fighting—one is to go on being interested in oneself under cover of that religion; the other, to go on being interested in oneself under cover of another religion. (Williams 1959, 63)

FELLOWSHIP

Word, Love, and Community

Psychologists, sociologists, and theologians agree on the interconnectedness of human beings and the centrality of verbal symbolization, making possible rational thought and language, to what is specifically human rather than merely animal about them. In fact, when Frederick II of Prussia wanted to find out what language children would naturally speak, he set aside a group of infants and forbade their guardians ever to speak in their presence. The babies simply died. Whatever one argues about this outcome occurring because the guardians may also have restrained affective expressivity and contact simply proves the centrality of speech to all phases of human relationships. It is not mere chance that the uniqueness of human beings and God's acts for them both are identified as "word"; rather, human rationality is a crucial part of the *imago Dei.* It follows that community is part of the intent of the Creator, not an awkward afterthought or expedient necessitated by self-preservation. This foundation is vital to the following discussion. Although we will be considering human solidarity and community in a basically "structural" way, I by no means intend to discount our willful, rational participation in it nor God's purpose for it. There is a difference between the biological necessity of having living people to produce people, the psychological necessity of communication and interaction to self-image, and the theological statement that it is not *good* for us to be alone (Gen. 2:18).

We were never intended to be alone. We cannot be human alone. We violate a greater whole and destroy our own being alone. By our very nature, we are not determined by our own boundaries and are not self-sufficient. In relationship to God, that lack of self-sufficiency may be felt as weakness, but as Paul comments, we may glory in that very weakness insofar as it opens us to God's power and activity (2 Cor. 12:9). In relationship to creation, that lack of self-sufficiency entails our crucial and individual importance in the great scheme of giving and receiving. Real giving denies self-interest; real receiving denies pride; so "individual importance" is killed and resurrected, established by being relinquished. That is the nature of fellowship: I am important not because *I* love me but because you do. And that, too, is the nature of grace.

Of course there can be community, of a sort, without love; we are tied together whether we like it or not (and without love, we may be fairly sure we will not like it). Then, as Sartre said, "Hell is other people." Ever since the Fall, knowing has preceded loving, which is the only way truly to know (Zizioulas 1975; see May 1972).[1] We thus know others as separate, as different, as objects for evaluation, as a threat, or as a means to our ends; and the false knowing blocks a true loving. As we know other people better, will we love them more? Yes, perhaps, but their otherness remains. As we love them more, will we know them better? Yes, perhaps, if we truly love *them* and not our image of them; but that knowing will hurt, because they too are fallen. The love bred by knowledge may be tainted by a touch of superiority or a touch of satisfaction in the other's weakness because it makes one feel safe or needed or valuable. The knowledge bred by love may leave one feeling disillusioned or betrayed. At the least—and at love's best—there will be pain, for love cannot meet sin without suffering; and the more love seeks to abolish sin, the deeper the suffering will surely be (see Frost 1954, 247).

---

[1] We noted above that the Hebrew ידע means "know," both in cognitive and in sexual terms.

Community and Suffering

Fellowship, or interconnectedness, brings suffering, whether that suffering is over against, with, or for one's neighbor. The suffering that is *over against* one's neighbor, one feels simply for oneself, as one person makes an impact upon another through worldly channels corrupted by sin and demonic distortions. One is persecuted or misunderstood, hated or betrayed, cheated or injured or deserted or neglected. The usual result is a sense of intense aloneness, of isolation, even a desire to withdraw and remain alone in order not to be hurt again—or else a desire to retaliate.

The suffering that is *with* one's neighbor comes when two or more are struck by the same tragedy or persecution or injustice, or when one deeply sympathizes or empathizes with another. This type of suffering creates solidarity, often against a common enemy. (If it does *not* create solidarity, as perhaps in a famine, what starts as suffering alongside but not with another quickly turns into competition.)

The suffering that is *for* one's neighbor is that which one can spare him by taking it upon oneself. A soldier throws himself on a grenade to save his company or a child gives her only coat to another who is cold or a father gives his own meal to a hungry child. In these cases one freely sacrifices oneself to reduce someone else's pain: one cannot make it vanish, but one can deflect the pain to oneself.

Unlike the suffering inflicted upon one, suffering with and for others is not inevitable. "You can hold yourself back from the sufferings of the world, this is something you are free to do and is in accord with your nature, but perhaps precisely this holding back is the only suffering that you might be able to avoid" (Laing 1969, 82, quoting Kafka). The loss of fellowship causes even more pain than does the suffering fellowship always entails. The more we hurt, the less we are willing to be hurt; but the imagined cure of withdrawal—or the release of revenge—is far worse than the disease. Here, as is so often the case, the natural, self-protective response breeds misery: evil spawns evil, just as power provokes power.

Let us engage in no sophistry: suffering is evil. In the writings of Paul, we find no clear source of suffering other than evil, despite all he says about God using suffering for good (Frost 1954, 214). Even in Hebrews and Revelation, the suffering counted as chastening was generally due to persecution. In any event, the *need* for chastening can hardly be counted desirable. We may affirm that any purpose of God lies *beyond* suffering, not in it. However, as in the face of temptation and other evils, we are fighting an adversary and not just learning self-discipline, so we should not expect the intensity of the battle to lessen. Suffering is evil—and suffering is inevitable. We will be struck, if not as a result of our sin, then because of our fellows'; and the more we avoid the former, perhaps the more we become a dartboard for the Enemy's target practice. Where either sin or suffering crosses the line to direct demonic influence is unclear (Mallory 1976), but in any event both are of Satan's design. What, then, can we do, besides become masochists and thereby affirm the Devil's destructive system? Or bat our brains against the inexplicability of good Omnipotence and evil actuality? ("If God is God He is not good, / If God is good He is not God; / Take the even, take the odd. . . ." [MacLeish 1956, 14].)

At least, as we considered in chapter 10, we can do our best by repentance and grace to avoid contributing to evil. Perhaps we may even bolster our spirits a bit by persuading ourselves that we cannot do without suffering. After all, suffering can bring out amazing qualities of courage and depth and compassion in persons; and as Mark Twain said, "The weakest of all weak things is a virtue which has not been tested in the fire" (quoted in Kehl 1976, 131). In a yet harsher vein, Nietzsche said, "I estimate the *power of a will* according to how much resistance, pain, and torture it endures and knows how to transform to its own advantage" (quoted in May 1972, 144–45). Suffering can be approached as something to conquer and use. That tactic, however, would appear to produce titanic pride rather than compassion and hence end up by increasing the amount of evil and suffering in the world. "Perhaps the demonic is present wherever power is exalted over compassion" (Nugent 1971, 75). In any case, suffering can teach and correct us. Furthermore, it may do wonders, as we suggested, to bind a group of persons together.

On the face of it, however, glorifying suffering does not do much to reduce it. At best, it enables us to cope a bit better and may help us to respond with less anger and bitterness. At worst, it reduces motivation to work against suffering, cheapens others' pain in our eyes, and breeds hardness instead of compassion. Now we would certainly agree that, when we experience suffering, we ought, while combating it, yet allow it to produce what fruit it can in our lives in terms of patience and courage and the like; and we should beware of allowing it to break off our fellowship with God and our neighbors. But what are we to do about our neighbors' suffering?

The two paths that we most generally advocate and follow are surely far from useless. First, some immediate comfort may be derived from another's sympathy and care. Furthermore, one who denies another his sympathy and practical care removes himself from fellowship and reduces his own humanity proportionate to the degree of that withdrawal. If suffering was simply natural, compassionate attempts to heal and restore the injured would be the only constructive course open to us. The question is frequently raised with regard to the Good

Samaritan, however (the paradigm for this sort of response), of how many times one picks up the injured off the road without dealing with the violence that has left them lying there. So, second, we insist that we must work for righteousness and justice on a larger scale rather than only engage in acts of mercy. (It is very much to the point in this connection that the judgment of the sheep and goats in Matt. 25 refers to *nations,* not just individuals; and in Revelation likewise, it is nations that are smitten, deceived, or healed.) Suffering often has corporate determinants with which we must deal.

Scripture insists upon corporate responsibility and justice. The question is how to approach such goals without perpetuating more evil—perhaps evil lesser in quantity, but evil nonetheless, as when we take one person's life to protect the lives of others. To refuse to do some evil in such instances is to put one's own technical purity ahead of one's love for one's neighbor, a bad bargain. In fact, the Devil really wins much more by our choice to be righteous on our own terms, for that choice not only lets Satan's destructiveness run rampant but, like withdrawal instead of sympathy, isolates us. Worse than just isolating us from our community, it isolates us from the God who has made clear that no one shall be righteous on one's own terms. The dilemma here is a truly dreadful one, Satan winning something either way. One is put in the position of having to become guilty—taking God's forgiveness on faith—in order to spare someone else.

It thus happens that what for the unbeliever is simply a pragmatic expedient becomes for the believer a sacrifice—which is as it should be. "Obedience to God implies to be given over to men; this is the foundation of the power to which the demons yield" (Schlier 1961, 44). The demons must yield not when power, or force (which is, after all, their own nature and tool), is used to overpower them and the expedient is considered good because of its effects; then their whole mode of being is justified and affirmed even as it is fought.[2] There is a subtle but infinitely great difference between that stance, which is directly or indirectly a means of self-preservation, and the love that makes one so given over to others that one will risk what to the good person is precious above all else, one's own goodness. The "good" person must become accursed and die—as indeed such a one always will, one way or another—for evil to be defeated, the defeat coming because love is greater than the terrors of evil. The risk lies in the fact that the line between love and mere self-willed pragmatism is finer than

---

[2] I certainly do not speak against exorcism here, which I conceive to be a function of Word and not a manifestation of Satan's means being used against him. We are not, at this point, talking about relating *directly* to demons at all but rather about combating their tactics as operative in human society.

fine, and the latter has no power over evil but carves it into one's own soul.

Thus the path we start on when we recognize that some evil must be done to curb evil forks almost imperceptibly a mere step from its beginning. Make no mistake: one or the other of the branches must be followed if sheer anarchy is to be avoided; and insofar as that accomplishment is the only goal, both branches lead to the same place. Evil is restrained. Only one branch makes inroads on it, though—the branch that causes the traveler pain.

Causes the traveler *pain?* Are we not interested in reducing, not increasing, suffering? Indeed we are. But if the source of suffering is the Enemy, it can be ultimately reduced only as he is defeated; and he is defeated only by the willingness of a Man, and henceforth of others through him, to do what is incomprehensible to any self-willed being: to give up one's own good for another's. "The enemy is powerless against this sacrifice, for he has no foothold or support in it for his self-willed nature" (Schlier 1961, 62).

> Here we have the witness, not only of great Christian thinkers and mystics but of myriads of simple Christian men and women, that that particular form of evil which we know as pain, both mental and physical, can, if it is offered to God by the sufferer in union with the suffering and death of Christ, be *used* as a positive means for the destruction of evil itself. Indeed, such is the coinherence of the human race and the Church in Christ that it would seem that the final triumph of God over evil, in which will be fulfilled the prophet's words "He shall look upon the travail of his soul and be satisfied," will include among the means by which it has been brought about the redemptive sufferings of Christ's members. (Mascall 1966, 155; see Col. 1:24)

The final way of dealing with suffering is therefore the only one that eventually defeats it: the paradoxical one of voluntarily taking it upon oneself—not, surely, as if doing so would make one good or strong or more acceptable to oneself or others or God, but only and always to spare someone else or enable that other one to be righteous (2 Cor. 13:5–9).[3] And only by so letting go of self-interest does one become

---

[3] Laubach (1958, 51) wrote, after a personal experience of pain that yet brought renewal, " 'God, how can we reconcile this need of pain with our effort to abolish all misery?' The answer seemed convincing to me. 'If you abolish the physical suffering of the world, there will still be disappointed love, yearnings which cannot be satisfied, which will leave hearts bleeding even as they do today. Mansions have as many burning hearts as do poorhouses. The things which drag men down to grossness and incessant selfishness must be wiped out. Then hearts will become sore over infinitely larger things than selfish needs. They will learn to bleed for a world with the heart of Jesus.' There will be more suffering than today, for only love knows how to suffer divinely. But the meanness of suffering for one's selfish disappointments will be gone, and we will see a magnificence and sublimity in suffering that will make us glad."

truly free, free precisely of that bondage to self that is the final and most deceptive form of slavery. Such freedom is redemptive for *others,* though, because of the coinherence of the human race and of the church in Christ (see chapter 3), because in mysterious as well as obvious ways we can suffer others' pain—if we will to do so. There is nothing automatic about it: accidental, incidental, unavoidable suffering, though sure to come, profits nothing for another's healing until freely accepted and offered to God.[4]

How does redemptive suffering work? We do not know, except on the obvious level where one gives up a coat or a meal. Indications of the reality of substitutionary interconnectedness appear on somewhat less blatant planes, however. Dionysius of Alexandria, in the early days of the Christian church, speaking of healings, said that "many who had thus cured others of their sicknesses, and restored them to strength, died themselves, having transferred to their own bodies the death that lay upon these" (quoted in Frost 1954, 109), and it is said that today as well, healers not uncommonly take on the pain of their patients (Moss 1974).[5] Who knows how far the principle may extend? Insofar as we are part of one body, by that very relatedness we do all suffer or rejoice together (1 Cor. 12:26), but the requirement goes deeper. The first thing Paul was told after his conversion was how much he would have to suffer for the name of Christ (Acts 9:16); and he later writes of suffering as a requirement for those who would be heirs of Christ (Rom. 8:17; Phil. 1:29). These statements are understandable enough, if unpalatable, where persecution was to be expected; but in the light of 2 Corinthians 1:5–7, they perhaps have a broader application:

> For as we share abundantly in Christ's sufferings, so through Christ we share abundantly in comfort too. *If we are afflicted, it is for your comfort and salvation;* and if we are comforted, it is for your comfort, which you experience when you patiently endure the same sufferings that we suffer. Our hope for you is unshaken; for we know that as you share in our sufferings, you will also share in our comfort. (Emphasis added)

And the letter to the Hebrews (11:39–40), speaking of the saints of old and hence extending the principle of fellowship in time, says, "And all these, though well attested by their faith, did not receive what was

---

[4] There may be a vital exception to this generalization (that for suffering to be used redemptively, it must freely and voluntarily be offered to God) in the suffering of the truly innocent, as of children, decried unforgettably by Dostoevsky (1923). Perhaps innocent suffering is as a rule used by God for good?

[5] Note particularly the occasion when Jesus said that he felt energy go out of him when another was healed (Mark 5:30). Interestingly, studies through Kirlian photography of healers generally show the healer's corona to be smaller after treatment and the patient's larger; but the energy may also go the other way. In one such case, a healer whose gift was originally identified by a fortuneteller had the energy go the wrong way once when he was engaged in healing for a television program and enjoying publicity and profit (Moss 1974).

promised, since God had foreseen something better for us, that apart from us they should not be made perfect."

Three vital questions arise when we consider our interrelatedness and the possibility of substitutionary suffering. First, is the church today so impotent to heal because it is unwilling to pay to the full the cost of discipleship (see Frost 1954, 202)? Second, if we actually can bear one another's burdens (Gal. 6:2), how much choice do we have as to which ones we pick up, and how do we do it when the burden is not a physical need or task? Third, may we say that all undeserved suffering has potential (or actual?) meaning and redemptive possibilities in the larger scheme of things when freely accepted—perhaps even, in some unknown way, a meaning that may serve those who have gone before us as well as those currently alive or those to live in the future?[6]

[6]For a most challenging treatment of this entire theme, see Charles Williams's theological novel *Descent into Hell* (1949), especially chap. 6, from which the following extended dialogue is excerpted.

"Haven't you heard it said that we ought to bear one another's burdens?"

"But that means—" she began, and stopped.

"I know," Stanhope said. "It means listening sympathetically, and thinking unselfishly, and being anxious about, and so on. Well, I don't say a word against all that; no doubt it helps. But I think when Christ or St. Paul, or whoever said *bear,* or whatever he Aramaically said instead of *bear,* he meant something much more like carrying a parcel instead of someone else. To bear a burden is precisely to carry it instead of. If you're still carrying yours, I'm not carrying it for you—however sympathetic I may be. . . . If you give a weight to me, you can't be carrying it yourself; all I'm asking you to do is to notice that blazing truth. It doesn't sound very difficult."

"And if I could," she said. "If I could do—whatever it is you mean, would I? Would I push my burden on to anybody else?"

"Not if you insist on making a universe for yourself," he answered. "If you want to disobey and refuse the laws that are common to us all, if you want to live in pride and division and anger, you can. But if you will be part of the best of us, then you must be content to be helped. You must give your burden to someone else, and you must carry someone else's burden. I haven't made the universe and it isn't my fault. But I'm sure that this is a law of the universe, and not to give up your parcel is as much to rebel as not to carry another's. You'll find it quite easy if you let yourself do it."

"And what of my self-respect?" she said.

He laughed at her with a tender mockery. "O, if we are of that kind!" he exclaimed. "If you want to respect yourself, if to respect yourself you must go clean against the nature of things, if you must refuse the Omnipotence in order to respect yourself, though why you should want so extremely to respect yourself is more than I can guess, why, go on and respect. Must I apologize for suggesting anything else?" (Pp. 98–99)

Williams is clearly going at the matter from the opposite direction, that of our willingness to be helped rather than to help; but that approach may give a part of the answer to the question of what a helper may pick up. In a profound sense we are privileged and honored to be allowed to suffer for another: the letting go and receiving help is often harder than the picking up and giving help. Even letting go is less difficult, though, when it is understood that everyone must both relinquish and bear for others. Furthermore, suffering for others within a larger purpose—or even the realization that there is a larger purpose that, whether or not one sees it, one's suffering genuinely *serves*—makes that which one experiences bearable in a way that isolated pain is not. Frankl (1963, xi) is fond of quoting Nietzsche to the effect that "he who has a *why* to live can bear with

The questions are rhetorical, yet at the same time they cry for some sort of practical response. The first has something to do with unreserved commitment to one another and to Jesus Christ, without regard to the cost; and the precise cost cannot be fully known—beyond the stark fact that the cost is one's life and all that one has (Luke 14:25–33)—because the command is simply to follow, without a designation as to where. The second involves less a heroic and self-congratulatory rescue mission that garners burdens "worthy" or "large enough" to be lifted than a willingness to serve in however inglorious or seemingly unnecessary ways. It also involves a willingness to stop playing hero in our own problems, to put down the packages that keep our own hands and minds occupied and to entrust them to another's faithfulness; else we are not free to serve. Both of these aspects may be suggested in Galatians 6:3, the response, one might suppose, to cavils raised about sharing burdens: "For if any one thinks he is something, when he is nothing, he deceives himself."[7] Here we choose both to give and to receive. The third question says something about our response to suffering that we do not choose and yet must face. It concerns freely, honestly, and without resentment or hostility offering it to God to be used in his larger purpose, in the assurance that, by so doing, someone, somewhere, sometime, and in a way known only to God, is spared.

Might not the end of these paths be a new vitality and strength for objective healing as well as a subjective freedom and an improved attitude? If we do not know, is it not because we have not tried? I suggest that the problem lies not in intellectual quibbles about how it could be possible that such a commitment or procedure or trust could work; those are a smoke screen hiding our deep, proud, selfish, and very, very frightened reluctance to commit, obey, and trust. Perhaps the means of becoming part of this intricate network of exchange and faith

almost any *how*." The suffering may be made *more* than just bearable, however. I think particularly of an individual known to me who raged for years against a situation that was seemingly purely arbitrary and surely unjust. Then in a moment of time it was revealed to this Christian—who was not inclined to idealize suffering or to rationalize or justify it—that, far from being a little personal tragedy, the struggle was indeed a cosmic one, of which that individual's pain was but a part. (Cf. 2 Kings 6:15–17 and also Mascall 1966, 129: "Scripture, tradition, and Christian experience combine in assuring us that the struggle against evil with which Christians on earth are concerned can be seen in its true proportions only against the background of a vaster and more mysterious conflict in the unseen world in which they too are caught up.") Healed of an agony of bitterness and self-punitive guilt, my acquaintance said again and again, with awe, that all the suffering was turned to glory. Most of us, having no vision of mutuality or of glory, are left to rage alone and nurse our hurt.

[7] Verse 5, "For each man will have to bear his own load" ($\phi o \rho \tau i o \nu$ rather than $\beta \alpha \rho o \varsigma$), has been taken by some commentators to refer to that which one person is capable of carrying by himself. However, the words do not normally differ sharply in meaning. In any case, we must take care not to presuppose that everyone can carry packages of the same size and shape that we can. If they could, trading might not help much.

and love is shown us in the exact proportion that we really want to know. And that is why most of us know so little.

* * *

Stranger: I don't understand a thing you are talking about.

Inquirer: I thought not.

Stranger: It's absurd. It's nonsense. Pure and simple nonsense.

Inquirer: Yes. I wish that we—that I—could be that foolish and pure and simple.

Stranger: You arrived at the first long ago. The only way to deal with suffering is to lessen one's own first.

Inquirer: That doesn't work very well; and it's you who argued that only what works, counts.

Stranger: Then you need to find out how to make it work. Except for the rare instance in which someone blows himself to smithereens on a grenade, a person's suffering and dying never saved anyone.

Inquirer: I disagree.

Stranger: Those sorts of people just make the living feel guilty—a cheap, post-mortem revenge. Masochists are sadists at heart. In fact, I think you want to make people feel guilty. But don't think that sort of stunt will work with me. I know better.

Inquirer: Or worse. You're right about the problem of guilt, though. We are all guilty. But we can be forgiven, if we will receive forgiveness. Moreover, if we want to learn how to heal, we need to learn not only how to suffer but also how to forgive.

Stranger: What! You'd sacrifice not only your own rights but the whole system of justice! Since the very beginning, I have upheld the law. Those who do wrong must be punished, and I'll do everything I can to see that it happens.

* * *

FORGIVENESS

Forgiveness and Righteousness

A genuine desire to relieve others of suffering and an ability to forgive go hand in hand, for there seems to be a law of sorts that, to will good for another wholeheartedly, one cannot at the same time be harboring any malice in one's heart. Indeed, the verse preceding the one about bearing one another's burdens reads, "Brethren, if a man is overtaken in any trespass, you who are spiritual should restore him in a spirit of gentleness. Look to yourself, lest you too be tempted" (Gal. 6:1). The idea is to help the fallen one by lifting what is too heavy for him, not to kick him because he is down and really should have been stronger. Perhaps he should have been, but he will not be strengthened by groveling in the mud. If one wants a child to be taller, she has to feed her, not tell her that she will have to stand in a corner and grow before she may have any dinner. Similarly, forgiveness appears to be a condition for growth: it must be offered or received before change will take place—either in the one who has offended or in the injured party.[8] And only through forgiveness can there be a true unity in a fellowship, without its being dissipated by "keeping score" on personal grievances.

It is a commonplace, affirmed (usually all too unthinkingly) every time we repeat the Lord's Prayer, that we are to request and expect no more forgiveness than we offer others. If someone was seeking pragmatic reasons for offering it (if it is possible to forgive from the heart for pragmatic, selfish reasons alone, which I doubt, since the heart attitudes of forgiveness and selfishness are opposite),[9] then that one should surely suffice. However, that reason is not the only one. The Bible strikingly associates forgiving others and being forgiven by God with extraordinary power in prayer: "Whatever you ask in prayer, believe that you have received it, and it will be yours. And *whenever you stand praying, forgive, if you have anything against any one*" (Mark 11:24–25; emphasis added).[10] The usual desire of our tit-for-tat hearts is not that our neighbor get mercy but that she get justice. Therefore God's infusion of life is denied us as well, and our prayers do not move mountains or even climb them; rather they are buried under a mound of

[8]It would be possible to argue, on the basis of Luke 17:3, that actual forgiveness by the injured party (though not the willingness to forgive) is contingent upon repentance by the guilty. However, the huge majority of Scriptures commanding us to forgive do *not* mention any preconditions for our act. I suggest that the process is *complete* only when the repentant sinner accepts forgiveness but that the injured party's relinquishing of all ill will is by no means meaningless in itself but is, indeed, required. I discuss below the issue of conviction of sin as a precondition of repentance.

[9]See also Williams ([1942] 1984, 52–53): "The first temptation of Forgiveness then is to procure, through its own operation, some immediate comfort. . . . Yet any haste after this comfort is apt to destroy the whole act of forgiveness. It may often be easier for us to forgive than not—easier because more comfortable; nor is it always wrong to do so. . . . But to pretend to forgive *for the sake of one's own comfort* is nonsense" (emphasis added).

[10]See Luke 17:4–6; Marshall 1974; chap. 3. Note also Job 42:10: "And the LORD restored the fortunes of Job, *when he had prayed for his friends*" (emphasis added). Under the circumstances, prayer for his friends could be no less than an act of forgiveness and good will of rather amazing proportions, especially when done before any restoration had taken place.

judgment. The good things, such as healing, that we would ask lie crushed under the rocks hurled at others.

The need for healing arises from sin and the activity of the Evil One. To have strength to heal, we must be forgiven, so that God's strength flows through us. To be forgiven, we must forgive the wrongs that have been done to us. To forgive wrongs done to us is to refuse Satan the foothold he gains when we harbor ill will in our hearts (2 Cor. 2:10–11). Thus, coming a long way around (but the only and therefore the shortest way), evil must be defeated within before it can be dealt with without. While in no way downplaying the truth of vicarious suffering, we must not lightly assume that our impotence to relieve suffering arises from some disinclination on God's part rather than from our sin and unforgiving spirits (see Frost 1954). Again and again we must remind ourselves that evil can be overcome only by good, not by more evil.

> If one man injures another, there are three ways in which evil can win a victory and only one in which it can be defeated. If the injured person retaliates, or nurses a grievance, or takes it out on a third person, the evil is perpetuated and is therefore victorious. Evil is defeated only if the injured person absorbs the evil and refuses to allow it to go any farther. (Caird 1956, 98)

One cannot absorb without forgiving, lest one's own spirit be poisoned. Forgiveness is the only remedy for the suffering that would set one over against her neighbors.

Clearly enough, forgiveness involves a change of attitude on the part of the injured party, a change that is doubtless psychologically healthy for her, whatever else it may do in opening up new possibilities in prayer. It enables her to let go of the past and focus her energies constructively.[11] When sincere and when received, forgiveness reopens the possibility for right relationships between the persons involved. Maybe, however, it does still more: "If you forgive the sins of any, they are forgiven; if you retain the sins of any, they are retained" (John 20:23). "Whatever you bind on earth shall be bound in heaven, and whatever you loose on earth shall be loosed in heaven" (Matt. 18:18; cf. 1 Cor. 5:3–5). These verses are spoken quite specifically of the church. We have in view the activity of the Holy Spirit, who is the bond uniting believers, assuring that ultimate forgiveness or retention of sin is an act of God rather than of persons. Still, a dreadful solemnity attends the thought that the church's actions may have eternal consequences, even if any individual would presume far too much if she believed that the

---

[11]This observation provides a major theme for Smedes's *Forgive and Forget* (1984). I accept the observation but agree with Williams (see n. 9) that personal gain is inadequate as a *motive* for true forgiveness.

grace or malice in her own heart could determine the fate of another's soul. We perhaps presume far too little about our interrelatedness, however, if we believe our heart attitudes are a strictly private matter having no impact on others.

The more individual, temporal analogue to the forgiveness or retention of sin in heaven may be blessing and cursing, whereby another's life here and now is affected by our good will or ill will. We are commanded to bless and curse not (Rom. 12:14): could it be that personal refusals to forgive are in effect curses that make an impact on others? At the very least, such refusals are judgments, and judging has clearly been forbidden us (Matt. 7:1; Rom. 2:1; 14:10; James 4:11–12).[12] By holding on to a judgment, we may not only freeze a person into a particular way of acting but also bind her by our interpretation of it—whether the interpretation is right or wrong. To forgive (in the human sense) is not to validate a person's actions but to let loose of our judgment of them and her. Perhaps the act of forgiveness in our own hearts, before or (if circumstances necessitate) even without the other's ever knowing that she has been forgiven, may thus have a cosmic resonance that provides an entirely new possibility, a new freedom, for her who has done wrong but has had no strength or perhaps no inclination to do otherwise.

We need not worry about undercutting righteousness by forgiving before we have evidence of another's repentance, as if God's law were protected only by our enforcing of it. "Enforcement," as a matter of the simple evidence of experience, does not write the law on anyone's heart, the only place it can do any good. As pastor Peter Marshall commented to his wife Catherine after many experiences of counseling persons in his church office, "Nothing—but nothing—is as difficult as for one human being ever to bring another person to the conviction of sin. Why, oh why do we ever try it?" (Marshall 1974, 37). Only the Holy Spirit can convict another of sin (John 16:8). If we are so very concerned about promoting righteousness, these words need to be emblazoned on our minds:

> The "doer of the law" has only one possible means of giving effect to the law, and that is by performing it himself. . . . It is only in this exclusive concentration upon one's own doing of the law, *without any other thought in mind,* that the law is given its due and is allowed to

---

[12] Altogether too regularly our difficulty in forgiving results from our need to guard *ourselves* from committing the very sins that we condemn in others. If we forgave certain wrongdoings, would we then lose control over our own impulses? This fear lies close to the heart of much of our most punishing behavior toward others. Also note scientist Ornstein's (1972, 153) serious consideration of the postulate that "blessing" can be a positive influence on another.

exercise its power also upon one's brother. (Bonhoeffer 1965, 44–45;
emphasis added)

If I speak in a sense of modeling, I do so with caution, for self-conscious modeling (letting the left hand know what the right hand is doing [Matt. 6:3]) is a form of unforgiving judgment and will be rejected as such.

Doing the law and forgiving are the only ways of giving the law effect—yet both of these are impossible of human achievement. Both are equally impossible because both demand a wholehearted love for God and neighbor, a complete trust in God's goodness and his ability to manifest it in our lives and the lives of others. Lest we cheapen them and make them a human possibility, it is perhaps not too much to affirm, "Pardon, . . . like love, is only ours for fun: essentially we don't and can't" (Williams 1949, 163). Such a comment says something about pardon (and love) that grates on our selfish souls. Its truth is shown by the way we recoil at the idea of pardon as "fun." Pardon, *fun*? When we have been hurt, should it give us joy—even that less sublime joy, *fun*— to forgive? Does pardon have a hint of warm, accepting laughter as well as a frightful solemnity? The first and freer mood is the harder for us to experience. Would it not be easier if we *really* wholeheartedly desired healing and good for the sinner and if we thought of pardon as the offering of a life-giving gift out of an abundant supply to which, after all, we have access strictly for the purpose of dispensing it? And would it not be easier if we were fully confident of God's intent and ability himself to restore, establish, and strengthen us (1 Peter 5:10)? The latter is the rub. It does not seem "fair" that the sinner should get off the hook so easily when we are still hurting—and all too likely cherishing the hurt. And in that mood, we would deign to be more just than God.

Unity and Healing

As long as we remain proud and judgmental, we block still another channel of God's power, beyond the forgiveness in our own lives that assures our prayers will be heard and answered and beyond the "permission" to change we may grant to others by releasing them from our condemnation. The third channel is the agreement, or "being of one mind," of the community, emphasized repeatedly by Paul as his great desire for the church (e.g., Rom. 12:16; 2 Cor. 13:11; Phil. 2:2; 4:2). Tellingly, being of one mind is particularly associated with humility and a desire of good for others. Members of a community with such a shared frame of mind are willing to absorb evil rather than return it or beat it off. In Peter's words, "Finally, all of you, have unity of spirit, sympathy, love of the brethren, a tender heart and a humble mind. Do not return evil for evil or reviling for reviling; but on the contrary bless, for to this you have been called, that you may obtain a blessing" (1 Peter 3:8–9).[13]

As long as persons are concentrating upon their rights and others' wrongs, as long as the tenor of a group is that of jockeying for position and earning status (whether the status is granted for "virtue" or for power or for a pleasing personality), harmony is destroyed, as if each piece in an orchestra were trying to play so loudly as to assure being heard. (In terms of this illustration, note that "being oneself" with excessive enthusiasm—even if perfectly on key—is harmful, almost if not quite as much as if cymbals were trying to take the part of a flute.) The natural reaction when one individual increases his volume is for everyone else to respond in kind, or else to respond in anger; and immediately there are competition and a loss of love. The explicit intent to forgive and restore is crucial to the maintenance of unity, particularly if it is necessary to correct one who errs (Matt. 18:15–17; Gal. 6:1).

The issue here is the necessity of unity for the church to have power to heal. In the early church, Lactantius noted that Christians sometimes failed at exorcism when there was discord among them; Cyprian noted the same for the healing of physical disease. Tertullian once asked rhetorically, "Then must the devil be understood to be stronger for injuring man, ruining him wholly? and must God have the character of comparative weakness, since He does not relieve man in his entire estate?" (Frost 1954, 92). We should not expect the complete annihilation of pain "before the time," but neither should we blithely assume that a specific instance of pain is inevitable and something about which nothing can be done, thereby exonerating the community from its ineffective ministry. The community no longer needs to look to its sinfulness and lack of accord if it assumes that remedying them would make no difference. Scripture speaks differently: "Again I say to you, if two of you *agree* on earth about anything they ask, it will be done for them by my Father in heaven" (Matt. 18:19; emphasis added).

Is this affirmation unrealistically easy? Perhaps it would be more difficult if we punctuated the Greek a bit differently and translated, "If two of you agree on earth about all things, whatsoever they ask will be done for them."[14] And of course the context of gathering in Christ's name (Matt. 18:20) is crucial. Perhaps the truth of the passage lies in the

---

[13] Cf. Paul (Rom. 12:14–17, 19), using words close to those of Jesus in the Gospels (see Matt. 5:44): "Bless those who persecute you; bless and do not curse them. Rejoice with those who rejoice, weep with those who weep. Live in harmony with one another; do not be haughty, but associate with the lowly; never be conceited. Repay no one evil for evil, but take thought for what is noble in the sight of all. . . . Beloved, never avenge yourselves, but leave it to the wrath of God; for it is written, 'Vengeance is mine, I will repay, says the Lord.'"

[14] The Greek text (unpunctuated) reads, εαν δυο συμφωνησωσιν εξ υμων επι της γης περι παντος πραγματος ου εαν αιτησωνται γενησεται αυτοις.

fact that we can get our wills fully together only by our wills becoming one with the will of Christ. Then indeed this perfect unity, even of two or three, may open the door to untold possibilities.

Maybe it is only and precisely in such a context that the church may claim the promise of James 5:14–16:

> Is any among you sick? Let him call for the elders of the church, and let them pray over him, anointing him with oil in the name of the Lord; and the prayer of faith will save the sick man, and the Lord will raise him up; and if he has committed sins, he will be forgiven. *Therefore* confess your sins to one another, and pray for one another, that you may be healed. (Emphasis added)

Note the curious relationship of sin and sickness here: there is no assumption whatever (as is also true in John 9:3) that a given sickness should be attributed to sin, though physical healing and forgiveness may be associated. However, mutual confession and the unity of prayer are counted the conditions for healing, as if healing will not take place as long as evil is granted a place in one's life and manages to isolate one from others. Healing concerns not just mending an individual's body but mending the body of Christ.[15] The weakness and disruption of the latter makes it impotent against disruption of the former. When one member of the body suffers, all members suffer together (1 Cor. 12:26); but when disunity, isolation, judgment, and discord break down this mutuality, no means of relieving the suffering remains. If one has a small cut on his finger and one's whole body, in one accord, mobilizes its resources, giving up whatever degree of energy necessary and sending it to reconstruct the injured tissue, healing will be rapid and relatively painless. Alternatively, the rest of the body could refuse its support on the assumption that, after all, each part has just enough to sustain itself in the style to which it is accustomed. That pesky injured finger is an insult to the body's health and efficiency and should be treated accordingly. Gangrene results, necessitating amputation: the offending member is dispensed with, but the whole body is maimed.

Whether suffering is simply physical or related to a specific sin, there is no way of rightly dealing with it except through a body brought together in restoring, forgiving love. This sort of healing and uniting is precisely the work of the Holy Spirit, who brings wills and structures into conformity with God through teaching, comforting, giving power to witness, and promoting maintenance of unity in the bond of peace. All

[15] "The righteousness of the Christian is never a mere sinlessness, relieved from all blemishes. It is not a thing pure and apart, but is a center of confidence, a direction of aspiration, a basic character of charity, lived within the framework of common liabilities" (Frye 1960, 104). The very commonness of the liabilities both enables and necessitates a loving, forgiving community.

of these activities are the opposite of the disintegrating, disorganizing, separating works of Satan, who lies and deceives, tempts and accuses, murders and depersonalizes. Wholeness cannot exist on a merely individual level. Wholeness always entails *reunion* as well as repair. And reunion means a fellowship willing to suffer, a forgiveness eager for unity.

Reunion is fellowship and suffering, forgiveness and agreement: a new body, over against all destruction and disruption.

12

A Paradoxical Way:

Prayer and Praise—Rejoicing

Stranger: Impossible.

Inquirer: What's impossible?

Stranger: You—and everything you're unloading on people. What you are demanding is unnatural. To suffer voluntarily and forgive unilaterally is absurd—inhuman. And to propose it is inhumane. People can't do it—and won't try, if they have any sense. Impossible. Absolutely unrealistic.

Inquirer: Yes; that's why it's so important. What is "natural" and "realistic" simply won't suffice. To be "realistic" is to labor and despair and die. It is to know that, naturally, "what is crooked cannot be made straight, and what is lacking cannot be numbered" (Eccl. 1:15).

> Vanity of vanities! All is vanity.
> What does man gain by all the toil
>   at which he toils under the sun?
> A generation goes, and a generation comes,
>   but the earth remains for ever.
> The sun rises and the sun goes down,
>   and hastens to the place where it rises.
> The wind blows to the south,
>   and goes round to the north;
> round and round goes the wind,
>   and on its circuits the wind returns.
> All streams run to the sea,
>   but the sea is not full;
> to the place where the streams flow,
>   there they flow again.
> All things are full of weariness;
>   a man cannot utter it;
> the eye is not satisfied with seeing,
>   nor the ear filled with hearing.

What has been is what will be,
and what has been done is what will be done;
and there is nothing new under the sun.
(Eccl. 1:2–9)

Stranger: Why stop there? I can quote Scripture too: "The fate of the sons of men and the fate of beasts is the same; as one dies, so dies the other. . . . Who knows whether the spirit of man goes upward and the spirit of the beast goes down to the earth?" (Eccl. 3:19–21). *You* don't. The law of gravity biases the odds against *anything* going up— as if there were any difference between up and down in the universe. It's all relative.

Inquirer: Actually, I prefer joy to gravity.

Stranger: What does that have to do with anything? *I* prefer gravity. Providing for my welfare is an extremely serious, down-to-earth business. It leaves very little time for flights of fancy and silly good humor. I find laughter nauseating.

Inquirer: And you're right that, by looking at the world, we deduce, what goes up, comes down. That's what I said in the first place. Being "realistic" is depressing—and thoroughly unnecessary, as I said not too long ago.

Stranger: That is absurd. You can't deny my—I mean, the whole natural order of things.

Inquirer: Quite true. I'm part of it and can't jump out of it. The Preacher knew that; and yet after his whole discourse on futility, he said, "Fear God, and keep his commandments; for this is the whole duty of man" (Eccl. 12:13). He seemed to think that that focus, doing everything with reference to God, makes a difference.

* * *

The crooked shall be made straight,
and the rough ways shall be made smooth;
and all flesh shall see the salvation of God.
(Luke 3:5–6)

This is the day which the LORD has made;
let us rejoice and be glad in it.
(Ps. 118:24)

PRAYER

Both of the last two chapters dealt with the impossible possibilities open to the children of God. Both were specifically aimed at discussing ways of defeating evil. Chapter 10 dealt with the individual and the construct "power," saying that the Enemy in his nature as power and as deceiver can be defeated only by God's Word as an alternative to force and falsehood and by human weakness as a denial of the ultimacy of this world's means. Evil perishes when we refuse to seek our own advantage by doing evil and refuse to give evil ultimate status by defining "the way things are" as simply necessary. Chapter 11 dealt with the community and an aspect of the construct "structure," saying that the Enemy in his nature as destroyer and isolator is defeated by a profound interconnectedness in which pain is healed through the resources and vicarious suffering of others and in which one's own hurt is not nurtured but is released through forgiveness. Evil cannot propagate itself when borne or absorbed. This chapter deals with the relating of everything in one's experience to God and the construct "will" and argues that the Enemy in his nature as liar and promoter of confusion, doubt, and misery can be defeated through a simple, single-minded, obedient focus of the will on God. This defeat occurs, not because of anything that will alone can do, but because of God's ability to transform evil to good.

Singleness of Mind

We have come full circle. We began by considering attention, intention, and focus as rather mysterious determinants of human acting and being, and on the same theme we shall close. Now, however, we are obviously going beyond scientific or philosophical epistemology in the narrower sense, for we shall speak about the paradoxical possibility of focusing not on the seen but on the unseen. And we shall point toward a confident, certain, unwavering focus that is pure and childlike and obedient. Not a Sunday school teacher but a great scientist said, "Whoever loses his simplicity becomes uncertain in the impulses of his spirit. Uncertainty in the impulses of the spirit is something that is incompatible with truth" (Heisenberg, quoted in May 1972, 62). Is this statement true because the impulses of the spirit, manifested in our will, are precisely spiritual and because spiritual truth is single?

No uncertainty attends the wisdom that comes from God (see James 3:14–17).[1] Uncertainty comes from the bulwarks of the enemy that are established in our hearts, bulwarks of doubt and false sophistication. With their protection we scornfully decry simplicity as a naive and

---

[1]Obviously, it does not follow that all one's felt certainties therefore come from God. If felt certainty were the criterion of truth, our attention would immediately be drawn away from God and toward our subjective state of mind—virtually always an unhelpful switch.

reprehensible failure to take seriously the complexity of any situation. Doubt and sophistication say that God of course could not or would not do what he says he will do: if he would, why has he given us so many resources to employ on our own? Obviously, we should look to them and not to him. It would be presumptuous and indolent to ask from his hand the daily bread that we ought to earn on our own. Oiled by half a truth (that those who do not work shall not eat [2 Thess. 3:10]), the lie slides into place and turns our eyes from God.

But again, where—and how—we look has everything to do with our fate:

> The eye is the lamp of the body. So, if your eye is sound [ἁπλοῦς, "single, simple, sincere, or healthy with a connotation of generosity"], your whole body will be full of light; but if your eye is not sound [πονηρὸς, "evil"], your whole body will be full of darkness. If then the light in you is darkness, how great is the darkness! (Matt. 6:22–23; cf. Luke 11:34–36)

In context, this RSV translation appears poor. The passage deals with the impossibility of a dual focus, specifically of serving God and mammon (v. 24), and the alternative to choosing God is worse than a mere lack of soundness—it is evil. The complex of ideas that "soundness" entails, however, proves instructive. For oneself, it indeed means health. With regard to one's neighbor, it concerns the generosity that comes from not clinging to worldly goods (cf. vv. 19–21). And both of these stem from one's relating to God in absolute loyalty and trust (vv. 25–33), single, simple, and sincere. Anything else is darkness, with which light has no fellowship (2 Cor. 6:14; 1 John 1:5–7). The contrast represents the alternatives of Christ and Satan. And note that, corresponding to our understanding of spirit and will, the light or darkness comes from within as well as without. What we are reflects what we look at, and what we look at reflects what we are.[2]

It results that we get what we really want. If we want human praise or our own self-conscious self-righteousness, we may have it—and no more (Matt. 6:1–6). If we desire to satisfy our lusts and make the finite ultimate, we may—and we will be given up to the conduct we have chosen and our senseless minds will be darkened (Rom. 1:21–31). If we insist on relying upon rigid rules about what is "possible" in the natural order, we may look at the raging waters on which (by faith, at the expense of nature's rules) we stand, instead of looking to Jesus—and go

---

[2]This dialectic would appear to be related to the distressing saying, "To every one who has will more be given . . . but from him who has not, even what he has will be taken away" (Matt. 25:29). So too, at the end, "Let the evildoer still do evil, and the filthy still be filthy, and the righteous still do right, and the holy still be holy" (Rev. 22:11). More and more we become what we are. Light conquers darkness, but darkness can only weave its own shroud.

down (Matt. 14:29–30). If we would follow someone who, comfortingly to our egos, can see no further than we, we may—and fall into the same pit as he (Luke 6:39). Or knowing that those who are fully taught will be like their teacher (Luke 6:40), we may look to Christ, with the result that "we all, with unveiled face, beholding the glory of the Lord, are being changed into his likeness from one degree of glory to another" (2 Cor. 3:18). We will be like him when we see him as he is; only by being like him *can* we see him as he is (see 1 John 3:2). The light we look to is also the light that shines in our hearts "to give the light of the knowledge of the glory of God in the face of Christ" (2 Cor. 4:6).

The more the light puts out the darkness—the better we know God—the less we can know of evil; for nothing is really known, as we have seen, except in the doing of it. Satan will be crushed under our feet not when we have spied out all of his activities but when we are wise as to the good but guileless babes as to evil (Rom. 16:19–20; 1 Cor. 14:20; cf. Matt. 10:16; Phil. 2:15). More and more we must become pure in heart. And more and more we must become actively obedient, which is likewise the result of God's working in us and enabling us (Phil. 2:12–13; Heb. 13:21). Thus even obedience is not as much a matter of a strenuous effort on our part—though it does entail serious work—as a sort of compulsion or, better, permission from God, with bestowal of his resources (Heim 1953a, 193). Purity and obedience come naturally from walking in the light, as a joyful privilege more than a painful duty. If we want them, we shall have them; for the asker, seeker, and knocker will receive, find, and have doors opened before him (Luke 11:9–10).[3] And the door that God holds open no one can shut (Rev. 3:8).

Prayer and Relinquishment

It can hardly be an accident that the passages we have just noted on singleness of purpose and on simple, persistent, believing request (Matt. 6; Luke 11), which are so essential to our becoming who we are meant to be, are also central to Jesus' teaching on prayer. Indeed, the gospel writers place his giving of the Lord's Prayer in this context. Not that our goodness or the articulateness or sheer quantity of our prayer (Matt. 6:7–8) can be used to manipulate God; far from it. As long as we desire to manipulate God, we do not really trust him, for the desire to manipulate presupposes that we think we know more about what is good for us than he does—the same sort of imagining that overcame Adam and Eve. We may rail much (and with seeming good reason)

[3] Lest what is basically plain and simple be made to appear facile and quickly disproved, we should note that the context of the passage and verb tense of "ask," "seek," and "knock" may be read to imply persistent, continuous action. The promise is not made to the spiritual dilettante.

about unanswered prayers; yet if we were honest, would we not also thank God that many unwise requests go apparently unheeded?

The point, though, is that effective prayer (see James 5:16) rests upon one's being rightly related to God, which is the biblical meaning of "righteousness" (צדקה in the Old Testament, δικιοσύνη in the New Testament). Those who never even think to put their requests before God, who make them for selfish, lustful ends, or who are double-minded doubters are not rightly related to God and will not receive (James 1:5–8; 4:2–3; cf. Matt. 21:21–22; Mark 11:23; John 14:13–14; 16:23). We must reemphasize the fact that Scripture associates double-mindedness, uncertainty, and instability, not with laudable intellectual integrity that refrains from overly quick judgments, but with impurity of heart (James 4:8), which in turn interferes with prayer.[4] It is as if such impurity short-circuits the flow between God and us or makes us refuse to believe that God promises to open a real door or leads us to try to push open the door by ourselves. "Behold, I have set before you an open door, which no one is able to shut; I know that you have but little power, and yet you have kept my word and have not denied my name" (Rev. 3:8). Not power on our part but faithfulness slips the key into the lock.

We do not come by this faithfulness easily. When we think of means of healing mind and body, we normally concentrate on perfecting various methodologies (which we conveniently may conceive as in our control). We too often see "spiritual" approaches as last resorts, dubious means suited only to hopeless cases. Indeed, the more favored we are with valuable healing techniques, the more difficult we usually find it to trust wholly in God—as difficult as it is for the rich man to find security in following Christ instead of in the worldly goods he has worked so hard to gain. After all, might not we see God most easily in what he has given? We console ourselves with that thought as an excuse for expecting to find him only there; and so we, the educated and gifted, experiment and manipulate with far more faith and fervor—and certainly with higher expectations and more clarity of purpose—than we pray.

> But the simple seem to feel God as easily as the heat of the sun or the kindness of a friend. The prayer which is followed by organic effects is of a special nature. First, it is entirely disinterested. Man offers himself to God. He stands before Him like canvas before the painter or marble

---

[4] Also cf. the usage of ἀκαταστασία and ἀδιάκριτος in James 3:16–17 with the closely related words in 1:6, 8. "What we suffer from to-day is humility in the wrong place. Modesty has moved from the organ of ambition. Modesty has settled upon the organ of conviction; where it was never meant to be. A man was meant to be doubtful about himself, but undoubting about the truth; this has been exactly reversed" (Chesterton [1908] 1959, 31).

before the sculptor. At the same time, he asks for His grace, exposes his needs and those of his brothers in suffering. Generally the patient who is cured is not praying for himself. But for another. Such a type of prayer demands complete renunciation—that is, a higher form of asceticism. The modest, the ignorant, and the poor are more capable of this self-denial than the rich and the intellectual. When it possesses such characteristics, prayer may set in motion a strange phenomenon, the miracle. (Carrel 1935, 144)[5]

And so the door *is* opened to a whole new world. When met by miracle, suffering and evil become something quite other than they appear; they are the backdrop for the glorious works of God (John 9:3).

The great work of God is to overcome evil, and the great channel joining us with God in that work is faithful prayer. No wonder prayer is the indispensable condition for both healing and exorcism in the synoptic Gospels (see Michaels 1976, 50). No wonder it may guard even the faith of another person against the wavering that gives access to Satan (Luke 22:31–32). No wonder it is the crucial accompaniment of the armor that allows one to stand firm against the wiles of the Devil (Eph. 6:11). No wonder nature itself must yield to it (James 5:17–18). After all, are not all the structures of the natural order like sentences formed from God's Word? Surely God may handle the syntax—control and reorder natural events—as he chooses. Or rather, the impact of prayer is a very great and impenetrable wonder. Why should it matter to the omnipotent Deity whether paltry humans pray? If all of creation belongs unquestionably to him, why should we have anything to do with what his acts in it will be? It would seem to be quite enough that we be given our own little sphere of free activity within that created order. And of course, in a sense we may choose and have just that. But we may have much more, for no good reason except that God has chosen to enter history and our hearts. Because he has done so, it matters urgently that all of nature be "referred back" to the Creator so that his presence is rightly manifested. We do that referring back when we pray.

Through prayer we may give everything into the hand of God with the sure knowledge that both what we ask and the one for whom we ask it rightly belong to God. In so doing we affirm that neither the one nor the other *does* rightly belong to the great determinist, destroyer, and economist, who would persuade us that certain means are never

---

[5] See Frank 1974, 72. Note also the words of William Temple (quoted in Brown 1984, 220): "We only know what Matter is when Spirit dwells in it; we only know what Man is when God dwells in him. . . . We find that if a man is thus united to God, Nature is his servant, not his master, and he may (so the story tells us) walk upon the water. . . . The stubbornness of lifeless matter is no necessary quality of matter. The machine-like character of the Universe, with its rigid laws and uniformities, is given to it by our unspiritual way of handling it; to a man in whom God dwells everything is plastic that he may mould it to God's purpose."

circumvented, certain damages are "natural" or never repaired, and what is given up or away always brings scarcity, because there can be no more than what is already.[6] In the realm of the reasonable and the possible, the Devil may have a field day, for a God limited by them is no bigger than Satan.

To whatever we would keep clutched in our own grasp or insist upon defining in our own terms, the Devil has access; for any "I am" or "it is," spoken in anything but a derivative sense after the "I Am" and "let there be" of the Creator, is sheer usurpation. What we wrest out of the Creator's hand, he has allowed to be fair game for all comers; but what we place back in his hand can be touched only as he permits. He and he alone knows the precise shape he has planned for what he has fashioned. Only through him can it be anything but distorted or disintegrated, however shiny the surface polished by another's effort.

Really to pray, then, is really to stand against the destructive work of Satan, without at the same time insisting upon his or our definition of the situation. Then he is forced in spite of himself to serve God's ends, deprived at every point of his standing as a rival who may do as he pleases. But let there be no mistake. The Enemy has done his work well. With the ally he has in our hearts, betraying us to the power he manifests in the world, he has made even a mustard seed's worth of faith desperately rare. How, indeed, can there be a single, simple, pure focus of eye and life and prayer when the traitor within turns always toward the darkness? Yet even a tiny mustard seed is enough; the smallest ray of light annihilates all the darkness it touches and starts the cycle that will finally put it entirely to flight. All things are possible with God (Matt. 19:26).

Nothing is impossible. Faith as a grain of mustard seed can move a mountain—or banish a demon or heal the sick. Nothing is impossible to believing prayer. And anything can happen. There remains a tension between "ask, and you will receive" and "thy will be done." Believing prayer may give up its right to define too precisely what constitutes the best outcome.[7] A frightening thought? Only if it is doubted that he with

---

[6] "The Devil is sterile. I [says the Devil] possess the will to create (hence my pride), but I am incapable of creating (hence my envy). And with envy raised to such a power as immortal minds can feel, I hate the Creator and His Creation. My greatest masterpiece is never more than a perversion—an ingenious disordering of Another's grand design, a perversion of order into chaos, of life into death. . . . Nothing enduring, as every craftsman knows, can ever be created without love. But I am as incapable of love as I am of goodness" (Chambers 1948, 84).

[7] In fact, what constitutes the best outcome cannot always be determined in this life. If it could, and if we could reliably "achieve" it by prayer, prayer itself would become only another means to our ends. So instead of providing tidy intellectual or practical proofs of its temporal efficacy, God leaves prayer as an open opportunity for relationship with him. And thus he leaves us free in our own sphere. For the time being, in response to prayer, he gives us first and foremost himself, who can be enjoyed only by love and not through

whom we have to do purposes the best for us; only if it is thought that he, too, is the sort of economist who can act only at someone's—at our—expense. If we were to trust him fully, then releasing all into his hand could bring nothing but perfect peace.

* * *

Inquirer: I know, you're going to say that answers to prayer are just coincidence. I'm tired of that response. My friends have commented, and I've noticed, that the "coincidences" strangely stop happening when we stop praying.

Stranger: That's not fair. Precognition is *my* territory. You're trying to walk all over my territory. You don't want me to have any territory at all. You're selfish, that's what. But I'll *prove* to you it's mine. I'll let *you* have some. How about that? I'll bet there are lots of things in your life you'd like different, right? Everybody has things he'd like to change.

Inquirer: Well, uh . . .

Stranger: And you don't have to go through all that prayer rigmarole, cleaning up your life and all that. What a drag!

Inquirer: Well, uh, I never quite supposed *I* could clean up my life . . .

Stranger: Of course not. And the great news is that you don't have to. You know those little self-indulgences of yours? I don't mind them at all. I'd be happy to help you enjoy them more.

Inquirer: But I don't *like* enjoying them!

Stranger: More's the pity. I promise I can help you. You're terribly inhibited and conflicted, I know, but that needn't last. I can show you lots of pleasures you have maybe never even thought of.

Inquirer: But I don't *want* them!

Stranger: Oh, come now, how could you possibly say that, when you don't even know what you're missing? That legalism just has to go. You'd judge and reject me, when I'm only working for your satisfaction. Ungrateful prig. Oh, but pardon me. Back to the subject. Don't you remember how often those neighbors of yours eat steak? Wouldn't you like to have it instead?

externals (even though external acts of grace may follow). I do not mean to deny that a gift of faith may be given for a particular outcome—an assurance that what one is asking is indeed the will of God and will certainly be accomplished when received by faith. I take such a specific assurance as a sovereign act of God that is a declaration of his will and is to be contrasted with our laying out a blueprint for our own will.

Inquirer: No, not instead; at least, I don't want to want it instead.

Stranger: All right, have it your way; it would taste better instead, but you can have it alongside if you insist. And you could be president of your company, all the branches of it. You could make lots and lots of money (yes, even give a little of it to your favorite charity) and be the marvel of all your competitors because your risky deals—which are never more than ever-so-slightly shady—never fall through. How about it?

Inquirer: What? You can't do . . .

Stranger: Oh, but I can. I've done it for lots of my *other* friends. Let me give you a free demonstration—and I offer lifelong credit. No security but your good name. There are no better terms available anywhere.

Inquirer: But what if I'm *not* your friend?

Stranger: You can be. It's easy. I make new ones every day. You don't have to obey me or anything to be my friend, the way that other one demands (John 15:14). Just "do your own thing," as they say. You don't like the way your life is—nobody does. And I've got the very quickest way to make it different.

* * *

PRAISE

Evil and Praise

For most people, life is indeed, in myriad petty or tragic ways, painful, frustrating, and unsatisfactory. Whether it is attributable to their heredity or their environment, their character or their circumstances, or the way these factors have impinged upon loved ones, much in their lives they would change if only they could—but they cannot. Discontent is no respecter of persons. The small island off the coast of Florida where some of the wealthiest people in the nation have winter mansions is known locally as "suicide island." And who are we to say that these "privileged" ones ought not to feel as they do, just because all the obvious reasons for despair are not in evidence. Who are we to say that only certain kinds of pain are "real." Somehow we suppose that people who have ready access to all the world's resources are freer than those who do not; and surely we see their deaths by their own hands as more blameworthy than the similar death of a ghetto dweller or a patient with a terminal illness. And it may indeed take more of a certain kind of sheer courage to endure the latter situations than the former. Perhaps having "too much" does breed softness and an unwillingness to cope—but that tendency is another issue. In any case, the most powerful among us often fail to ward off despair.

Along with discontent and despair, tragedy respects no one's status in life. Here we somehow count it "more tragic" when someone with a "great future" ahead of him is struck down by accident or disease than when a slum dweller whose name no one but the local welfare agency will ever know suffers the same fate. We feel as if more is "wasted" in the one case than the other and count fate all the more cruel and arbitrary because of it. But is the loss less for the loved ones of the latter than the former? Hardly.

Suicides and unavoidable blows from outside of one are the extremes at which futility at the personal level comes into the sharpest focus.[8] Here we see it stark and unmasked, without the cloaking busyness and pressures that make daily futilities and annoyances seem necessary—or necessarily ignored. In the rush to get to tomorrow, we assume that things will be different then. But what if they are not? *Then* would one go on—and on and on—or go mad?

To speak in this way just after talking about the infinite power of God and the unlimited possibilities for his action when we are rightly related to him in prayer may seem strange in the extreme. I do not intend to deny my basic premise that we may fully trust God when we place everything in his hand. But despite my cautions against presuming too surely that we have what is good for us neatly and finally figured out when we pray, the fact remains that we tend to pray because we want something changed—even because, we hope, God himself wills that something be changed. Nothing whatever is wrong with such a petition; it is one major point of praying. We usually pray to ask God to act in one way or another (to heal, to direct, to provide, to forgive), and if God acts, things happen. If he has said that he will answer prayer, and if we believe it, is that not the end of the matter? Not quite. It is not that easy. There are implications to placing all in God's hand.

If we give everything securely into God's control—with no corners reserved for self-will or territory posted with No Trespassing signs behind which the Enemy lurks—it follows that we must thenceforward *receive* everything from his hand.[9] From nowhere else can it come. Shall

---

[8] In a world of mass starvation, oppression, torture, and terrorism, it may seem perverse to speak of any individual case as an extreme or even to spend time on the evils afflicting individuals. Evil in our world takes such monstrous forms and futility gets such a stranglehold on entire populations that it sometimes seems as if people of good will can make no other choice than to give themselves wholly to the larger political struggle. I respect that viewpoint but would still argue for the appropriateness of taking seriously the evils closest to us, lest we lose track of our neighbor in our (necessary) fight for humanity. Even in this sphere, we could gain the whole world and lose our souls.

[9] Here again, I speak only of one's attitude in one's own case. Never are we justified in

we accuse him of giving a stone for bread or a serpent for a fish (Matt. 7:9–10)? That question is easy to ask, but what of the fields of our lives that are strewn with stones, peppered with vipers? Have I not insisted that the Enemy has prepared those fields as proper ground for the weeds that he sows (Matt. 13:25)? I have indeed and would say no differently now—except that even the Enemy can touch the believer only as God allows. Satan could not plague Job until God let him through the hedge he had set around him (Job 1:10; cf. Luke 8:32, where demons had to ask Jesus' permission even to enter into swine). Satan indeed has resources that he uses to his ends, as I have been at pains to insist. But he can only *use* them: they do not finally belong to him.

> He uses them against the unregenerate at his own whim; and he uses them against the children of God whenever the Lord takes down the hedge and permits him to hurl their force against the believer. In this sense they are acts of God for a believer but they are always acts of the devil for the unsaved. (Barnhouse 1965, 147)

Thus we come to another paradox: the believer may truly praise God for all things (Eph. 5:20), even the ones he most desires to have changed.[10]

Now it could be charged that we are talking the most patent nonsense: how on earth can one struggle with all his might and all his faith against that which is, by every definition known to him, evil and at the same time give thanks and praise to God for what he would do anything to be rid of? Scripture plainly forbids calling evil good (Isa. 5:20), so it would seem that we were involved in sophistry or an exercise in mental hygiene or an experiment with positive thinking. Or "praising God" may become a sort of gimmick, carrying the covert or overt assumption that, by praising God for what we do not want, we will get what we do want. Or the words "praise the Lord" may be uttered

dismissing another's pain as simply "God's will" for that person. Anything breaking the network of mutuality comes from Satan.

[10] See Isa. 54:16–17 and Rom. 8:28, which reads, "We know that in everything God works for good *with those who love him, who are called according to his purpose*" (emphasis added); this restriction is significant. Offensive as the thought is to many, the words of Eph. 5:20 are clear: it reads "always and for [ὑπέρ] everything giving thanks," not "*in* [ἐν] everything." One may take the words as hyperbole or make assumptions as to what they "obviously could not" apply, but one can get no comfort from the text as it stands. There are not even any textual variants offering a more reasonable reading. It *is* important, though, that the thanks be given "in the name of our Lord Jesus Christ," who is the one who puts evil to flight. Those words provide a context that prohibits the object of thanksgiving from gaining any independent status. (Cf. 1 Thess. 5:16, 18, which reads, "Rejoice always, . . . give thanks *in* all circumstances.") It is curious that the only place in the New Testament where rejoicing is *discouraged* is Luke 10:17–20, where the disciples delight that the demons are subject to them. The sort of rejoicing in triumph that can slide over into pride or magic is dangerous (Richards 1974). Rejoicing is to be in what *God* does, not in what one thinks one has oneself done. Thus the occasion for it is always less that which is seen than the purpose that God has; and if one is confident of God's overarching purpose for everything, then all may be cause for thanksgiving.

cheaply as a sort of pseudopious profanity, roughly translatable as "Oh, damn!" Unfortunately, the success stories in the popular literature of people who have praised God in adversity tend to foster these distortions. By no means do I suggest that such is the intent of the popular literature or that whatever genuine miracles have been reported have occurred when praise has been used as one more way to manipulate God. To the contrary, I would affirm that the basic concept is biblical and right when it springs from believing trust in God's loving sovereignty.

Resting thankfully in that sovereignty does in some unknown way clear the path for God's working. Again, though, that very truth breeds the error of focusing on successes instead of on God. We substitute the lesser good for the greater and lose both. Praise cannot serve as a means unless it is first an end (and according to the Book of Revelation, it certainly will be, at the last, an end). Thus we find the curious phrase "sacrifice of praise" (Heb. 13:15). Even more than being "for" anything, whether the object is pleasant or painful, praise is a way of acknowledging God and laying ourselves before him. Most of all it is a sacrifice when the circumstances would seem not to warrant it.

To view praise as sacrifice may help to combat one's subjective disinclination to praise, since sacrifice is not expected to be painless. However, that formulation hardly counters the objective, moral objection to offering praise for evil situations. On the face of it, it would seem that one was presenting such a sacrifice to a hungry Molech who was morally unworthy, a God who might be praised for his arbitrary and incontrovertible strength but scarcely for his love. Indeed, that conclusion would easily follow if events had but a single determinant. In chapter 3 I argued that such is precisely *not* the case; that, for instance, what Joseph's brothers meant for evil, God meant for good. Likewise Pharaoh was raised up—presumably through quite normal means—in order that God's power might be shown and his name be proclaimed (Rom. 9:17).

Above all, in the cross of Christ we see several levels of determinism.[11] On the first level function the designs of people—through religion, politics, and the passion of the crowd. Behind the surface manifestations of that level lie the rulers of this present darkness. The Antichrist can corrupt religion not because he presents himself as radically different from Christ but because of his diabolical resemblance to him that permits a successful masquerade. The principalities and powers twist and absolutize politics and the state. And in the heart of the average person, something drives an irresistible compulsion to

---

[11] For the following discussion see Stewart 1951, to which I am greatly indebted for content and format.

perpetrate heinous evil. On another level, the will of Jesus, given over to obedience to God, yet freely chose death (John 10:18). Jesus did not die the death of a mere victim who had nothing to say about the fate that overtook him. Rather, his death was an attack upon and victory over the principalities and powers (Col. 2:15; see also Heb. 2:14–15). And on a third level, the Cross had its source in the purpose of God the Father himself (Acts 2:23): "The divine sovereignty is such that the hostility of the ἄρχοντες [principalities] and ἐξουσίαι [powers] is compelled to subserve God's ends and not theirs" (Stewart 1951, 300). All dualism is finally overcome. Thus we can see that we may never stop with the lowest-level determinant of an event if we wish to know what it means. At its lowest, the Crucifixion provides the great example of all time of the fact that evil cannot bear good and will do anything to be rid of it. If that word were final, the situation would indeed be worse than hopeless; for a good God, dead, cannot even be placated, as can an evil one, alive. We praise God for what we see in the Cross, because it is a part of what lies beyond it.

God with Us

If we were only computers handling a pyramiding scheme in which all the losses at the bottom did not erase the gains at the top or in which the human quality of events was irrelevant to the ends in view, perhaps we could look coolly at "levels of explanation" and nod agreeably that it all comes out for the best in the end and that therefore we ought to be thankful. But we are not computers. We are human beings who react with uncomprehending rage at evil, even when we know that we, too, are guilty of it. And we rage at a God who, "from his perspective," barred to us, engineers a good at our expense. We rage—until somehow we realize that he took our perspective and has engineered good at *his* expense. He is "God with us," not just "God beyond us." He is *with* the sparrow that falls, not just distantly observing it with a billion-mile telescope.

> Jahweh stands out from the world of abstractions, of symbols and generalities; he acts in history and enters into relations with actual historical beings. And when God the Father [*sic*; "God" or "God the Son"] "shows" himself in a radical and complete manner by becoming incarnate in Jesus Christ, then all history becomes a theophany. (Eliade 1957, 153)

God has not created the world as a toy for his amusement. He himself has chosen to live and bleed in his world. Could he have done differently? A vain question, for he did not. What matters is that, in "the larger picture," what is distinctively human in pain and suffering and temptation and anger is not set at nought but is known to the heart of

God. We may praise him for evil in our lives, knowing that he who is not evil but wholly good (and to whom the evil must therefore be all the more alien than to us, who share all too freely in it) takes that evil upon himself for us. We praise God for what we see because we know him to be present in the midst of it. Is it hard for us to see him? No harder for us than for Jews and Romans and Greeks in the first century to see God in a common criminal hanging on a cross.[12] And for that terrible evil, no believer may fail to thank God.

We may truly thank and praise God for all that befalls us if we trust his purpose and know that he will not abandon us to situations more stressful than we can bear, whatever the appearance may be (1 Cor. 10:13). If we know that truth (and really only if we know it), we become free to follow wherever our commitment leads. And if we know that God's purpose is loving and good and that his presence is unfailing, our daily life can take on the aspect of an adventure instead of a treadmill or a chamber of horrors. The horrors are there, all right, and must be battled; but they are also more (and less?) than they appear and cannot best be fought with the despair or hatred or grumbling that lies in the Enemy's province. Even terrible trials can become an opportunity to see what God will do, to see his glory manifested. And we may expect to be surprised. What the philosopher of science Polanyi says of science at its best—and does himself apply to Christianity (1964, 198)—gives a feeling for both the humility and the excitement of the adventure of faith:

> Thought can live only on grounds which we adopt in the service of a reality to which we submit. (1967, xi)

> The responsible choices made in the course of scientific enquiry . . . are made by the scientist: they are his acts, but what he pursues is not of his making; his acts stand under the judgment of the hidden reality he seeks to uncover. . . . In these intensely personal acts, therefore, there is no self-will. (Pp. 76–77)

> To trust that a thing we know is real is . . . to feel that it has the independence and power for manifesting itself in yet unthought of ways in the future. (P. 32; see also 1964, 311)

[12] I am saying here that evil of whatever sort is at bottom an attack on God that he sustains (at least up to the point of its being consigned to hell) and may, at his cost, redeem. In this way we may see him in evil. I am aware of Amos 3:6 ("Does evil befall a city, unless the LORD has done it?") but do not take it as a counterinstance. God is probably the only Father who can rightly say when punishing his children, "This hurts me more than it hurts you." The passage is explicitly speaking of punishment, not of moral evil. I compare it to Jer. 45:3–5, where Baruch is complaining about his own sorrow and pain, and the Lord responds that he is breaking down what he has built, plucking up what he has planted. The implication is that the evil he is doing wrenches him in a way that Baruch cannot even fathom. (To hear only a statement of arbitrary sovereignty would appear to violate the tenor of the passage as well as the revealed character of God.)

If we wish to know rightly, we cannot second-guess what God may reveal to us of his reality. This very act of submitting to a reality greater than we can perceive, however, means precisely that we must not absolutize slavishly the one that we *do* perceive. "Whatever rules of rightness a person tries to fulfill and establish—be they moral, aesthetic, or legal—he commits himself to an ideal; and again, he can do so only within a medium blind to this ideal" (Polanyi 1964, 334).[13] A person can know his ideals not by looking at the medium, then, that knows nothing of them, but only by freely pursuing them (see Polanyi 1964, 337; John 7:17). It follows that "the indwelling of the Christian worshipper is therefore a continued attempt at breaking out, at casting off the condition of man, even while humbly acknowledging its inescapability" (Polanyi 1964, 198). Although we cannot escape our condition, Scripture tells us that God continually breaks through the limits of that condition.

> God . . . gives life to the dead and calls into existence the things that do not exist. In hope he [Abraham] believed against hope. . . . He did not weaken in faith when he considered his own body, which was as good as dead because he was about a hundred years old, or when he considered the barrenness of Sarah's womb. No distrust made him waver concerning the promise of God, but *he grew strong in his faith as he gave glory to God,* fully convinced that God was able to do what he had promised. (Rom. 4:17–21; emphasis added)

The result was not just peace of mind but a son—Isaac, whose name means "laughter."[14] Faith had grown not through what was seen, but through giving glory to God.

The Transformation of Evil

So "we rejoice in our sufferings, knowing that suffering produces endurance, and endurance produces character, and character produces hope, and hope does not disappoint us, because God's love has been

---

[13] See also Wink 1984, 114: "The universe itself is blind to its own principle of cohesion."

[14] The barren old woman
eavesdrops in her bitterness
upon the old man and the Lord,
and hears the promise of fruit
upon her withered vine.
Clinging to the corner where she listens
she titters
like the crackling bonfire
of autumn vegetation.
God hears her tittering
and has the last laugh
in the imposition of a name.
    (Slotten 1971, 317)

poured into our hearts through the Holy Spirit which has been given to us" (Rom. 5:3–5). The first part of this passage sounds perfectly sensible and natural, setting forth the benefits potentially available through suffering and a "good attitude." The conclusion, however, is not the dictum of mental hygiene, Follow these instructions and everything will be better, whether it is better or not. The conclusion is that our hope will not end in disappointment. No final futility or inescapable evil can overtake us. No terror is larger than God's love or can overwhelm the power of the Holy Spirit. Even the great sea monster Leviathan, symbol of the great, dark, evil power lurking in the depth of oceanic chaos, is but a creature made to play in God's pond (Ps. 104:26). Should we not then take evil seriously? Oh yes, indeed, but never so seriously—never with such lack of faith—that it can put out the light of praise and rejoicing in our lives. Or quench the laughter. The sound of the sureness of God's victory, heard beyond every sob and moan, is the ring of laughter in his heart. His signature on a life, if first of all love, is likewise joy. "In the world you have tribulation; but be of good cheer, I have overcome the world" (John 16:33).

How can we make such an affirmation? By looking at the Cross?

> The really tragic force of the dilemma of history and of the human predicament is not answered by any theology which speaks of the Cross as a revelation of love and mercy—and goes no further. But the primitive proclamation went much further. It spoke of an objective transaction which had changed the human situation and indeed the *kosmos* itself. It spoke of the decisive irrevocable defeat of the powers of darkness. (Stewart 1951, 294)

Always in looking at the Cross, we must keep the Resurrection in view. The Resurrection is the event in which, not theoretically or abstractly but actually, evil was *overcome* by good (Rom. 12:21). Real victory cannot be, though, a mere annihilation of evil, for the simple reason that evil is not a second and autonomous principle over against God but stems from the revolt of his own creatures. I suggest, therefore, that "overcoming" involves finally the *transformation* of evil to good. The thought is not an easy one. We understand much more readily how good may be transformed to evil, in the ways we have considered earlier. We have personally experienced that transformation. The movement in the other direction—involving reconciliation and restoration and maybe even a greater and fuller good than that which was lost—is far more mysterious. We have hints, surely, that the rebellious powers themselves are not wholly lost but will be brought back to their true purpose (Col. 1:16, 20). Not everything that currently serves Satan is ultimately damned. By itself, however, this truth relegates the triumph all too exclusively to the future. The question is what difference Christ's

251

presence makes *now*. It must somehow be possible that even evil can be made other than it is if evil is not to win all of earthly life "before the time" for itself.[15]

A thing in itself obviously cannot be more than itself. I have argued, however, that only by drawing artificial barriers can we conceive things "in themselves." I have spoken in terms of "dimensions" and "levels of explanation," thus always considering a larger context. Now we must go one step further. The only final way of overcoming evil, the only means of transformation that changes the very character of the evil itself and does not merely use evil means to achieve good ends (a practice that we have said is self-defeating for persons and that we do not attribute to God) or that does not redefine evil from a broader perspective, is for the higher to put itself—in a substitutionary, sacrificial manner—in the place of the lower. Only so can evil no longer find a resting place. It may roam restlessly and disruptively for a time, but the time is limited. Even now, for the believer, its power can never defeat God's ends (see 2 Cor. 13:8).

Ultimately, of course, God achieves his ends for humankind because Christ, in his death, put himself in our place. He took our death upon himself. Death could not hold him and hence cannot hold those who are in him. It is transformed into a gateway to life. If there were no other result, however, the world would still be penultimately abandoned to the Devil—lost—and only by leaving it could we taste what would seem to be something of a Pyrrhic victory. Christ did even more than conquer the physical death at the end of earthly life, the mark of the Enemy's triumph; he left his Spirit to conquer the daily spiritual dyings and to fight the daily spiritual battles of the Creation. Because of the presence of the Holy Spirit, we do not stand alone in the evil age; we cannot despise and reject the world, and we may not affirm impotence against evil. The Holy Spirit is a transforming power—God's power at work here and now. It is he who makes possible all that we have said must happen.

The Holy Spirit opens our hearts to God's Word and works through our weakness. He is transforming *us*, remaking us, planting his fruit and gifts within us, so that God's character, will, and power may be manifested. He is "Christ in [us], the hope of glory" (Col. 1:27). Without him there is no renewal. The Holy Spirit is the Comforter who strengthens us in suffering and provides a bond of unity among believers

---

[15]That there is a state—hell—where those who perpetrate evil remain what they are, I do not deny. It is appropriate to say no more than that that state is hell—separated by a great gulf from the merciful working of God. However, from the theological affirmation that there is a hell, we do *not* deduce God's inability to use what persons consigned to it have done on earth. (Perhaps hell concerns more the willful than the structural aspect of evil. Although structures may ultimately serve God's purposes, individual wills may not.)

(Eph. 4). He is transforming the *church* in order that it may grow in mutuality and maturity as the body of Christ. Without him there is no reunion. The Holy Spirit prays for us when we lack words and wisdom (Rom. 8:26) and makes praise to rise up in our hearts, even against all logic, in recognition of the active, present greatness of God. He is preparing the *world* to be transformed into the kingdom of God. Without him there is little cause for rejoicing.

But *with* him who gives eyes to see and hearts to believe, we can affirm that the whole of salvation history is the story of God's paradoxical bringing of good out of evil. Samson's riddle was no riddle: its answer could in no way be derived from our common experience. "Out of the eater came something to eat. Out of the strong came something sweet" (Judg. 14:14). It is not natural to get honey from the belly of a marauding lion. Nor is it natural that life should come back into—and ever afterward, out of—the dead body of the Lion of the tribe of Judah (Rev. 5:5). Out of death comes life. Those who would save their lives will surely lose them. Those who lose their lives for the sake of the gospel will find them. But even the losing can be good because of the joy that is set before us; and we can taste the joy now because he with whom we die is already alive and victorious, dwelling in and among us. So we may already receive all things from his hand with praise in our hearts. By no manipulation of science or magic, by no logical syllogism or irrational reversal, but by the alchemy of God, in which his gold is sufficient to take the place of all dross, evil is being transformed to good. The impossible is accomplished: the crooked is made straight. And in this we rejoice.

Rejoicing is prayer and praise that is simply focused: a new heart, over against all duality and division.

Renewal: a new mind. Reunion: a new body. Rejoicing: a new heart. Behold, he makes all things new.

* * *

Stranger: No, no, no, NO! It's not true. It's a lie. You're wrong. He can't. He doesn't. He won't. You don't *want* to die and suffer and pray. Nobody does. I'll show you another way. I'll give you long life and health and wealth and power and pleasure and satisfy all your desires and . . .

Inquirer: Be silent. And in the name of Jesus, be gone.

* * *

Behold, he makes all things new.

Appendix: The Paradoxical Way and Psychotherapy

Much has been written in recent years by Christians about the practice of clinical psychology and about psychological counseling in general. Some have sought to adopt a slightly modified secular psychology. Others have endeavored to fill the counseling process with specifically Christian content. Still others have roundly anathematized the whole discipline. Rather than propose a fully developed fourth alternative, I offer a *perspective* governed by the theological commitments articulated in the preceding pages. Although some of those pages rest heavily on clinical psychology, many of them have the ring of sermons. The therapy hour is not a tent meeting in which sermons may be preached. It is, however, part of a life in which their essential thrust may be lived. In my view, the sermons *must* be lived in one's counseling, for excluding God from any part of one's life, explicitly or tacitly, violates the singleness and simplicity of the entire relationship and has all the consequences of a pencil-sized hole in a dike. I offer here a few reflections on the paradoxical way of Christian faith as it relates to psychotherapy.

WORD, WEAKNESS, AND PSYCHOTHERAPY

The reader must be assured that I propose no "rules," nor can my perspective be defined in terms of a binding preference for one therapeutic technique over another. Rather, I explore once again the question of ends and means, with the assumption that God cannot be made one apart from the other. He is neither a means to our ends nor an end to be reached by our means. But for that reason, it is no simple matter for the believing therapist to maintain her integrity with an unbelieving client, for she knows that "the sons of this world are wiser in their own generation than the sons of light" (Luke 16:8 RSV). She knows that she may sometimes be able to do greater temporal "good" of the sort the unbeliever seeks more efficiently by the world's means than by God's. Has she a duty to use worldly means to make happier the person who has bartered the kingdom for this world? Why not a little adultery to release someone's inhibitions and make him "healthier"? But who knows when the exchange is final. And who knows the outcome, even relatively short-term, of strengthening the Destroyer's grip on the

255

world by looking at it as he does. The good of anyone but himself is never the Devil's aim, however convenient a bait it may be.

The difficulty is increased by the fact that, as I have indicated, the therapist cannot preach to her client, and not just because of professional ethics. More important ultimately, to preach in the therapeutic context carries connotations of "validating" God's Word in terms of worldly criteria and seems to imply a secular force behind the proclamation (i.e., "psychology says religion is good for you," with "good" in such a statement implicitly conceived in a temporal, empirical sense). Not that the gospel lacks power in this life, but those who grasp at it simply to please their therapists or to exert power will likely not get what they bargained for. There is always danger of either therapist or client falling into a magical view of faith (see Tournier 1960), a danger increased by the known effects of "belief" ·in general (see chapter 2 above).

That tendency may be somewhat counteracted by the affirmation that God normally uses means and that the means of psychotherapeutic techniques can hardly be excluded from those that he deigns to employ. Except insofar as a method goes against God's Word or is depersonalizing, it surely cannot be counted a priori as a pagan or demonic means.[1] Surely we ought to affirm the Calvinistic dictum that whatever is genuinely good in this world stems from, and is rightfully claimed for, God. Here the danger lies less in magic than in considering "nature," as seen through the orders we discover or impose, to be more trustworthy than God because we find it more reliable, more predictable, and certainly more manageable than God's intermittent intervention. Sanctioning *use* of all legitimately available knowledge emphatically does not entail sanctioning a comfortable *reliance* upon any technique whatever.[2] And not so incidentally, as in every realm, the more power involved in a method, the greater the temptation to idolatry. The more "effective" the therapist, the greater her need of God, lest her power become demonic. Furthermore, as Tournier (1960, 112) sensitively states, "In everything we do for the good of a person's soul we run in some degree the risk of taking God's place there."

These extended prolegomena speak only superficially to the question of what the therapist may offer the client and scarcely touch the implications of Word and weakness. They tell us only that to make

---

[1] A caution from Barth (1958, 541) at this point is that gymnastics employed to figure out the "meaning" of a command or law quickly become illegitimate. In his words, "A child versed in this pseudo-theology might argue as follows. My father says: Go to bed. He means that I am tired. He does not want me to be tired. But I can dissipate my tiredness by going out to play. Therefore, when my father says: Go to bed, he really means: Go out to play."

[2] The qualifying adverb "legitimately" is important. I certainly do not consider the occult and the "dark things of Satan" to be permissible sources of knowledge.

Word central does not mean "preach" and to know that God utilizes weakness does not mean "sit on your hands and ignore every tool God has provided." What more positive view may they give us of health? What path do they frame for therapy? (And we must remember that end and way are all of a piece.) My suggestions at this point focus not on overcoming specific inabilities and obstacles but on providing a conceptual set to govern particular decisions and on guarding against trading a pathological manifestation of a basically valid commitment for a symptom-free manifestation of a basically false commitment.

First, against determinism, anything can happen. Nothing need be considered inexorably fixed for all time, frozen by past determinants and kept solid by current environment. God's Word provides power for change, and repentance provides freedom to change. One need not justify where he is if he does not feel helpless to move; and one may not justify where he is if he realizes that "none is righteous, no, not one" (Rom. 3:10). To be willing to let go of pathological securities is to take a giant step toward renewal. Because Word makes new possibilities and does not simply manipulate what is, we may have hope.[3]

Second, against magic, idolatry, and pragmatism, victory and visible health are not one-to-one correlates of holiness or the final test of the success of a process of psychotherapy—or the success of a life. Defeat or suffering is not a sure sign that one is inadequate or that one is being punished. While salvation, when consummated, will entail the end of pain, it does not follow that current comfort equals salvation. Thus, while both therapist and client seek relief from the suffering that cripples (as Christ himself sanctioned, by healing and by providing bread for the hungry), yet they will not consider exchanging righteousness for a pair of shoes.[4] They will not count "success" as proof over against God's Word (Deut. 13:1–3). They will seek to trust God's strength as entirely sufficient, however bleak the circumstances. The ability to persevere and to refrain from self-condemnation under adverse conditions is a sign and requirement of renewal. Because Word sustains us and works through weakness, we need not be defeated by failures but may have faith.

Third, against "self" as a beginning and ending point, "fulfilling" us and protecting our "rights" is something God has said *he* will take care of; our task is to serve him and fulfill the needs of our brothers and

---

[3]To recognize one's guilt before God and give up one's self-righteousness is *not* the same thing as to be self-condemnatory. The latter is another form of self-righteousness and pride that will not accept forgiveness and grace. Self-condemnation is a tool of Satan in that it blocks rather than fosters change. Interestingly, even biological vulnerability is thought to be increased by feelings of helplessness and hopelessness (Frank 1974, 55).

[4]"I will not revoke the punishment; because they sell the righteous for silver, and the needy for a pair of shoes" (Amos 2:6).

sisters. He *will* provide for us: he has certainly demonstrated extravagantly that we *matter* to him, that we are important and valuable; but he has made it just as clear that "I" makes a perfectly terrible center for the universe. Even practically speaking, the reply to the statement, "I don't see why you don't enjoy [or 'fulfill' or 'assert'] yourselves" is, "Because, sooner or later, there isn't anything to enjoy in oneself" (Williams 1949, 64). To realize that fact quickly is to avoid untold frustration in the pursuit of that original imagined good, one's own independent pleasure and self-sufficiency.[5] The ability really to see God is the ultimate sign of renewal (1 John 3:2; Rev. 22:4), and to see one's neighbor, the penultimate sign (1 John 4:12). Because the Word given us is Love, we may love.

Hope and faith and love: what better paths to health—and signs of health?

FELLOWSHIP, FORGIVENESS, AND PSYCHOTHERAPY

"Health" cannot be had in isolation. Affirming that "I" makes a terrible center for the universe leads us directly to our concerns for community. Indeed, because fellowship is central to the very nature of creation, I therefore see isolation from others as an absolutely central problem.[6] The truly isolated person (not the simply introverted person) lacks the most basic access to resources for healing as well as for gratification, despite the supposed and actual advantages isolation offers by protecting one from certain kinds of suffering. If the restoration of community (and that vital medium of mutuality, communication) is crucial, and if community is seen in organic terms more than just as the coordination of essentially separate individuals, then much may be said in caution against any procedure that tends to promote satisfaction with separateness and maximally autonomous "self-fulfillment," against tendencies toward "viewing the landscape of reality from the perspective of the self, [so that] all falls into place in terms of convenience and acceptability to the individual" (Frye 1960, 106). To say that other people are not reliable and cannot be counted on as sources of sustenance and reward is no truer than to say that (apart from God

---

[5] Again, to make such a statement is not to ignore the frequency with which "altruism" is really pathological and self-aggrandizing; "trusting God," an excuse for laziness, passivity, and failure to develop the gifts God has given one; and relinquishment of "rights," weak, manipulative, and productive not of charity but of hostility and resentment. Counterfeit coin is no proof against the real; indeed, it could not exist without the genuine article. I am not suggesting an exchange of pragmatism for blind naivete but a replacement of cynicism (the root of pragmatism?) with a hungering and thirsting after righteousness.

[6] Boisen (1936) sees the essential evil in mental disorder not in the conflict but in the sense of isolation or estrangement. We might go a bit further and say that there is more than a "sense" of estrangement; the break from community is all too real.

himself, who generally works through people) they are the only sources available. Making independence rather than interrelatedness central may briefly dull pain—possibly because the thought of one's own "rights" can be rather intoxicating—but it goes against the intent and fact of the created order.[7]

Furthermore, if the therapist's view of community is such that he believes suffering does or can have redemptive meaning, that belief will lead him to consider the *nature* of a given instance of suffering and not the mere *fact* of pain. Such a view of suffering certainly does not make it unimportant. Neither does such a view deny that suffering may often be self-imposed—a direct result of one's own wrongdoing, or a means of self-punishment for one's evil impulses that at the same time may allow one to indulge them, or a desperate attempt at self-discipline and self-control (see Boisen 1936, 202–4). This view most certainly *does* deny that suffering is necessarily evidence of one's guilt and God's punishment, or that it is necessarily gratuitous. The possibility of redemptive suffering may come into focus particularly when, hard as it may be to distinguish sequences, suffering has more set off pathology than the reverse, or when environmental circumstances apparently allow no escape from very real pressures and tragedies. It is also at issue in another sense, however, when a person who sees himself as having done wrong in thought or deed comes for help: he may need forgiveness and someone to pick up his load, to take on his suffering (if indeed the hurting one really wants to give up the burden, which is by no means always the case).

So, we must also consider the need of the distressed person to forgive and receive forgiveness. I said in chapter 10 that the first step toward renewal is willingness to let go of one's rigid definition of oneself and one's aims. Just as essential is a willingness to stop clinging to that other form of self-justification, judgment of others, however much they may have wronged one. One cannot budge while tied to the past by

---

[7] The argument is scarcely intended to favor parasitic relationships, which also go against the structure of our calling to give as well as receive—though nothing says we ought to give to him from whom we have received or can expect to receive, but rather the reverse (Luke 6:32–35). (The real problem is not a bit of parasitism—my thumb is something of a parasite on my body—but the fact that the "host" is usually not healthy enough to handle it without aggravating both his own and the hanger-on's problems. Parasites with really healthy hosts probably do not often come to see psychotherapists!) The healthy person is not the one who carefully balances what goes out with what comes in in every relationship, so that he does not come out short, but the one who can give (and receive) without keeping score. In the case of persons who are psychologically ill, relationships are by definition distorted, and the person is presumably unable in one way or another to make a healthy response (not too surprising a state of affairs, since most of us reasonably "healthy" people are also unable or unwilling to do so). Our procedures thus need to be governed by our ultimate vision of health rather than by a proximate, pain-killing expedient. Our lack of truly healing procedures is as much a commentary on the state of society and the church as it is on psychotherapy.

grievances; and maybe the wrongdoer is bound by the same chain. Not only does Scripture insist that we will be forgiven as we forgive, but also we thwart our ability to conceive and receive forgiveness for ourselves by harboring malice. Even though the initial act of forgiveness comes from beyond us, it withers and dies if it stops with us, instead of flourishing and bearing fruit by being passed on. By choosing not to forgive, we choose slowly but surely to poison ourselves with our own venom.

With regard to the psychotherapist and the therapeutic interaction, some stickier issues must be raised—or, perhaps we should say, the same issues in a stickier form. First, can healing occur without communion, with the therapist acting simply as a projection screen or a mirror or an M & M dispenser? How does an artificial relationship, deliberately guarded from becoming too real lest the client become dependent, promote health?[8] The answer is easy enough if personal insight, growth, self-control, and the like are all that is at stake, and far be it from us to decry any of these: they can be positively good. But they are thoroughly unsatisfactory ultimate goals. While they may enable better relationships and may remove certain barriers, they leave the focus on the self instead of on one's God and one's neighbor. They may provide some additional personal resources, such that, analogically, the cymbals that once could not be heard now can be. Still, the cymbals are not much good without the orchestra, and they are still less good if they are playing to their own sheet of music. Then they will just be rejected again, able to make a big noise but still alone. I certainly do not say that such is the intent of the major forms of psychotherapy, but is it the common result of an artificial relationship? Perhaps the real goal is to be able to *give* love, not primarily to *receive* it (i.e., to have our needs met; cf. 1 Cor. 10:24: "Let no one seek his own good, but the good of his neighbor"). We reach the goal only through receiving love, *not*— whatever the popular literature insists in contradiction to 1 John (especially 1 John 4:19)—by painfully learning to love ourselves.[9]

---

[8] I do not wish to imply that allowing a client to become dependent is desirable when the professional relationship cannot legitimately gratify the dependency, when there can be no supposition of real mutuality.

[9] Much as the New Testament demonstrates the infinite value of persons in God's eyes, and much as we are thus taught to value others, and much as we may rightly deduce that we ourselves are of infinite value to him, nowhere does the New Testament teach that proper self-esteem is a precondition for anything whatever. Indeed, we are to be realistic, not self-deprecating (Rom. 12:3; Gal. 6:4), but even here the context puts this realism over against pride. One could plausibly argue that the biblical writers were simply not attuned to the problem of self-hatred. However, self-hatred is usually manipulative or a sort of independent pride in reverse. The very word shows its center of attention. Perhaps the word the self-hater needs to hear is that it is not his business to judge himself (1 Cor. 4:3–4) but to be a trustworthy steward (vv. 1–2), that he is to turn his attention from himself to his task.

There are pressing professional, personal, and practical barriers to the therapist's unreservedly loving and giving himself to his patients in the way that Christ enjoined us to love one another. Is it surprising, then, that so few get well?

Second, even if a therapeutic contract formally excludes real communion, the therapeutic relationship still has some of the structural characteristics of a field. In fact, one prominent therapist likens it to a field of force (May 1972, 88). He has found in his own practice that sometimes an action or feeling is required of which the client is incapable, but healing may yet take place if the therapist expresses it. Here on a small scale we may see the whole substitutionary schema in action, but kept neatly within the therapeutic hour. The intervention illustrates a truth of interrelatedness without giving it its natural scope. To express a feeling is one thing—and very possibly a helpful one. However, the therapist makes a business of seeing suffering people; and what is he to do about a seemingly endless stream of suffering?

The Bible leaves no room for those who would be impersonal, detached, and merely efficient in "handling" the evil and pain in this world. Do we want to help others without suffering and dying? God could not. How presumptuous, cheap, and puerile can we be? It seems to be a principle of life that *hurt must be borne by someone;* merely letting it loose provides no final cure. I suggest, then, that it may be flatly wrong for us as Christians to promote the opening up of more pain than we are personally willing to become involved in, not because unspoken pain is going to go away, but because a client's personhood is even more ultimate than his pain.[10] "Treating" the latter abstracted as much as possible from the former fails to honor the unique individual God has created. He becomes instead a mere appendage of his problem. (I am not persuaded that, ipso facto, removal of pain enhances personhood. Obviously the latter is not only desirable but also a goal taught by Jesus himself. But evil does not just disappear; it must be transformed by good. See Rom. 12:21 and chapter 12 above.) Furthermore, the therapist becomes hardened. Hardness is the antithesis of love, and it often stems from facing more suffering than we have the power of love to bear and redeem.

We thus come to the dichotomous proposition that those who would see many people must be either very hard or incredibly well supplied with love, a proposition complicated by the measureless prodigality of love, which cannot be divided and administered in prefabricated lots. To say that we are responsible only "to" and not "for" one another is often a

---

[10] Even a pagan shaman may consider that he must lay himself on the line in dealing with evil (Frank 1974, 63).

slippery way of denying our indissoluble bond with one another.[11] Is it not impractical, inefficient, and even impossible to demand that we love our clients so much that we take their sufferings upon ourselves? Does not this slippery path have the pits of martyr and messianic complexes on either side? Of course. Jesus had neither, but we are not he and need often to be reminded of that fact. Nonetheless, the simple fact that the biblical God is a personal God makes what we are as persons and what we do with other persons made in his image of absolutely incalculable importance.

Our conclusion can only be that to be a channel of God's love is simply not a human or psychotherapeutic possibility. We may look with wonder at what is entailed. We may hunger and thirst after God's righteousness. We may study and listen and obey as best we know how. Nonetheless, God's gracious action is always an awesome event, never a managed objective. Even the ability to give, to be humbly open, and to bear other's burdens comes as a gift rather than an achievement. All the same, it is a gift somehow and strangely correlated with our wholehearted desire to be so endowed.

PRAYER, PRAISE, AND PSYCHOTHERAPY

Only because of my belief in God's grace and faithfulness can I write as I have; and only because of that belief dare I say to the Christian client who reads these lines, "Don't be afraid. He who has begun a good work in you *will* complete it (Phil. 1:6). Trust him, in therapy and out. And pray. And give thanks. And rejoice."

Likewise to the Christian therapist I would repeat, "Don't be afraid. Don't be afraid that nothing can be done and that the whole scene is of no account." One can find reasons enough, if one wants reasons, for feeling discouraged and helpless and hopeless in the face of the problems and life situations of many clients, whether or not those clients are believers. It is easy enough to be overwhelmed by evil and to feel impotent because of it. Therapists are not known for a low suicide rate. They too need to pray and praise and rejoice. They too need healing.

I consider these personal implications of chapter 12 to be the most vital ones, from which all the others follow; yet there are a few more general lines of thought that bear directly upon the therapeutic relationship. One resembles the point made when considering weakness and not doing evil or using evil means. Here the caution takes the form of a warning against deliberately experiencing evil. Often we make the assumption that we ought not to reject that which we have not

---

[11] Cf. Philem. 18, where Paul is willing to have any debt Onesimus may have incurred charged to his own account.

experienced or at least carefully investigated or that, if we were strong enough, we would not need to fear evil. We can disprove the former by taking an extreme case: surely we will not profit by long contemplating murder, much less doing it, before we reject it! The latter must be answered just by admitting that we are not strong enough. Not one of us is so good that she cannot be burned by evil; and there is no protection for her who presumptuously sticks her hand into the fiery furnace. Many steps in life cannot be retraced; lost innocence cannot be regained—and innocence is lost in thousands of little ways, not just by a single dramatic bite of forbidden fruit. Thus arises the paradox that the person walking in the light knows less and less of evil. If the therapist believes that persons take on the shape and expression of what they pursue and attend to, she ought carefully to consider any activities or foci that she might advocate. Experience for its own sake—one of the idols of our time—has precious little to recommend it. She who looks for fresh-water springs in the middle of the ocean—and keeps on tasting the brine to test her hypotheses—will simply perish. To build up a tolerance for evil is to put out one's eyes so as to feel more at home in the dark.

Another issue has to do with the place of prayer. With respect to the therapist's work, it has two aspects. First, of course, the therapist should actively place the client in God's hands, with specific intercession for the client's particular needs. The believer may readily agree with this obligation—but all too often actually fails to pray. She who believes in the God of the impossible as well as the possible will not hesitate to make petition for needs of whatever stripe—physical, psychological, or spiritual. She will *expect* God to work because she knows that her prayers are heard. She would not be overly surprised if one of her clients was soundly saved, healed, and delivered. (She might even do a bit of serious soul-searching if she *never* had a patient saved or healed or delivered, because she need not doubt that such is consonant with God's will.) Second, and equally obvious, the therapist should pray for guidance for her own words and actions. I do not mean merely that she invites God to "do his thing" while she independently does hers. Such a thought is far too perfunctory. She ought rather to seek to be so attuned and sensitive that she might anticipate God's revealing problems and providing the words that will be healing and redemptive in a given case.[12] Woe betide her who attributes such revelation solely to "clinical

---

[12] An educator, chairperson of his department at a major university, shared a specific instance with me of such revelation of problems. A young man from out of town, whom he had never met, was coming to see him for counseling, and they were to have only one hour together. Before the hour began, two areas of difficulty were shown by God to this man. He bided his time, but after fully forty-five minutes had passed, the youth's remarks had come nowhere near these areas. Taking the bull by the horns, my friend broke in and

intuition": Herod was struck dead for accepting adulation himself and failing to give proper glory to God (Acts 12:22–23). Prayer is a matter both of specific intercession and of an ongoing relationship with God that leaves one always open and ready for what he would say and do.

Finally, the therapist's own affirmation of life and attitude of praise may shine in who she is and be a source of strength and hope. Certainly she will never use Romans 8:28 as a bludgeon (in fact, she would probably never refer to such a verse at all) or blithely praise God for tragedy in a client's life from which she, the therapist, is safely dissociated. To do so is not just cheap but cruel. Her own measure of peace and confidence, though, may serve as a quiet light that will not be hidden. Whatever she herself suffers, she need not be ashamed; for she knows whom she has believed and is fully confident that God is able to keep what she has entrusted to him (2 Tim. 1:12 KJV).[13] She need never despair. She need never fear that pain and tragedy are either final or meaningless. She need not protect herself too much. She learns how to live in learning to die, and how to die in learning to live. She knows that the enemy is vanquished. Better yet, she knows that evil is being transformed to good. Because of her confidence, peace, and joy, laughter will filter through her love.

said in effect, "Yes, yes, but what about this and this?" Almost knocked over by astonishment, the young man owned the truth about his problems. (Not so incidentally, he ended up being saved and psychologically healed.)

[13] In this verse, the pronoun μου may be translated either as an objective genitive ("What has been entrusted to me" RSV) or as a subjective genitive (the KJV reading). I prefer the KJV but would argue that the RSV interpretation is simply the other side of the same coin.

Bibliography

Aaronson, S. 1974. Shadow and substance. *The Sciences* 14 (5): 11–18.

Alland, A. 1962: "Possession" in a revivalistic Negro church. *Journal for the Scientific Study of Religion* 1:204–13.

Ansbacher, H. L., and Ansbacher, R. R. 1956. *The individual psychology of Alfred Adler.* New York: Basic Books.

Anshen, R. N. 1972. *The reality of the Devil.* New York: Dell.

Arndt, W. F., and Gingrich, F. W. 1957. *A Greek-English lexicon of the New Testament and other early Christian literature.* Chicago: University of Chicago Press.

Auden, W. H. 1976. *Collected poems.* Ed. E. Mandelson. New York: Random House.

Aulén, G. 1935. *Christus victor.* Trans. A. G. Herbert. London: S.P.C.K.

Bannister, P. 1976. Objects flew through the air and a broken clock chimed. *National Enquirer* Jan. 6, 5.

Barber, T. X. 1969. *Hypnosis: A scientific approach.* New York: Van Nostrand Reinhold.

Burnhouse, D. 1965. *The invisible war.* Grand Rapids: Zondervan.

Barth, K. 1958. *Church dogmatics.* Trans. G. Bromiley. Vol. 4, pt. 2. Edinburgh: T. & T. Clark.

Basham, D. 1972. *Deliver us from evil.* Washington Depot, Conn.: Chosen Books.

Bass, C. B. 1976. Satan and demonology in eschatological perspective. In *Demon possession,* ed. J. W. Montgomery. Minneapolis: Bethany Fellowship.

Bauer, P. 1967. *Wizards that peep and mutter.* Westwood, N.J.: Revell.

Bauernfeind, O. 1964. νικάω. In *Theological dictionary of the New Testament,* vol. 1, ed. G. Kittel, trans. and ed. G. Bromiley. Grand Rapids: Eerdmans.

Baumgärtel, E., and Schweizer, E. 1968. πνεῦμα, πνευματικός. In *Theological dictionary of the New Testament,* vol. 6, ed. G. Friedrich, trans. and ed. G. Bromiley. Grand Rapids: Eerdmans.

Bazin, G. 1952. The Devil in art. In *Satan* (a compilation), series ed. Père Bruno de Jésus–Marie, trans. Malachy Carroll et al. New York: Sheed & Ward.

Bennett, D. J. 1976. Deliverance. Letter reprinted in Presbyterian Charismatic Communion *Newsletter* Jan.–Feb., 9–10.

Berger, P. L. 1969. *A rumor of angels.* Garden City, N.Y.: Doubleday.

Berkof, H. 1962. *Christ and the powers.* Scottsdale, Pa.: Herald.

Berkouwer, G. C. 1961. Satan and the demons. *Christianity Today* June 5, 770–71.

Berne, E. 1964. *Games people play.* New York: Grove Press.

Blackburn, T. R. 1973. Sensuous-intellectual complementarity in science. In *The nature of human consciousness,* ed. R. E. Ornstein. San Francisco: Freeman.

Boisen, A. T. 1936. *The exploration of the inner world.* New York: Harper.

Bonhoeffer, D. 1965. *Ethics.* New York: Macmillan.

Bonnell, J. S. 1956. Jesus and demon possession. *Theology Today* 13:208–19.

Boring, B. G. 1957. When is human behavior predetermined? *Scientific Monthly* 84:189–96.

Bourguignon, E. 1968. World distribution and patterns of possession states. In *Trance and possession states,* ed. R. Prince. Montreal: R. M. Bucke Memorial Society.

Bowers, M. K.; Brecher-Marer, S.; Newton, B. W.; Piotrowski, Z.; Spyer, T. C.; Taylor, W. W.; and Watkins, J. G. 1971. Therapy of multiple personality. *International Journal of Clinical and Experimental Hypnosis* 19:57–65.

Brooks, P. 1971. Delivered from oppression. *Christian Life* May, 33:27ff.

Brown, C. 1984. *Miracles and the critical mind.* Grand Rapids: Eerdmans.
Brown, F.; Driver, S. R.; and Briggs, C. A. 1972. *A Hebrew and English lexicon of the Old Testament.* Oxford: Oxford University Press.
Brown, R. 1965. *Social psychology.* New York: Free Press.
Brown, R. M. 1976. The need for passion. Baccalaureate address, Claremont Colleges, California, June.
Buzzard, L. R. 1976. Introduction. In *Demon possession,* ed. J. W. Montgomery. Minneapolis: Bethany Fellowship.
Caird, G. B. 1956. *Principalities and powers.* Oxford: Clarendon Press.
Carrel, A. 1935. *Man, the unknown.* London: Hamish Hamilton.
Carrigan, R. L. 1970. The revival of astrology—its implication for pastoral care. *Pastoral Psychology* 21:7–17.
Cassidy, M. 1975. Stars, fortunes, and spirits. Taped lecture, Aug. 11.
Chambers, W. 1948. The Devil. *Life* Feb. 2, 77–85.
Chandler, R. 1975. It's the witches' day to howl. *L.A. Times,* Oct. 31, part 2, 1–2.
Chein, I. 1972. *The science of behavior and the image of man.* New York: Basic Books.
Chesterton, G. K. 1959 [1908]. *Orthodoxy.* Reprint. Garden City, N.Y.: Image Books.
Collins, G. R. 1976. Psychological observations on demonism. In *Demon possession,* ed. J. W. Montgomery. Minneapolis: Bethany Fellowship.
Cristiani, L. 1962. *Evidence of Satan in the modern world.* Trans. C. Rowlang. New York: Macmillan.
Daane, J. 1973. *The freedom of God.* Grand Rapids: Eerdmans.
DeCharms, R. 1968. *Personal causation.* New York: Academic Press.
Deikman, A. J. 1969a. Deautomatization and the mystic experience. In *Altered states of consciousness,* ed. C. Tart. New York: Wiley.
_____. 1969b. Experimental meditation. In *Altered states of consciousness,* ed. C. Tart. New York: Wiley.
_____. 1973a. Biomodal consciousness. In *The nature of human consciousness,* ed. R. E. Ornstein. San Francisco: Freeman.
_____. 1973b. The meaning of everything. In *The nature of human consciousness,* ed. R. E. Ornstein. San Francisco: Freeman.
Delling, G. 1964, αρχη. In *Theological dictionary of the New Testament,* vol. 1, ed. G. Kittel, trans. and ed. G. Bromiley. Grand Rapids: Eerdmans.
_____. 1971. στοιχεῖον. In *Theological dictionary of the New Testament,* vol. 7, ed. G. Friedrich, trans. and ed. G. Bromiley. Grand Rapids: Eerdmans.
Demon experiences in many lands. 1960. Chicago: Moody Press.
Dostoevsky, F. M. 1923. *The brothers Karamazov.* Trans. C. Garnett. London: William Heinemann.
Douglas, J. D. 1971. Charming power of witchcraft. *Christianity Today* Mar. 26, 15:621–22.
Ebon, M. 1974. *The Devil's bride.* New York: Harper & Row.
Eccles, J. C. 1953. *The neurophysiological basis of mind.* Oxford: Clarendon Press.
Edwards, J., ed. 1949 (1817). *The life and diary of David Brainerd.* Newly edited by P. E. Howard, Jr. Chicago: Moody Press.
Eeden, F. van. 1969. A study of dreams. In *Altered states of consciousness,* ed. C. Tart. New York: Wiley.
Eliade, M. 1957. *Myths, dreams, and mysteries.* Trans. P. Mairet. London: Harvill.
Erikson, M. H., and Kubie, L. S. 1939. The permanent relief of an obsessional phobia by means of communications with an unsuspected dual personality. *Psychoanalytic Quarterly* 8:471–509.
Evans, R. 1970. The lure of the black arts. *His* Apr., 9–12.
Ferguson, M. 1975. *The brain revolution.* New York: Bantam.
Fish, J. M. 1973. *Placebo therapy.* San Francisco: Jossey-Bass.
Fletcher, J. 1966. *Situation ethics.* Philadelphia: Westminster Press.
Foerster, W. 1964a. δαίμων. In *Theological dictionary of the New Testament,* vol. 2, ed. G. Kittel, trans. and ed. G. Bromiley. Grand Rapids: Eerdmans.
_____. 1964b. ἐξουσία. In *Theological dictionary of the New Testament,* vol. 2, ed. G. Kittel, trans. and ed. G. Bromiley. Grand Rapids: Eerdmans.

Bibliography

—————. 1971. σατανᾶς. In *Theological dictionary of the New Testament*, vol. 7, ed. G. Friedrich, trans. and ed. G. Bromiley. Grand Rapids: Eerdmans.

Foerster, W., and von Rad, G. 1964. διάβολος. In *Theological dictionary of the New Testament*, vol. 2, ed. G. Kittel, trans. and ed. G. Bromiley. Grand Rapids: Eerdmans.

Frank, J. D. 1974. *Persuasion and healing*. New York: Schocken Books.

Frankl, V. 1963. *Man's search for meaning*. Trans. I. Lasch. Boston: Beacon Press.

Freeman, H. E. 1971. *Angels of light?* Plainfield, N.J.: Logos.

Frost, E. 1954. *Christian healing: A consideration of the place of spiritual healing in the church today in the light of the doctrine and practice of the ante-Nicene church*. London: Mowbray.

Frye, R. M. 1960. *God, man, and Satan*. Princeton: Princeton University Press.

Gasson, R. 1966. *The challenging counterfeit*. Plainfield, N.J.: Logos.

Gazzaniga, M. S. 1973. The split brain in man. In *The nature of human consciousness*, ed. R. E. Ornstein. San Francisco: Freeman.

Gershman, R. 1975. Case study. L.A. County—University of Southern California Medical Center, Grand Rounds, Aug. 19.

Goddard, H. H. 1926. A case of dual personality. *Journal of Abnormal and Social Psychology* 21:170–90.

Grad, B. 1970. Healing by the laying on of hands: Review of experiments and implications. *Pastoral Psychology* 21:19–26.

Gregory, A. K. 1974. Introduction. In *Possession, demonical and other*, by T. K. Oesterreich, trans. D. Ibberson. Secaucus, N.J.: Citadel.

Gregory, R. L. 1966. *Eye and brain*. New York: McGraw-Hill.

Gribbin, J. 1984. *In search of Schrödinger's cat*. Toronto: Bantam Books.

Gruenthaner, M. J. 1944. The demonology of the Old Testament. *Catholic Biblical Quarterly* 6:6–27.

Gruenwald, D. 1971. Hypnotic technique without hypnosis in the treatment of dual personality. *Journal of Nervous and Mental Disease* 153:41–46.

Grundmann, W. 1964. δύναμαι, δύναμις. In *Theological dictionary of the New Testament*, vol. 2, ed. G. Kittel, trans. and ed. G. Bromiley. Grand Rapids: Eerdmans.

Harder, G. 1968. πονηρός. In *Theological dictionary of the New Testament*, vol. 6, ed. G. Friedrich, trans. and ed. G. Bromiley. Grand Rapids: Eerdmans.

Harper, M. 1970. *Spiritual warfare*. Plainfield, N.J.: Logos.

Hastings, J., ed. [1898] 1951. *Dictionary of the Bible*. Reprint. Vol. 1. Edinburgh: T. & T. Clark.

Haynes, R. 1961. *The hidden springs*. New York: Devin-Adair.

Heim, K. 1953a. *Christian faith and natural science*. Trans. N. H. Smith. New York: Harper.

—————. 1953b. *The transformation of the scientific world view*. Trans. W. A. Whitehouse. New York: Harper.

—————. 1961a. *Jesus the Lord*. Trans. D. H. van Daalen. Philadelphia: Muhlenberg Press.

—————. 1961b. *Jesus the world's perfecter*. Trans. D. H. van Daalen. Philadelphia: Muhlenberg Press.

Heuvel, A. H. 1966. *These rebellious powers*. London: S.C.M. Press.

Heywood, R. 1961. *Beyond the reach of sense*. New York: Dutton.

Hill, H. 1974. *How to live like a king's kid*. Plainfield, N.J.: Logos.

Hincks, E. Y. 1896. The meaning of the phrase τὰ στοιχεῖα τοῦ κόσμου in Gal. iv.2 and Col. ii.8. *Journal of Biblical Literature* 15:183–92.

Hobart, R. E. 1934. Free will as involving determinism. *Mind* 43:1–27.

Hoffman, B. R. 1970. Beyond the intellectual. *Pastoral Psychology* 21 (Sept.): 41–53.

Hume, D. 1926 (1777). *Concerning human understanding*. Chicago: Open Court.

Huxley, A. L. 1952. *The devils of Loudun*. New York: Harper.

Immergluck, L. 1964. Determinism-freedom in contemporary psychology: An ancient problem revisited. *American Psychologist* 19:270–78.

Jackson, B. 1976. Reflections on the demonic: A psychiatric perspective. In *Demon possession*, ed. J. W. Montgomery. Minneapolis: Bethany Fellowship.

Jacobs, D. R. 1966. Christian theology in Africa. Unpublished manuscript, Mt. Joy, Pa.

James, W. 1961 (1902). *The varieties of religious experience.* New York: Collier.

Jung, C. G. 1963. *Memories, dreams, reflections.* New York: Pantheon Books.

————. 1973. Synchronicity: An acausal connecting principle. In *The nature of human consciousness,* ed. R. E. Ornstein. San Francisco: Freeman.

Kallas, J. 1966. *The Satanward view.* Philadelphia: Westminster Press.

————. 1975. *The real Satan.* Minneapolis: Augsburg.

Karlins, M., and Andrews, L. 1972. *Biofeedback.* Philadelphia: Lippincott.

Kaufmann, W., ed. 1954. *The portable Nietzsche.* New York: Viking Press.

Kehl, D. G. 1976. The cosmocrats: Diabolism in modern literature. In *Demon possession,* ed. J. W. Montgomery. Minneapolis: Bethany Fellowship.

Kelly, H. A. 1970. Death of the Devil? *Commonweal* 93:146–49.

Kildahl, J. P. 1964. A case of iatrogenic demon possession. *Journal of Religion and Health* 3:272–74.

Kinlaw, D. F. 1976. The demythologization of the demonic in the Old Testament. In *Demon possession,* ed. J. W. Montgomery. Minneapolis: Bethany Fellowship.

Kitchen, K. A. 1973. Magic and sorcery. *The new Bible dictionary,* ed. J. D. Douglas. Grand Rapids: Eerdmans.

Koch, K. 1965. *Christian counseling and occultism.* Grand Rapids: Kregel.

————. 1973. *Demonology past and present.* Grand Rapids: Kregel.

Koestler, A. 1967. *The ghost in the machine.* New York: Macmillan.

————. 1973. *The roots of coincidence.* New York: Vintage Books.

————. 1974. Order from disorder. *Harpers* 249 (1490): 54–62.

Krippner, S. 1975. *Song of the siren.* New York: Harper & Row.

Krippner, S., and Davidson, R. 1970. Religious implications of paranormal events occurring during chemically-induced "psychedelic" experience. *Pastoral Psychology* 21 (Sept.): 27–34.

Kuhn, T. S. 1970. *The structure of scientific revolutions.* Chicago: University of Chicago Press.

Laing, R. D. 1969. *The divided self.* London: Tavistock Publications.

Langton, E. 1942. *Good and evil spirits.* New York: Macmillan.

————. 1949. *Essentials of demonology.* London: Epworth Press.

Laski, M. 1962. *Ecstasy.* Bloomington: Indiana University Press.

Laubach, F. C. 1958. *Letters by a modern mystic.* Westwood, N.J.: Revell.

Lee, R. B. 1968. The sociology of Kung bushman trance performances. In *Trance and possession states,* ed. R. Prince. Montreal: R. M. Bucke Memorial Society.

Lépée, M. 1952. St. Teresa of Jesus and the Devil. In *Satan* (a compilation). New York: Sheed & Ward.

LeShan, L. 1973. What is important about the paranormal? In *The nature of human consciousness,* ed. R. E. Ornstein. San Francisco: Freeman.

————. 1974. *The medium, the mystic, and the physicist.* New York: Ballantine.

Lewis, C. S. 1947. *The abolition of man.* New York: Macmillan.

————. 1949. *Transposition.* London: G. Bles.

————. 1961. *The Screwtape letters.* New York: Macmillan.

Lewis, I. M. 1971. *Ecstatic religion.* Middlesex: Penguin.

Lhermitte, J. 1963. *True and false possession.* New York: Hawthorne Books.

Libassi, P. T. 1974. The powerful and the inglorious. *The Sciences* 14 (5): 24–30.

Ling, T. O. 1961. *The significance of Satan.* London: S.P.C.K.

Linthorst, A. 1973. Discerning pathology is not enough. *Psychotherapy: Theory, Research, and Practice* 10:359–61.

Lovelace, R. 1976. The occult revival in historical perspective. In *Demon possession,* ed. J. W. Montgomery. Minneapolis: Bethany Fellowship.

Luccock, H. 1974. Materialist's version of twenty-third Psalm. In L. W. Althouse, The psychic and man's religion. Address at North Carolina Retreat of Spiritual Frontiers Fellowship, Lake Junaluska, North Carolina, Aug. 21.

Ludwig, A. M. 1968. Altered states of consciousness. In *Trance and possession states,* ed. R. Prince. Montreal: R. M. Bucke Memorial Society.

Bibliography

————. 1969. Some general views on altered states of consciousness. In *Altered states of consciousness,* ed. C. Tart. New York: Wiley.

Ludwig, A. M.; Brandsma, J. M.; Wilbur, C. B.; Bendfeldt, F.; and Jameson, D. H. 1972. The objective study of a multiple personality. *Archives of General Psychiatry* 26:298–310.

McAll, R. K. 1976. Taste and see. In *Demon possession,* ed. J. W. Montgomery. Minneapolis: Bethany Fellowship.

McCasland, S. V. 1951. *By the finger of God.* New York: Macmillan.

Mackay, D. M. 1967. *Freedom of action in a mechanistic universe.* London: Cambridge University Press.

MacLeish, A. 1956. *J. B.* Boston: Houghton Mifflin.

Magny, C. 1952. The Devil in contemporary literature. In *Satan* (a compilation). New York: Sheed & Ward.

Mallory, J. D., Jr. 1976. Response. In *Demon possession,* ed. J. W. Montgomery. Minneapolis: Bethany Fellowship.

Marshall, C. 1974. *Something more.* New York: McGraw-Hill.

Martin, M. 1976. *Hostage to the Devil.* New York: Reader's Digest Press.

Mascall, E. L. 1966. *The Christian universe.* London: Darton, Longman & Todd.

May, R. 1969. *Love and will.* New York: Norton.

————. 1972. *Power and innocence.* New York: Dell.

Melhuish, G. 1973. *The paradoxical nature of reality.* Bristol: St. Vincent's Press.

Michaels, J. R. 1976. Jesus and the unclean spirits. In *Demon possession,* ed. J. W. Montgomery. Minneapolis: Bethany Fellowship.

Mischel, W., and Mischel, F. 1958. Psychological aspects of spirit possession. *American Anthropologist* 60:249–60.

Moeller, C. 1952. Introduction. In *Satan* (a compilation). New York: Sheed & Ward.

Montgomery, J. W. 1974a. Exorcism: Is it all for real? *Christianity Today* July 26: 1183–86.

————. 1974b. The occult: Demonology. *Christian Ministry* 5 (6):23–27.

————. 1975. *Principalities and powers.* Minneapolis: Dimension Books.

————. 1976. Commentary on hysteria and demons, depression and oppression, good and evil. In *Demon possession,* ed. J. W. Montgomery. Minneapolis: Bethany Fellowship.

Morosco, R. 1974. Conceptions of spiritual powers in the Pauline corpus. Ph.D. diss., Fuller Theological Seminary, 1974.

Morris, L. L. 1973. Devil. In *The new Bible dictionary,* ed. J. D. Douglas. Grand Rapids: Eerdmans.

Moss, T. 1974. *The probability of the impossible.* Los Angeles: Tarcher.

Motyer, J. A. 1973. Urim and thummim. In *The new Bible dictionary,* ed. J. D. Douglas. Grand Rapids: Eerdmans.

Muggeridge, M. 1974. Living through an apocalypse. Address given at the International Congress on World Evangelization in Lausanne, July.

Murphy, G. 1970. Phantasms of the living and of the dead. *Pastoral Psychology* 21:13–18.

Nevius, J. L. 1893. *Demon possession and allied themes.* Chicago: Revell.

Newport, J. P. 1976. Satan and demons: A theological perspective. In *Demon possession,* ed. J. W. Montgomery. Minneapolis: Bethany Fellowship.

Nugent, D. 1971. The Renaissance and/of witchcraft. *Church History* 40:69–78.

Oesterreich, T. K. 1974. *Possession, demonical and other.* Trans. D. Ibberson. Secaucus, N.J.: Citadel.

Ornstein, R. E. 1972. *The psychology of consciousness.* San Francisco: Freeman.

Owen, A. R. G. 1964. *Can we explain the poltergeist?* New York: Garrett.

Peck, M. S. 1983. *People of the lie.* New York: Simon & Schuster.

Penfield, W. 1975. *The mystery of the mind.* Princeton: Princeton University Press.

Penn-Lewis, J. n.d. *War on the saints.* Fort Washington, Pa.: Christian Literature Crusade.

Peterson, W. J. 1973. *Those curious new cults.* New Canaan, Conn.: Keats.

Philpott, K. 1973. *A manual of demonology and the occult.* Grand Rapids: Zondervan.

Polanyi, M. 1964. *Personal knowledge.* New York: Harper Torchbooks.

————. 1967. *The tacit dimension.* Garden City, N.Y.: Anchor.

Prince, R. 1968a. Can the EEG be used in the study of possession states? In *Trance and possession states,* ed. R. Prince. Montreal: R. M. Bucke Memorial Society.

———. 1968b. Possession cults and social cybernetics. In *Trance and possession states,* ed. R. Prince. Montreal: R. M. Bucke Memorial Society.

———. 1968c. Preface. In *Trance and possession states,* ed. R. Prince. Montreal: R. M. Bucke Memorial Society.

Pruyser, P. W. 1969. Calvin's view of man: A psychological commentary. *Theology Today* 26:51–68.

Rengstorf, K. H. 1971. σημεῖον. In *Theological dictionary of the New Testament,* vol. 7, ed. G. Friedrich, trans. and ed. G. Bromiley. Grand Rapids: Eerdmans.

Richards, J. 1974. *But deliver us from evil.* New York: Seabury Press.

Ricouer, P. 1969. *The symbolism of evil.* Boston: Beacon Press.

Robenson, W. n.d. Taped case study related by W. Robenson.

Roheim, G. 1955. *Magic and schizophrenia.* New York: International Universities Press.

Rose, L. 1971. *Faith healing.* Middlesex: Penguin.

Rougemont, D. 1945. *Talk of the Devil.* London: Eyre.

Russell, B. 1938. *Power.* London: G. Allen & Unwin.

Ryle, R. J. 1907. The neurotic theory of the miracles of healing. *Hibbert Journal* 5:572–86.

Sargant, W. 1959. *Battle for the mind.* New York: Harper & Row.

———. 1974. *The mind possessed.* Philadelphia: Lippincott.

Schlier, H. 1961. *Principalities and powers in the New Testament.* New York: Herder & Herder.

Schmidt, R. P., and Wilder, B. J. 1968. *Epilepsy.* Philadelphia: Davis.

Schrenk, G. 1972. θέλω, θέλημα, θέλησις. In *Theological dictionary of the New Testament,* vol. 8, ed. G. Friedrich, trans. and ed. G. Bromiley. Grand Rapids: Eerdmans.

Seesemann, H. 1968. πεῖρα. In *Theological dictionary of the New Testament,* vol. 6, ed. G. Friedrich, trans. and ed. G. Bromiley. Grand Rapids: Eerdmans.

Shulman, B. H. 1968. *Essays in schizophrenia.* Baltimore: Williams and Wilkins.

Skinner, B. F. 1971. *Beyond freedom and dignity.* New York: Knopf.

———. 1972. On having a poem. *Saturday Review* 55:32–35.

Slagle, A. 1974. Psychiatrist seeks evidence of reincarnation. *Miami Herald,* Aug. 25–28.

Slotten, R. 1971. The divine wit of miraculous conceptions. *Christian Century* Mar. 10, 317.

Small, L. 1973. *Neuropsychodiagnosis in psychotherapy.* New York: Brunner/Mazel.

Smedes, L. B. 1984. *Forgive and forget.* San Francisco: Harper & Row.

Smith, A. 1975. *Powers of mind.* New York: Random House.

Smoker, D. 1961. Teaching the law of sorcery in Exodus to African Christians. Master's thesis, Fuller Theological Seminary, 1961.

Steiner, C. M. 1975. *Scripts people live.* New York: Bantam.

Stewart, J. S. 1951. On a neglected emphasis in New Testament theology. *Scottish Journal of Theology* 4:292–301.

Stinnette, C. R. 1955. Demonic possession in modern man. *Pastoral Psychology* 6:35–42.

Stringfellow, W. 1969. The demonic in American society. *Christianity and Crisis* 29:24–48.

Swinburne, R. 1970. *The concept of miracle.* London: Macmillan.

Tart, C. T. 1969. Psychedelic experiences associated with a novel hypnotic procedure, mutual hypnosis. In *Altered states of consciousness,* ed. C. T. Tart. New York: Wiley.

———. 1973a. Preliminary notes on the nature of psi processes. In *The nature of human consciousness,* ed. R. E. Ornstein. San Francisco: Freeman.

———. 1973b. States of consciousness and state-specific sciences. In *The nature of human consciousness,* ed. R. E. Ornstein. San Francisco: Freeman.

Taylor, W. S., and Martin, M. F. 1944. Multiple personality. *Journal of Abnormal and Social Psychology* 39:281–300.

Thornton, E. E. 1974. The mystic consciousness (or getting high on God). *Christian Ministry* 5 (6): 3–7.

Thornton, T. C. G. 1972. Satan—God's agent for punishing. *Expository Times* 83:151–52.

Tillich, P. 1963. *Systematic theology.* Vol. 3. Chicago: University of Chicago Press.

Tippett, A. R. 1976. Spirit possession as it relates to culture and religion. In *Demon possession,* ed. J. W. Montgomery. Minneapolis: Bethany Fellowship.

Tournier, P. 1960. *A doctor's casebook in the light of the Bible.* New York: Harper & Row.

Underhill, E. 1961. *Mysticism.* New York: Dutton.

Unger, M. F. 1953. *Biblical demonology.* Wheaton, Ill.: Van Kampen Press.

————. 1971. *Demons in the world today.* Wheaton, Ill.: Tyndale.

Van Der Walde, P. H. 1968. Trance states and ego psychology. In *Trance and possession states,* ed. R. Prince. Montreal: R. M. Bucke Memorial Society.

Walsh, C. 1971. *God at large.* New York: Seabury Press.

Watson, G. 1972. *Nutrition and your mind.* New York: Harper & Row.

Wayman, A. 1968. The religious meaning of possession states. In *Trance and possession states,* ed. R. Prince. Montreal: R. M. Bucke Memorial Society.

Weldon, J. 1975. Taped conversation on TM.

White, J. 1976a. Commentary on psychological observations on demonism. In *Demon possession,* ed. J. W. Montgomery. Minneapolis: Bethany Fellowship.

————. 1976b. Problems and procedures in exorcism. In *Demon possession,* ed. J. W. Montgomery. Minneapolis: Bethany Fellowship.

White, V. 1953. *God and the unconscious.* Chicago: Regnery.

Wiesinger, A. 1957. *Occult phenomena.* London: Burns & Oates.

Wilkinson, J. 1967. The case of the epileptic boy. *Expository Times* 79:39–42.

Williams, C. [1942] 1984. *The forgiveness of sins.* Reprint. Grand Rapids: Eerdmans.

————. 1949. *Descent into hell.* Grand Rapids: Eerdmans.

————. 1959. *Witchcraft.* New York: Meridian Books.

Wilson, W. P. 1976. Hysteria and demons, depression and oppression, good and evil. In *Demon possession,* ed. J. W. Montgomery. Minneapolis: Bethany Fellowship.

Wink, W. 1984. *Naming the powers.* Philadelphia: Fortress.

Wolberg, L. R. 1972. *Hypnosis: Is it for you?* New York: Harcourt Brace Jovanovich.

Woods, R. 1971. *The occult revolution.* New York: Herder & Herder.

Woodward, K. L. 1974. The exorcism frenzy. *Newsweek* Feb. 15.

Wright, J. S. 1973a. Divination. In *The new Bible dictionary,* ed. J. D. Douglas. Grand Rapids: Eerdmans.

————. 1973b. Possession. In *The new Bible dictionary,* ed. J. D. Douglas. Grand Rapids: Eerdmans.

Wright, L. E. 1960. Are demons outmoded? *Journal of Religious Thought* 18:5–21.

Zilboorg, G., and Henry, G. W. 1941. *A history of medical psychology.* New York: Norton.

Zizioulas, J. D. 1975. Human capacity and human incapacity: A theological exploration of personhood. *Scottish Journal of Theology* 28:401–48.

Zuck, R. B. 1971. The practice of witchcraft in the Scriptures. *Bibliotheca Sacra* 128:352–60.

Zucker, W. M. 1969. The demonic: From Aeschylus to Tillich. *Theology Today* 26:34–50.

Zuesse, E. M. 1971. On the nature of the demonic: African witchery. *Numen* 18:210–39.

Scripture Index

OLD TESTAMENT

NEW TESTAMENT